For Better or Worse?
Women and ZANLA in
Zimbabwe's Liberation Struggle

For Better or Worse? Women and ZANLA in Zimbabwe's Liberation Struggle

by

Josephine Nhongo-Simbanegavi

WEAVER

W

—PRESS—

Published by Weaver Press,
Box 1922, Avondale, Harare. 2000

© Josephine Nhongo-Simbanegavi, 2000

Typeset by Fontline, Harare.

Cover design: Danes Design, Harare

Distributed in Europe and the USA by African Books Collective
Unit 13, Kings Meadow, Ferry Hinksey Road, Oxford OX2 0DP, UK

And in South Africa by David Philip: Cape Town, Johannesburg and Pietermaritzburg.

*The author and publisher would like to express their gratitude to MS Zimba-
bwe and SIDA-SAREC, Harare for their generous donations, which made the
publication of this title possible.*

ISBN: 0-7974-2105-X
ISBN-13: 978-0-7974-2105-9

About the author

Born Josephine Elizabeth Nhongo in Bikita in 1965, Dr Nhongo-Simbanegavi went to St Dominics Secondary School and St Ignatius College in Chishawasha. She later enrolled at the University of Zimbabwe where she graduated in 1989 with a BA Hons. in History. Between 1993 and 1997, she studied at Oxford University from where she obtained her doctorate. Her thesis, 'Zimbabwean Women in the Liberation Struggle: ZANLA and its Legacy, 1972-1985', provided the background to this book. Currently, she is a lecturer in the History Department at the University of Zimbabwe. She is married to Blessed Simbanegavi and has two children.

Acknowledgements

In the first instance, my thanks go to all the women who willingly shared their experiences with me and gave me valuable insights into what happened during Zimbabwe's liberation struggle. I also owe thanks to Professor Ngwabi Bhebe, whose academic and administrative support was a great encouragement to me. To Professor Terence Ranger, who supervised my doctoral research at Oxford, I will always be indebted. He has continued to give his professional guidance and support and this has been crucial in enabling me to get my work into print. Rtd Air Chief Marshall Josiah Tungamirayi, a former ZANLA commander and a fellow researcher, humbly acknowledged the need for his Party to open up the ZANU Archives to historians to evaluate the war in which he personally participated. I hope his dream of seeing the documentation of the war properly catalogued and preserved will be fulfilled. I deeply appreciate too, the personal commitment shown by my publisher, Irene Staunton, to see this publication through. In many ways she was more than just a publisher. Many thanks also go to Virginia Knight, who did the first edits to my manuscript, and to Shelagh Ranger, who read the final proofs. I thank my husband Blessed too for his moral and logistical support in the last stage of the process of writing this book. I would also like to register my gratitude to the various organisations who provided financial support at various points, from the inception of this study through to its publication. In particular, I received assistance through the University of Zimbabwe from SIDA/SAREC; and through Oxford University, from the Beit Trust and the ORISHA Studentship Fund. I was also assisted by the Danish organisation M.S, through my publishers at Weaver Press. Due, however, to limitations of space, I am not able to mention the many others who offered me practical and moral support. You know who you are, may it suffice to say a big thank you to you all for your generous assistance.

This work is inspired by all those women and men who have taken a leaf from the experience of the violence of the 1970s. May your quest for peace and dignity today heal our country's wounds and create a safer Zimbabwe for future generations. To young Zimbabweans, and especially to my children, Kumbirai and Ruvimbo, I dedicate this book.

Glossary of Shona and other terms used in the text

Dagga — Indian hemp, otherwise known as marijuana

Chef — A term coined during the Zimbabwean war to refer to someone holding a senior position of authority and now in common usage in independent Zimbabwe to refer to the same in politics and in the workplace

Chimbwido — A civilian aide to liberation war fighters engaged to carry out menial tasks

Ambuya — The Shona word for grandmother, also used respectfully to address any elderly woman or one with skills associated with old age and wisdom

Lobola — The brideprice paid by the groom's family to the family of his prospective spouse

Mujibha — An informant engaged by liberation forces to spy and report on the activities and movements of Rhodesian security forces

Povo — Term adopted by ZANLA from FRELIMO to refer to the people, or the masses

TTLs — Tribal Trust Lands

Vashandi — The Shona word for workers used during the war in reference to the Marxist and Soviet-oriented political leanings of ZIPA.

ZANLA — Zimbabwe African National Liberation Army

ZANU — Zimbabwe African National Union

ZIPRA — Zimbabwe People's Revolutionary Army

ZAPU — Zimbabwe African People's Union

ZIPA — Zimbabwe People's Army

Map 1: ZANLA's Operational Zones

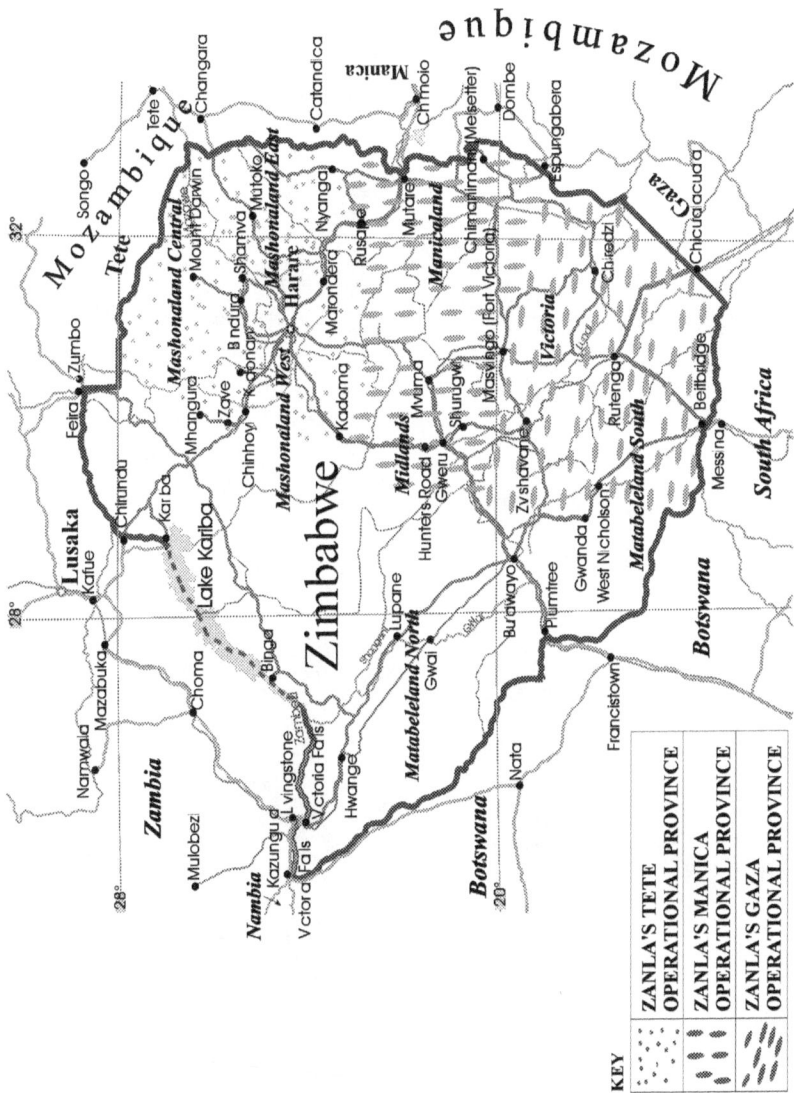

KEY

ZANLA'S TETE OPERATIONAL PROVINCE	
ZANLA'S MANICA OPERATIONAL PROVINCE	
ZANLA'S GAZA OPERATIONAL PROVINCE	

Map 2: ZANLA's Liberated Areas

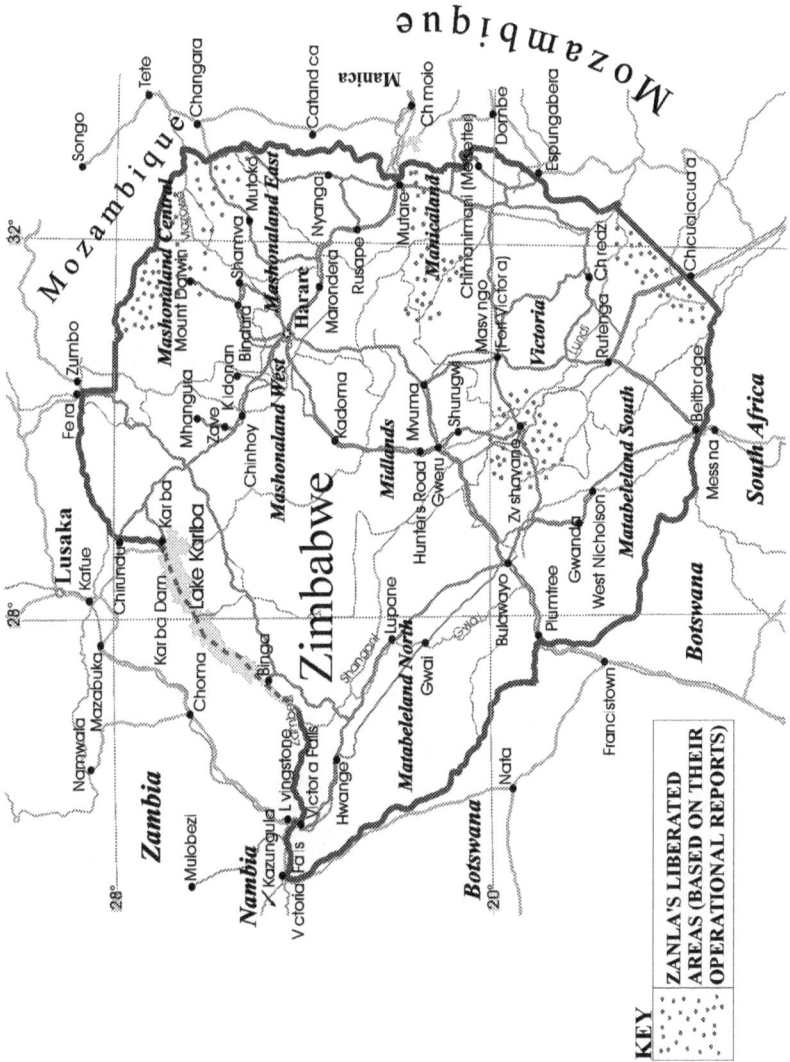

KEY

ZANLA'S LIBERATED
AREAS (BASED ON THEIR
OPERATIONAL REPORTS)

xi

Contents

Foreword

The ZANLA guerrilla war was one of the best documented in history. Every guerrilla group had a recorder whose task it was to make regular reports back to Mozambique. These reports - in English, 'the language of the revolution' - recorded military engagements, interactions with the people, breaches of discipline. Once in Mozambique they were analysed and synthesised by Political Commissars. Some of these commissars, the unsung heroes of the war, ventured into Zimbabwe to try to re-impose control on 'rogue' guerrilla groups, and their experiences were later recorded in reports. Within Mozambique a prolific correspondence was carried on between party organisations and the camps.

Only a fraction of this mass of documentation survived the war. Some fell into Rhodesian hands as a result of 'contacts' inside Zimbabwe. Many more were seized during Selous Scout raids on the camps in Mozambique. The capture of these documents was as much the object of Rhodesian raids as the killing of guerrillas. In 1980 thousands of the captured documents were shredded or incinerated in Harare; others were sent down to South Africa to help its army to train for guerrilla war.

But much *did* survive. After 1980 the ZANLA papers were bundled together and packed into cases to be sent back to Zimbabwe. They arrived; were unpacked; and piled up in a series of ramshackle locations. The new ZANU PF government did not trust the National Archives, which alone had the capacity to sort and catalogue the documents. To this day the papers remain in a rich confusion. No one knows quite what is in them, or how to find again a document previously unearthed.

Such a situation is frustrating to historians but it also offers them great opportunities. No one has censored the ZANLA papers or withdrawn sensitive information from them. There are many finds to be made.

Dr Josephine Nhongo was the first scholar to have free access to the ZANLA Archives, which form the main source for this book. It will soon become clear to readers that she found remarkable things - denunciations of the party leadership by dissident guerrillas; complaints by women combatants and refugees; frank reports of indiscipline and brutality among some guerrilla groups inside Zimbabwe. Her book offers a uniquely frank and well documented account of a guerrilla war.

That is its first claim to importance. The second is that Dr Nhongo's focus is on a topic often written about but seldom understood - the experience of women within ZANLA. After 1980 there was much rhetoric about women's role in the war. it was claimed that they had formed a large proportion of the fighting forces and that they had won equality of status and esteem. Dr Nhongo's evidence shows that these claims distorted reality. Women were always subordinated and marginal during the war; and after it they continued to experience discrimination, both in 'traditional' society and in 'revolutionary' politics. Dr Nhongo's book is one of the most important studies ever written of gender in a liberation war.

Dr Nhongo also carried out many interviews with female ex-combatants to trace what happened to them after 1980. And this brings me to the book's third claim to importance. It makes a remarkable contribution to history but it also helps us to understand the present.

Today the term 'ex-combatant' has taken on a whole range of new meanings. The violent role of men claiming to be ex-guerrillas before the June 2000 elections; their demands for priority in the distribution of the land they occupied; their threats, both to the government and to the opposition - all these brought about a wholesale re-evaluation. Letters began to appear in the press not only denouncing the conduct of so-called 'veterans' in 2000 but also denying that they were heroic in the 1970s. Young people especially were weary of re-iterated claims that the guerrilla war entitled Robert Mugabe and his ministers to rule.

It seems a bad moment for a book on the guerrillas to appear. But no one should be misled into dismissing it as 'just another book on the war'. Dr Nhongo does not glorify the struggle. What is more, her book helps us to understand one very important dimension of the present crisis.

Many people have asked, as they read reports of attacks on opposition supporters or of farm occupations, 'Where are the women?' Many male veterans have stood aside from or criticised the violence. But hardly any female ex-combatants have been involved at all. The women one sees on television have been bussed in to dance and sing; none of them has taken a decision; none of them stand to benefit from the fast track redistribution of land.

Why is this? Dr Nhongo provides some answers, even although her book was written well before the current crisis. One answer is that women were never allowed to make policy during the liberation war nor to take command of men. Another answer is that most women were 'demobilised' after the war, returning to civilian life and the 'command' of their husbands. Already, in the early 1980s, violence had been entirely masculinised. There were no female 'dissidents'; no female members of the Fifth Brigade. but the main answer is that during the 1970s the problem of gender was never analysed or confronted within ZANU PF ideology or guerrilla education.

The Women and Land Lobby group have shown that the current land occupations and redistributions have not benefitted women at all. hardly any female-headed households have been allocated land in the 'fast-track' settlement schemes. Women do much the most work in rural agriculture but receive by far the least reward. Households are now being settled on land which has no infrastructure; men will leave in search of urban employment; women will face a greater poverty than before. The Women and Land Lobby group call for the suspension of resettlement and for a national dialogue about how women can be involved in a positive and successful reclamation of the land.

Dr Nhongo's book does not show that such a national dialogue is impossible, but it shows for how long it has been needed and for how long it has been postponed.

Terence Ranger
Department of History
University of Zimbabwe
November 2000

Introduction

The bitter, armed struggle of African nationalists against the white minority government headed by the Rhodesian Front, lasted eighteen years but eventually lead to negotiations and a general election. Zimbabwe achieved its independence when the Zimbabwe African National Union Patriotic Front (ZANU PF) won the election in 1980 and formed a new government. The two guerrilla armies that had confronted the Rhodesian forces were ZANU's military wing, the Zimbabwe National Liberation Army (ZANLA), and the military wing of the Zimbabwe African People's Union (ZAPU), the Zimbabwe People's Revolutionary Army (ZIPRA).

With the new government, a legend developed about the role of African women in the liberation war. The ZANU PF régime propagated this myth in collaboration with feminist scholars. At the time, both Zimbabweans and outsiders perceived women as having played a major role in winning the war and, by 1979, the female component of ZANLA's total armed forces had significantly risen. According to the official line, the leadership were initially unwilling to deploy women to operational zones to engage in combat with enemy forces. Eventually, they overcame their reluctance and indeed the rhetoric would seem to indicate that many had become convinced of the female soldiers' equality with their male comrades. For example, Edson Zvobgo, Minister of Local Government and Housing in the newly formed government, recounted the war-time experiences that had revolutionised official thinking on this matter:

> In the early days of the struggle, there were women in the ZANLA forces but they were custom bound. They did the cooking, they carried arms over the border so that the men could fight... By 1977 we had a crisis on our hands... We had 10,000 women trained exactly like men, but we could not face the reality that they too could fight. They rebelled and they did go out and fight. We have grown because of that and our mentality has changed.[1]

ZANU PF's alleged transformation of attitudes towards women was proclaimed in a series of public declarations throughout the war. The Party chroniclers cited the grand Congress of ZANU women in Mozambique in May 1979 as the critical climax of the history of the women's struggle: on that occasion the ZANU leadership professed to bury patriarchy. Women had won the right to a new status on the battlefield.

Soon after its establishment in 1980, the new government introduced a series of legal measures designed to ensure women's newfound status. Since then, exponents of the legend have been divided between those who believe that significant advances for women

---

[1] 'Oppression of Women is Dead', the Chronicle, Bulawayo, 22 May 1980.

have been achieved since 1980, and those who see a reversal of the 'gains' made during the war.

Though for a time the view that women had advanced during the struggle was influential, it was insecurely based, with hardly any testimony from rank-and-file ZANLA women. The orthodoxy depended on statements by a few elite spokesmen and women. The continuing chauvinism of male Zimbabwean discourse since 1980 - as well as the history of patriarchy under colonialism - makes it clear that even heroic participation in war was not likely to effect rapid and major changes in gender relations.

Newly available evidence offers a much more complex and nuanced account of women's participation in the liberation war. A mass of archival and oral material reflects the experiences of rank-and-file ZANLA women and of women civilians. In particular, ZANU's archives in Harare - an extraordinarily rich, if greatly disorganised, source - have become available. This book is therefore an unorthodox account of the war based largely on the testimonies of women participants and ZANU's administrative documents. It does not discuss the experience of ZIPRA women.

The picture that emerges from this research is similar to other studies of guerrilla and liberation wars. From the early 1970s, ZANLA deliberately recruited women, but not for combat duties. ZANLA leaders allocated women roles as cooks, nurses and, above all, as porters and carriers. Although the chefs and 'veterans' sexually exploited many women, the party sought to elaborate and enforce puritanical rules about sexual relations and marriage. These drew on supposed 'customary law' and on Christian mission teaching. They also flirted with socialist ideas.

The political and structural framework of ZANLA was limited in scope and did not offer women enough opportunity to think through new roles. The Party's understanding of history was centuries of 'feudal' patriarchy. It offered women no role models. The colonial-constructed customary law offered them no assistance other than 'tradition'. After the suppression of the young radicals of the Zimbabwe People's Army (ZIPA),[2] little or no attempt was made to develop a theory or ideology of revolutionary war.

By 1979, when attempts were again made to elaborate an ideology of liberation in response to disciplinary problems at the front, the war was drawing to a close and little

---

2   ZIPA, an attempt by junior officers in ZANLA and ZIPRA at the close of 1975 to unite the two main nationalist organisations, failed, as a military union, to bring about the political integration of their leaders. The ZIPA coalition collapsed, and the leadership was disbanded by chefs in ZANU between 1977 and 1978. As they watched the persecution of their comrades, even educated fighters learnt that keeping quiet was wise.

time remained to do more than articulate politically progressive slogans at elite level. These bore little relation to the day-to-day experiences of ZANLA women. Although some women were, by then, fighting as armed guerrillas, they never constituted more than a small component of the total ZANLA forces. Mostly they were deployed in 'liberated' or 'semi-liberated' zones as porters, nurses and political commissars. Their presence in operational zones merely served to extend the frontiers of their 'auxiliary' operations rather than represent a change in their roles. Having been assigned duties, which the leadership viewed as non-pivotal in the dispensation of the war, the situation climaxed in an ironic way for ZANLA women. Having been viewed as a supporting refugee population in Mozambique, during the 1980 cease-fire, many women with military training were kept out of the guerrilla Assembly Points, being once again defined as 'refugees' rather than 'combatants'. As such they were sent back into the country to campaign for ZANU PF in preparation for the February 1980 elections.

The actual role of women during the war makes it abundantly clear that ZANU had hardly laid any foundation for a significant transformation of gender relations during the struggle. Gender reforms were never on the movement's practical agenda.

Nevertheless, the war was an extraordinary time for women. Teenagers who crossed the border into Mozambique found themselves in totally unexpected and unprecedented circumstances; women who remained in the rural areas had to play many new and demanding roles. Even if women guerrillas did not constitute a major proportion of the ZANLA army and were largely deployed in 'liberated' or 'semi-liberated' zones, this was the first time in Zimbabwean history that women had fought as soldiers.

As well as documenting a 'heterodox' and, for many Zimbabweans, a rather iconoclastic account of the nationalist struggle, this book seeks to make other contributions. Although it focuses especially on the experience of women, it is one of the few studies so far, to make extensive use of the ZANLA archives, illuminating the overall history of the guerrilla war in eastern and central Zimbabwe where ZANLA deployed its forces. Thus, it offers a new periodisation for the phases of the war during the 1970s; distinguishes between 'liberated', 'semi-liberated' and 'contested' zones; and discusses the crisis of guerrilla discipline in the late 1970s much more fully than in previous studies.

Moreover, while this study closes in 1985, the issues that it grapples with have a strong bearing on current political developments. The ruling party, ZANU PF, is calling upon those who fought in the war to re-mobilise over the land question. Some ex-guerrillas have moved onto white owned commercial farms. It is important to look at how female ex-guerrillas have responded to this sometimes violent development. As the book will show, the majority of the women who participated in the liberation struggle were very disappointed with the way in which they fared after the war, with many failing to receive any recognition for their contribution to the realisation of independence. The majority ended up designated as refugees and were excluded from the benefits extended to veterans of the war; many simply picked up from where they left off, rebuilt their lives and contributed to the new Zimbabwe without demanding compensation.

The immediate question that arises is whether these women would consider it worthwhile to make sacrifices for another nationalist cause - which is what the recent farm occupations are claimed to be. While it appears on the surface that this action involves both male and female guerrillas, there is evidence that women have not responded as enthusiastically as the men.

Indeed a women's land-rights lobbyist, Abigail Mugugu, argues that women are not benefiting from the government's fast-track land redistribution scheme. Very few female-headed households have been allocated land under the current exercise. In fact, she argued that only a small percentage of ex-combatants are part of the crowds of dancing, chanting women, who have been appearing on television, supposedly supporting the land invasions.[3]

Indeed there are some suggestions that the majority of these women are acting on coercion or they are a 'rented crowd'. While there might not be enough testimony to support this, what is conspicuous is the absence of women's voices in the public statements made by veterans in support of the occupations. The only female voices are those of ZANU PF's traditional spokeswomen, a few highly placed women. How much do we learn from them about women's perceptions of current events, and, to what extent, can that be used to assess the level of women's involvement in decision-making, especially with regard to the long-term implications of the land occupations.

The gender-determined power relations of the war period are useful in helping us analyse women's current position.

Josephine Nhongo-Simbanegavi
November 2000

---

[3]   Abigail Mugugu, 'Women Farm Workers', Land Stories Seminar, UNESCO Zimbabwe Film and Video Training Project, Harare, 9th October, 2000.

CHAPTER ONE

Myths of Female Liberation

Introduction

During the war, ZANU and ZANLA mythologised their support for gender equality. Subsequently, writers used their official propaganda to argue that women had emerged from Zimbabwe's war significantly emancipated and investigation by researchers on gender issues was done using this misleading data from the nationalist struggle.

The party's official position regarding women's liberation

In reconstructing ZANU and ZANLA's official line on gender, reference will primarily be made to ZANU's official organ, the *Zimbabwe News*. This monthly bulletin left readers in no doubt as to the Party's commitment to women's liberation. Generously illustrated, it carried pictures of formidable-looking women, often in situations defying traditional notions of femininity. Women were shown 'in action' in military training exercises, operating mounted guns, aiming to shoot, or receiving military briefings in the war zones. Captions applauding the revolutionary transformation of ZANLA men and women, all a result of the nationalist forces' unity of purpose, accompanied such pictures. ZANU proudly announced this supposed development:

> *ZANLA fighters and ZANLA WOMEN'S DETACHMENT FIGHTERS, ...in the war zone. In the true spirit of a [sic] waging a People's War ZANU has united the people of Zimbabwe in action and blood in the battlefield.*[1]

---

[1]   *Zimbabwe News,* Vol. 8, No. 7, July 1974, p.10.

Others proclaimed:

Women's physical participation is a major step forward in our bid to create a society of equals.[2]

According to official proclamations, the emergency situation had totally transformed women's lives and their political consciousness in the camps. A caption under a picture of dancing women pointed out: 'Even when dancing guns are always in hand.'[3]

ZANU had enough 'proofs' of female emancipation, upon which it could congratulate itself. The pictures showed women in trousers, marching aggressively with their guns – the living testimonies of the Party's success in a great revolutionary experiment:

The ZANU Revolution has produced a new kind of woman: proud, confident and totally liberated through armed struggle and ideological education.[4]

Over time, the claims became bolder. 'Our women are women of action', proclaimed the title of an article based on an interview with the leader of the ZANLA women, Teurai Ropa. It recorded:

Teurai Ropa (her name means 'spill blood'), 23, ZANU's fire-eating Secretary for Women's Affairs and in her own right a seasoned guerrilla, symbolizes the level of ideological and revolutionary development that has taken place in... the Party's history.[5]

Another article explained why ZANLA regarded women's emancipation and their involvement in the struggle as essential:

No revolution can claim to be successful if more than half of the exploited people, that is women, are not liberated. Indeed for it to be victorious, the revolution must of necessity involve women.[6]

ZANLA considered it vital to address women's issues during the war of liberation. The leadership proclaimed that no compromises would be made about that.

As ZANU gradually achieved recognition as an authentic liberation movement its members started receiving invitations from sympathetic countries, especially those in the former Eastern Bloc. ZANU exploited such occasions to spread the story of its success with gender reform. In 1978, Ropa attended the Eighth Congress of the Women's Union of Albania. In her address to the gathering she declared:

---

[2]   Ibid., Vol. 8 No. 9, September 1974, p. 14.
[3]   Ibid., Vol. 9, Nos. 5 & 6, July-December 1977, p. 11.
[4]   Ibid., p. 27.
[5]   Ibid., Vol. 10, No. 1, January-February 1978, p. 21.
[6]   Ibid., p. 23.

Women comrades are represented at every level of our organisation from the National Execu-
tive through the Central Committee, High Command, General Staff down to every level of the
ZANLA forces... We have won our rights and place in the Revolution not by anyone's pity, but
through our determination, devotion, and bravery... To be fair, however, we owe a lot to our
progressive male comrades, who have stood by us, fought for our rights, allowed us the degree
of freedom to contribute to the best of our abilities for the National cause. [7]

ZANU's propagandists declared that ZANLA women derived their inspiration from Nehanda, a spirit medium who the colonial government incarcerated and executed for allegedly participating in a resistance movement against them at the close of the nineteenth century. Proclaiming her 'an exemplary freedom fighter'[8], the ZANLA fighters also referred to her fondly as 'Comrade Nehanda' in recognition of what was supposedly her Marxist revolutionary stance.[9]

Building on this 'history', Robert Mugabe, the Party leader, was able by May 1979 to outline with much satisfaction the progressive developments his organisation had implemented in relation to women's emancipation. Reiterating Ropa's claims in Albania the previous year, Mugabe assured his audience that women were represented at every level in the ZANLA structure:

Although in the High Command there is only one woman, Comrade Sheba Tavarwisa, who is
Deputy Secretary for Education and Culture in Central Committee, in the General Staff there
are now scores of women officers, while in the Army generally several thousands of cadres
gallantly serve in one role or another. [10]

He also emphasised his party's commitment, as a socialist organisation, to the cause of elevating women:

If women are not drawn into public service, into political life, if women are not torn out of their
stupefying house and kitchen environment, it will be impossible to build even democracy, let
alone socialism. [11]

Many scholars succumbed to these high-sounding declarations and accounts given by ZANU's publicity organs. Staffed with some of the party's most élite members, these organs distributed propaganda to the international community and to the field operational zones.

---

[7] Ibid., Vol. 10, No.2, May-June 1978, p. 31.
[8] Ibid., p. 31.
[9] Ibid., p. 65.
[10] Robert Mugabe, 'The Role and History of the Zimbabwean Women in the National Struggle', in *Women's Libera-*
tion in the Zimbabwean Revolution: Materials from the ZANU Women's Seminar, Xai Xai, 21 May 1979, ZANU,
San Francisco, 1979, p.15.
[11] Ibid., p. 19.

In the camps, however, distribution of the *Zimbabwe News* was limited, with most readers just scanning it to see if their pictures had been published.[12]

When researchers have used this propaganda, the resulting histories have sometimes been quite alien from the real life experiences of those concerned. Some women written about have not even been able to recognise themselves in these rather too scholarly accounts. One female ex-combatant commented bitterly:

> We have seen books and newspaper articles that are supposedly about us. We do not know where the writers obtained their information, they never talked to us.[13]

Many interpretative problems emanate from a general assumption that as capitalist colonial institutions fall apart, national liberation wars automatically enhance women's status. After absorbing the rhetoric, scholars often go into the field with high expectations. Rather than confronting the truth when findings prove otherwise, they sometimes ignore the compelling evidence to the contrary and publish what they would have wished to see.

Official propaganda and earlier scholarship on gender reforms

Sister Aquina K.H. Weinrich produced one of the earliest works that reflected and perpetuated the false view that ZANU made major efforts to redress gender imbalance during the war.[14] Although her publication only appeared in 1979, she says she carried out her assessment in the years 1972-75, in the early years of the war. Weinrich emerged with an extremely positive appraisal of both the situation of women in the ZANLA camps in Mozambique and the prospects for their social and political standing after the war. She included a discussion of this matter in wider research on women's experience of racial discrimination in Rhodesia. To stress racial issues she downplayed aspects of black women's exploitation by black men.

Although Weinrich gave the period of her field research as 1972 to 1975, she is not clear when exactly she conducted the interviews with ZANLA women[15], whether she did

---

[12] The *Zimbabwe News* was prepared and compiled by those who worked in the offices. Those who dealt with day-to-day issues in the camps do not seem to have made significant use of it as literature for political education lessons. Towards the end of the war, political commissars were urging people to put it to greater use rather than just admiring how well their pictures had come out. In the operational zones, some forces only started reading it seriously in 1979, when they were confronted with politically conscious supporters who were seeking clarifications on issues they did not understand.

[13] Interview with Margaret Dongo, Parliament Building, Harare, 10 March 1992.

[14] A.K.H. Weinrich, *Women and Racial Discrimination in Rhodesia*, UNESCO, 1979.

[15] As she says she gathered her materials from Mozambique, the only possible time for this would be 1975 after ZANLA had moved from Zambia. But she says she got clearance and assistance from the ZANU Central Committee. The Central Committee members were all imprisoned then and they did not even supervise the movement of their forces to Mozambique. They were not released until 1976.

them herself and what assistance she received from the ZANU Central Committee.[16] The direct testimonies she used in her book came from publications produced between 1977 and 1979 (most by nationalist activists), where one would have expected her to make such citations from her own interviews.

The manner in which she discussed the findings of her research suggests that a group of carefully selected women received questionnaires to which they gave responses to achieve a pre-determined result.[17] This would explain why, for example, the respondents reflected a higher level of education than the overall situation among Zimbabwean women at the time, as Weinrich herself remarked.[18] This is probably because only literate women could have filled out the questionnaires. The data collection method employed here significantly skewed the facts.

The only points where the responses differed were the individuals' personal details; things like age, exact education, what field of training they had received, and their home background. For questions regarding the experience of the war, and women's perceived position in the future Zimbabwe, their assessments were suspiciously uniform. They all claimed, for example, that everything was equal between men and women in the camps.[19] Strikingly, even at this stage in the war, they all had a clearly defined feminist position on certain matters. None, for example, would have bridewealth (*lobola*) paid for her after the war![20]

On the whole, the production of the materials that Weinrich used are so contrived that we do not learn much about individual opinions; rather, we learn the official position on the matters raised.[21]

There is need to consider Weinrich's personal career to understand her position on the issues in question. She was a Catholic nun in the Dominican Order and had served with the Catholic Commission for Justice and Peace in Rhodesia. In fact, it was she who helped Mugabe to escape to Mozambique in 1975 after the Rhodesian government released him from prison. During his stay in prison, Weinrich visited him and had become a great admirer of his. Later, the Rhodesian government deported her from Rhodesia and this ena-

---

[16] Weinrich, *Women and Racial Discrimination*, see Introduction.
[17] Ibid., p. 44.
[18] Ibid.
[19] Ibid.
[20] If the interviews were conducted in 1975 as we suggested, ZANLA had just arrived in Mozambique, and the limited political lessons, which had been taught to recruits in Zambia, made no reference to gender reforms.
[21] The book was actually written from Tanzania where she was then working after having been expelled by the colonial government from Rhodesia.

bled her to express her sympathies with ZANU's position more clearly. She became a socialist convert and worked closely with ZANU's Central Committee, where she helped draft their policies. Her loyalties clearly lay with ZANU and Mugabe, and she worked to help them achieve domestic and international acceptability.[22] Her conclusions about ZANU's position on women seem to have been based on what she understood Robert Mugabe to stand for, that is the creation of a socialist state, which Weinrich herself also advocated.[23]

Although such publications were essential to gain the support of the international donor community for the liberation movements, they did not do justice to history. They fed into ZANLA's propaganda machinery, helping the organisation provide more 'proof' of their commitment to gender reforms.

Perhaps her most useful contribution was her findings on Protected Villages (PVs) where she recorded the deplorable conditions, the difficulties women faced in trying to provide for their families' domestic needs,[24] the camp guards' demands for women's sexual services and related problems.[25] Weinrich's favourable assessment of the women's position in ZANLA camps was probably meant to be contrasted with the abominable situation of the women in the PVs.

Ruth Weiss is another researcher on Zimbabwean women's experiences who, like Weinrich, was deported from Rhodesia by the colonial government. Published soon after the war, her work has also been instrumental in sustaining the myth that ZANU showed substantial commitment to women's emancipation during the war. Although she acknowledged lack of progress for women in independent Zimbabwe, she did not know where to place the blame. Remembering women's massive contribution to the struggle, she asked: 'But what, I wondered, happened after the war?'[26] With all the evidence she seems to have come across in her research, perhaps she should have asked a much more basic question: what happened during the war?

---

[22] The author thanks Professor Terence Ranger for this clarification on Weinrich's background.
[23] Weinrich's position was clearly spelt out in her *African Marriage in Zimbabwe*, published by Mambo Press in 1982, but researched and written earlier. She adopts a combined Marxist and liberation theology approach and suggests 'that in the present situation of Zimbabwe all the elements for a profound re-appreciation of every aspect of social and religious life are present. The country finds itself in a revolutionary situation and there is little doubt that the old colonial Rhodesia will be based on an ideology which is totally different from that of the past. The ideologues of the Zimbabwean liberation movements are predominantly Marxist... Consequently the forms under which marriage and family life will be expressed will differ from those of the past, not only from those of the tribal past but also from those brought by Christian missionaries.' (pp.xi-xii).
[24] A.K.H. Weinrich, 'Strategic Resettlement in Rhodesia', in *Journal of Southern African Studies*, Vol. 12, No. 3, April 1977, pp. 211; 220-21.
[25] Ibid., pp. 224, 226.
[26] Ruth Weiss, *The Women of Zimbabwe*, Kesho Publications, London, 1986, p.13.

Weiss apparently became trapped in a self-created problem, ascribing too much importance to the stories of the war's official heroines. She compromised lesser voices to sustain her success story.

In one instance, Ruvimbo, a female ex-guerrilla, told Weiss that women engaged in transporting war materials before 1973 finally 'demanded' some training in self-protection as their duties exposed them to enemy attacks.[27] Weiss' analysis did not question why the women should demand something that should naturally have been given them, according to ZANU's rhetoric.

In another testimony, a former commander revealed unsettling occurrences in the camps, disconcerting issues that Weiss surprisingly ignored. She told Weiss that:

> Firstly it was traditional that men should be obeyed by women... But when discipline was good, when relationships were good, women began to feel not only equal to men but the same as men. The question of sex did not arise... Where difficulties arose, it was often with leaders... who felt that it was their right to demand the services of women as semi-servants or semi-wives at their base camp. Some women would go along with this, either because they loved the man, or because they felt that they could gain some advantage from an association with a leading comrade.[28]

Curiously, Weiss does not explain how such blatant abuses of power and seniority by the male leadership could possibly have created an environment conducive to the social elevation of women. Women's complaints of sexual abuse by senior male guerrillas abound in ZANLA's administrative records. Some leaders manipulated their position as keepers and distributors of basics in a situation of extreme scarcity. This issue of sexual abuse had a strong bearing on the direction that the women's movement took as the war raged on.

In her desire to show that things had changed, Weiss carefully selected her proofs of 'success', like: Mrs Julia Zvobgo, who 'stood for Parliament and was elected' and who became the treasurer of the newly formed Zimbabwe National Women's Organisation and also an executive member of the ZANU PF Women's League; Mrs Teurai Ropa Nhongo (now Joyce Mujuru), who became Minister of Women's Affairs (although the government soon dissolved the ministry); and Mrs Sally Mugabe, who was Deputy Secretary of ZANU PF Women's League and the wife of Robert Mugabe.[29]

While these officials gave glorious versions of gender equality in the struggle, some-

---

[27] Ibid., p.80.
[28] Ibid., p.95.
[29] Ibid., pp.13-24.

times they differed with each other. Mrs Mugabe claimed that men and women always reached unanimity on what to do when a woman became pregnant and how the child would be cared for.[30] Mrs Zvobgo, on the other hand, said she became aware of women's resentment of the practice of sending them to Osibisa, the camp created for expectant and nursing mothers. She also clarified that it was ZANU policy that women could not use contraceptives.[31]

Freedom Nyamubaya, herself an ex-ZANLA guerrilla, describes the depressing atmosphere in Osibisa Camp in one of her poems. Her vivid account leaves her readers in no doubt why women hated it.[32] Thus decisions to send women there could not have been made amicably as implied by Mrs Mugabe.

While élite views are important, they should be carefully applied when dealing with the experiences of less prominent women, especially those who did not have husbands in such important positions as those presented by Weiss.[33]

Some informants 'spoke in tongues'. Tainie Mundondo told Weiss for example:

there was no difference between men and women… there was only one difference: men were better trained in the use of arms than women. But a woman officer was treated with the same respect as a man.[34]

Such contradictory statements were also encountered in the research for this project. These statements need to be viewed partly against loyalty to the organisation and the feeling among some people that criticising the liberation movement was being disloyal to one's nation.

The differences in responses to enquiries on such matters also arise from variants such as education or age among the guerrilla recruits. Older or more educated women were probably less vulnerable to exploitation than the younger girls, or illiterate women. Such factors may also have sharpened their ability to identify and articulate exploitative or sexist tendencies.

---

[30]   Ibid., p.20.
[31]   Ibid., p. 94.
[32]   Freedom Nyamubaya, 'Osibisa', in *On the Road Again: Poems from the Liberation Struggle*, Zimbabwe Publishing House, Harare, 1985, pp.66-67.
[33]   General Rex Nhongo (now Solomon Mujuru), was ZANLA Chief of Operations, and at Independence became the Zimbabwe National Army Commander (now retired); Eddison Zvobgo was ZANU's Publicity Secretary and later became Minister of Legal and Parliamentary Affairs. He still holds a ministerial post in the ZANU PF Government; Robert Mugabe was the Party's General Secretary, later becoming its President. Now he is President of Zimbabwe.
[34]   Weiss, p.90.

In her novel *Woman in Struggle*, 'Ropa Rinopfuka' Mahamba sought to capture the promise of non-pressured love relationships that ZANLA held out for young women.[35] In this novel she related the fictional experience of a girl whom guerrillas saved from a forced marriage. The girl followed the guerrillas to the liberation struggle where, in the spirit of comradeship, she shared with male colleagues in the camps, experiencing real emancipation. Most women's experiences were less romantic, however. They did not always enter voluntarily into war-time relationships with men.

Gender in other studies on Zimbabwe's liberation struggle

Some of the major academic accounts of the nationalist struggle that emerged after Independence have also contributed to our understanding of women's involvement and gains in the war. Among them are the scholarly writings of Terence Ranger on peasants and David Lan on spirit mediums.[36] Ranger argued that there was, in principle, a clear consensus between the peasants' agenda in the nationalist struggle and the causes advocated by the guerrilla movement. Although the voices of elderly men predominated in politics in the district of Makoni as well as in Ranger's work, women, in fact, constituted the majority of the peasant population. Recording the implications for generational and gender relations of the guerrillas' presence among civilians in the operational zones, Ranger wrote:

> Men in their fifties, ...who were used to controlling a flock of dependent women... now found that the initiative had passed to young men with guns. These young men called upon the unmarried women of Makoni to act as their cooks, informants and messengers and in these latter two roles, teenage girls were able to exercise a good deal of power, for the first time in Makoni's history.[37]

The young women became politically visible due to their ability to gain audience with the guerrillas. The guerrillas, in turn, used their information to assess the amount of support they had among the local people.

Later, Ranger points out, both young men and women abused their positions and challenged the traditional authority of the elders by cohabiting, without approval from their parents, with the guerrillas in their mountain hide-outs. The society viewed this rather

---

[35]   Irene Mahamba, *Woman in Struggle*, Zimfep, Harare, 1986.

[36]   T. O. Ranger, *Peasant Consciousness and the Guerrilla War in Zimbabwe: A Comparative Study*, James Currey, London, 1985; David Lan, *Guns and Rain: Guerrillas and Spirit Mediums in Zimbabwe*, James Currey, London, 1985.

[37]   Ranger, *Peasant Consciousness*, p. 207.

licentious sexual behaviour as something that only misguided youth enjoyed, with the support of guerrillas of questionable character and legitimacy. The weakness of the youth's power base became evident when both they and the guerrillas found themselves quickly shoved back into their places once the war was over.[38] Because their war-time 'power' depended on the collusion of 'misguided' young men with guns, they had no legitimate authority to reinforce or sustain their position.[39]

The women had nothing to show for their pains in the war; neither did they entertain any hopes about the future. Ranger comments from his earlier paper on the women of Makoni that:

> those who saw or predicted change all thought it had been or would be for the worse... in spite of their contributions, their efforts are hardly recognised or acknowledged.[40]

David Lan looked at the way ZANLA used spirit mediums in Dande to legitimate the cause of the guerrilla movement. He intricately analysed the importance of gender and generation in defining the spirit mediums' framework of operation. During the war, when the mediums engaged in direct dialogue with young male strangers, they compromised on generational and kinship rules. They made no such compromises with pregnant and menstruating women, however, and thus excluded women from certain activities and places. This meant that the women guerrillas had to cope with occasional obstacles in their field operations. Lan's material on ZANLA's tacit rule on menstruating and pregnant women has interesting implications for our understanding of women's experiences as soldiers in ZANLA.

Ranger acknowledged that many guerrillas were sexually active in the operational zones, in spite of the mediums' injunctions. Lan, however, simply laid out the mediums' rules without assessing how the guerrillas implemented them. Lan did not attempt to take to task the fighters' and their *mujibhas'* claims that they upheld medium-enforced sexual codes.[41] Such claims need challenging in order to fully understand the threat posed to women by the presence of young, armed men in their villages.

Gradually, however, research from a later phase began to challenge more openly some of the widely held assumptions about women's roles and about gender relations during the war. Irene Staunton collected testimonies from women whose accounts showed that, al-

---

[38] Ibid., p. 292.
[39] Even if we discount the matter of authority, it is still debatable how much the young women could personally be considered to be powerful, especially when they had no control of the processes that so intimately touched their lives.
[40] Ranger, 'Women in the Politics of Makoni', Manchester University, Seminar paper, p. 32., 1981
[41] Lan, *Guns and Rain*, p. 158.

though in principle most people supported the cause of the war, the methods used by the guerrillas were not always considered appropriate.[42] Guerrilla relations with young women, for example, featured as a major point of bitterness.

Even more daring accounts followed later. In Norma Kriger's presentation of her research in Mutoko District in northern Zimbabwe, she challenged the theory that nationalist consciousness was the major reason the peasants supported the guerrilla war. She argued that local struggles were more important and that, faced with the challenge of an undefeated colonial state, ZANLA had to use coercion to secure the full co-operation of the peasants. Challenging nationalist claims that female emancipation had been on their agenda, she explained:

> Female participation during wars in roles from which they are normally excluded is not sufficient evidence of changing attitudes to women.[43]

Also discounting claims that guerrillas promoted better gender relations in their areas of operation, Kriger wrote:

> Guerrilla attitudes and behaviour to women could not have made them suitable promoters...
> of family unity and new standards of morality that prohibited divorce and adultery and made it mandatory for men to marry women who bore their children. [44]

Kriger did not have enough evidence on sexual discrimination and abuse in the camps and, unfortunately, could only speculate that things did not seem entirely harmonious between male guerrillas and their female comrades.

Although Kriger rightly questioned the liberation movement's ability to emancipate women, she did not match that perception with similar aptitude in her assessment of peasant women's political consciousness. The peasants' nationalist perspectives (often overzealous) are critical in explaining why gender-based struggles were successfully thwarted during the war. The presence of the colonial state, which Kriger acknowledged, was crucial in fostering and sustaining a spirit of revolt among the peasants. Kriger's problem in this matter lay in the fact that her informants were vocal about guerrilla abuses but kept curiously quiet about colonial deprivation and incidents of Rhodesian violence. In that respect, Kriger's theory that women's agendas were disjointed during the war underlies another, implying benignity on the part of the colonial authority.

---

[42]   Irene Staunton, *Mothers of the Revolution: The War Experiences of Thirty Zimbabwean Women*, James Currey, London, 1990.

[43]   Norma J. Kriger, *Zimbabwe's Guerrilla War: Peasant Voices*, Cambridge University Press, New York, 1992, p.195.

[44]   Ibid.

CHAPTER TWO

Mass Mobilisation and Recruitment: 1972 to 1976

Introduction

From the beginning of ZANLA operations in north-eastern Zimbabwe in 1972 to the time of the ZIPA onslaught in 1976 the military impinged on the daily schedules of the local men and women and boys and girls. However, the recruitment of women, for instance, did not essentially alter gender relations in the local communities. Militarisation and mobilisation did not bring changes in the gender division of labour, and in male-female power relations. The geographical and social spaces created by the incidence of war in Zimbabwe did not change how women were perceived and how they perceived themselves.

By the close of 1972, ZANLA attacks had intensified in the north-east, bringing home to the Rhodesian authorities the threat of widespread upheaval. Both sides began fervent propaganda campaigns, prominently featuring women, to legitimate their cause. Among other things, both parties said they were acting to protect society's vulnerable members, that is women and children, from the abuses of the other side. As reflections on that earlier period show, such abuses were rampant, with most evidence incriminating the Rhodesian government forces and their agents.

Although the claims of both sides must be investigated, simply distinguishing the perpetrators of the alleged crimes from those who protected the victims is not sufficient. It is necessary to understand how the propaganda thrived on certain patriarchal beliefs and how, in turn, it reinforced them.

Believing that men had an inborn capacity for violence (which could be harnessed for positive ends), both sides called upon men to fight. They presumed the reverse of women, who were supposedly averse to violence, embodying kindness and fragility. In turn, women qualified as providers of care and comfort, and recipients of male protection. Both the indigenous people and the European settlers' traditional perspectives revealed these views. Men or women who took actions that were not socially identified with their sex received as much attention in white society as among the African population.

These are the ideas around which both the nationalist armies and the Rhodesian security forces reorganised the communities in the countryside for war-time functions: men beget war; women support them. Such thinking shaped gender relations in the African as well as in the European cultural context.

Looking at women who joined the guerrillas, they all came from different backgrounds and brought with them different sets of expectations. While pre-war gender relations hardly changed, it is undeniable that the act of joining the war had considerable implications for the social and political ideas of the communities from which the women came. Soldiering, after all, had always been regarded a male occupation.

Initiations into the culture of protest

Women, like men, were involved in peasant resistance strategies and nationalist demonstrations in the late 1950s and early 1960s. Discussing peasant agency in Makoni in the pre-war period, Ranger gave a lively account of what one District Commissioner deemed a 'typical Mashona campaign of disorder and disobedience'.[1] This campaign, which involved destroying cattle dips and burning crops on settler farms,[2] was not just a male affair. Women took an active part in it too.[3]

Government agents used less force in responding to women's action than they did when men were the activists, reflecting the commonly held view of who really were regarded as the more serious threat to the colonial state's survival. Women got rough treatment when the authorities detected male involvement behind their actions, harassing women to coerce their men to co-operate with the state's programmes.[4]

---

[1] T.O. Ranger, *Peasant Consciousness and the Guerrilla War in Zimbabwe: A Comparative Study*, James Currey, London, 1985, p. 152.
[2] Ibid., pp. 152- 71.
[3] Also see Robert Mugabe, 'The Role and History of the Zimbabwean Women in the National Struggle', in *Women's Liberation in the Zimbabwean Revolution, Materials from the ZANU Women's Seminar Xai Xai, 1979*, ZANU, San Francisco, 1979, pp. 13-14.
[4] Ibid., pp. 36-37.

Noting that the risk of reprisals was lower when resistance action was conducted by women, male nationalist activists decided to keep a low profile. Instead, organised groups of women increasingly conveyed grievances pertaining to the welfare of Africans to the colonial state. Ruth Weiss recorded interview accounts referring to the involvement of largely illiterate rural-based women in the demonstrations organised by urban men in the early 1960s.[5] Unlike men and middle-class women who feared losing jobs, rural uneducated women participated more enthusiastically in public expressions of disapproval of state programmes.[6] In most of rural Zimbabwe, men and women had received their initiation in mass action against the state long before they saw the guerrillas.[7] Thus Seri Jeni, one of Staunton's informants, explained what she had witnessed in the Guruve area, in northeastern Zimbabwe:

> During those years in Guruve there was plenty of politics. Those were the years when ZAPU started. Everyone, men and women were involved in the party. The police would come to arrest them... Then those who had not been arrested lay in the road to prevent the trucks from moving.[8]

Vacillating attitudes: nationalist ideas on mass involvement

However, attitudes towards female involvement continually shifted as the techniques of the nationalists vacillated between the use of sporadic attacks and the adoption of fully militarised and mechanised warfare. Combined with the mass protests, the nationalists organised sabotage operations using gangs of young men armed with light weapons, including petrol bombs. The saboteurs relied on a civilian intelligence network. However, after the disasters of 1964[9], ZANLA's leadership decided that the operations being conducted by their small sabotage units inside Rhodesia stood a better chance without civilian involvement, and they became even less willing to involve women. Thus the organisation's clandestine recruitment exercise for the rest of the decade after 1966 mostly targeted Zimbabwean men living in neighbouring countries. To a lesser extent, they also secretly recruited men from Rhodesia, luring them with false promises that they would secure jobs in the neighbouring countries. Instead the desperate job seekers were enlisted for quasi-mili-

---

[5]   Ruth Weiss, *The Women of Zimbabwe*, Kesho Publications, London, pp. 11-15.

[6]   Ibid., p. 12.

[7]   Ranger, *Peasant Consciousness*, p. 171.

[8]   See Irene Staunton, *Mothers of the Revolution: The War Experiences of Thirty Zimbabwean Women* James Currey, London, 1990, p. 2.

[9]   In 1964, a group of ZANLA fighters code-named 'the crocodile gang' mounted attacks on farms in Melsetter (now Chimanimani). Although they managed to kill one farmer, their operation was frustrated by in-house squabbles and the enemy gathered abundant intelligence on their civilian supporters resulting in several arrests. See T. O. Ranger, 'Violence Variously Remembered: The Killing of Pieter Oberholzer', *History in Africa*, 1998. Also, *Zimbabwe News* , December 1988, p. 28.

tary training. As these young men hardly received any political orientation, the new approach yielded no better results.

After ineffective sporadic sabotage operations, the leadership re-designed more serious strategies, encompassing full-scale war. By the end of the 1960s, they had become undoubtedly convinced that a 'self-contained' struggle, or one that excluded the masses, would never achieve anything. A protracted war was essential to achieve nationalist independence, and for this, they needed the co-operation of the rural population.

Laying the groundwork for full-scale war

The lessons learnt from past mistakes were first tested in north-eastern Zimbabwe, where by December 1972 ZANLA had started intensive military operations. According to David Lan's findings in Dande, upon entering the operational zones the guerrillas first had to approach the spirit mediums to have their operations in that area made legitimate.[10] The spirit mediums were both male and female, as religion was one aspect of the indigenous people's lives in which women could wield influence. The nationalists professed to be acting in the name of Zimbabwe's national spirits, among them the female spirit of Nehanda, the heroine of the 1896-97 primary resistance movements. In 1972, the ZANLA guerrillas actually took the woman who was then the Nehanda spirit medium with them to Mozambique, so that she would not be harassed or killed by the Rhodesian soldiers. They also wanted her guidance on how to conduct the war. [11]

Once the guerrillas had received the blessings of the ancestors, they would make contacts with the leaders of the area, the power élites of the living world, who were men. The guerrilla commanders asked the men, as the heads of their families, to surrender their sons[12] to ZANLA for training as nationalist soldiers. Coming to operate in an area where they had no political base at all, the going was not easy for the ZANLA guerrillas. Although the local peoples had participated in political action earlier they had been organised by members of ZAPU rather than ZANU. Testimonies relating to the period make this clear.

In the early 1970s ZANU had no such political background when its forces arrived in the country to pave the way for intensive engagements with the enemy. Being largely unknown in the area, ZANU's options for opening up north-eastern Zimbabwe for guerrilla war were

---

[10] David Lan, *Guns and Rain: Guerrillas and Spirit Mediums in Zimbabwe*, James Currey, London, 1985, pp. 147-48.

[11] Ibid., p. 5; David Sweetman, *Women Leaders in African History*, Heinemann, Oxford, 1984, p. 97.

[12] ZANU (PF) Archives, File: Defence Secretariat, Doc.: Manuscript of Interview with Josiah Magama Tongogara (Secretary for Defence) by Edson Zvobgo (ZANU Information and Publicity Secretary), 16 October 1978.

16

quite limited. Recalling their strategies between 1969 and 1971 and how they had to resort to planting their own men in rural families to start political and military mobilisation, Josiah Tongogara, ZANLA's Chief of Defence, explained in an interview in 1978:

> We used to go to villages, pick out these die hards, replace them with our trained comrades. We got to an old man and said, "How many boys do you have?". He said "I have got five." And we said, "Give us 3." We replaced them with three. Then the Rhodesian Intelligence would get there and say, "How many children do you have? " And he would say 5. They would register them as the children of that old man. [13]

Once placed in families like this, the guerrillas behaved in ways that did not arouse suspicion. They designed their operations to fit into the rural household's activities, ensuring as little disruption as possible and respecting the conventions governing relations between the male and female members and the younger and older generations of their host communities. They had to behave as children to their 'fathers' and 'mothers', and as brothers to their 'siblings'. Their success depended on maintaining pre-existing gender and generational patterns.

As the exercise got to the recruitment stage, Tongogara's account highlights how ZANLA still operated within pre-war parameters, which deemed warfare a male occupation. Thus, their initial recruitment exercise focused on men. However, as demands arose for women's services at the rear, they expanded their recruitment to include both sexes. The guerrillas' great need to secure female recruits required them to observe strict sexual codes to pacify the rural patriarchs. By doing so, they could gradually extort concessions from the elders to entrust ZANLA not only with their sons but their daughters too.

As young women joined the armed struggle they passed over to the patronage of a new set of patriarchs, the nationalist leaders. A promise by the guerrillas to defer to spirit medium-enforced sexual codes may have cultivated a relationship of trust with the rural power élites and served to allay their concerns regarding the chastity of their female wards who were leaving home to join the guerrilla army. But this is not to say that they stopped worrying about this issue.

Mass mobilisation

The rallying point for the nationalist campaign was land, land that had been appropriated by the white settlers. Indigenous men and women each needed land for different reasons.

---

[13] Ibid.

For men, the recovery of lost lands would once more increase their political and social influence in their communities. For women, their need for land arose 'from the concrete conditions of women's positioning within the gender division of labour'.[14] In that structure, women were responsible for feeding their families. Land was crucial in their ability to fulfil this role, and therefore the guerrillas' promise to deliver it went a long way in explaining ZANLA's general success in securing rural women's co-operation.

The obvious question that arises is how the people of north-eastern Zimbabwe saw their position with regard to land. David Lan noted that in Dande, the first area the guerrillas infiltrated, many people had settled there after being dispossessed of their lands in Chiweshe.[15] These newcomers obviously welcomed the prospect of recovering their lost lands, and the promise of such a development was also popular with the original Dande inhabitants who had to share their own land with the dispossessed communities.

This pattern obtained in many parts of the country, where land awards to white Rhodesians returning after World War II had displaced thousands of African families. In the Eastern Highlands, bitter struggles were going on with Chief Rekayi Tangwena who was resisting government orders to move his people off their land. Tangwena's people had simply been told that their land now belonged to settler farmers who were alleged to have bought it. From his position as a male leader, Tangwena argued to prove that he was worth the titles he held:

> If the Government is honest about its claim that the chiefs are the only African leaders, they should prove this to the world by leaving me on my father's land.[16]

Thus, as in Dande, such people wanted to learn what part they could play in the struggle to ensure the return of the lands lost to the colonial population. Once this common ground was articulated, the guerrillas could then spell out everybody's roles in the struggle.[17]

---

[14] Maxine Molyneux, 'Mobilization without Emancipation: Women's Interests, the State and Revolution in Nicaragua', in *Feminist Studies*, Vol. 11, No. 2, 1985, p. 233.

[15] Lan, *Guns and Rain*, p. 12.

[16] Julie Frederikse, *None but Ourselves: Masses vs. Media in the Making of Zimbabwe*, Zimbabwe Publishing House, Harare, 1982, p. 77.

[17] David Maxwell has documented a similar pattern in north-east Nyanga, where 'Manyika' immigrants evicted from 'white' lands introduced nationalism and later became the first allies of guerrillas. See D. Maxwell, *Christians and Chiefs in Zimbabwe, A Social History of the Hwesa People*, IAI, Edinburgh University Press, 1997. The same processes took place in north-western Zimbabwe on an even larger scale. See Jocelyn Alexander and Terence Ranger, 'Competition and Integration in the Religious History of North-Western Zimbabwe', *Journal of Religion in Africa*, (28.1.98). In all these cases, just as in the Dande and Mt Darwin, guerrillas mobilised the evictees by appeal to their nationalism and the long-term residents by appeal to their traditions.

Women's wartime duties: forward with the Cooking Stick!

For women, as 'parents', or more specifically as 'mothers', one of their main tasks was to ensure that 'their sons', the guerrillas, did not go out to fight on empty stomachs. Food was a prime requirement for the fighters, whose own stocks from the rear bases barely covered the journey across the border. Once the guerrillas were inside their operational areas, the rural women were expected to extend their motherly care to these fighters living in the bush.

The slogan of the day became: 'Forward with the cooking stick!' This was accompanied by similar slogans glorifying the role of mothers. Clearly, such slogans bestowed a new importance on women's roles. Women were being urged to take their social duties seriously and to understand that without their co-operation as cooks and mothers, there would be no nationalist fighters and, by extension, there would be no nation. Without the restoration of the nation, the deprivation arising from national subjugation (such as land alienation) would continue.

Initially, the guerrillas approached men with their requests for food. Then the men would instruct their wives to cook it. Often, young girls escorted by men would carry the food to the guerrillas' hiding places in the bushes or in the mountains. Later, as the fighters were spending more and more time in these new operational zones, the young girls would take warm bath water to the guerrillas, as well as pick up their clothes for laundry.[18]

Men's war-time duties: roadwork and 'hunting' activities

In sabotage operations, men's labour was crucial. If the guerrillas needed trenches dug across the roads to stop soldiers from using them, they would call upon the men. They would also use male labour to dig pits to bury landmines on these roads to make them inaccessible to Rhodesian forces and other government agents. Such strategies were meant to paralyse the colonial administration in the long run.

Apart from these duties, civilian men conducted 'hunting' operations into nearby white farms. Once the raiders had made it out of the settler farms, young women could join them to drive the looted cattle quickly to the relative safety of the villages. To the guerrillas, cattle raiding was mainly a nationalist strategy to undermine the settler economy, but to the rural

---

[18] Interview with Mildred Dengu, Sunningdale, Harare, 14 March 1992; interview with Mrs Zurukwa, Dotito, Mt Darwin, 14 May 1992.

population it was much more – it eased the burden of feeding the guerrillas. The rural people also saw it as compensation for the loss of their own animals at the hands of the Rhodesian authorities.

Rhodesian confiscation of indigenous cattle also had wider social implications. In Shona society, the possession of cattle had been important in the social construction of manhood. Cattle were also important in many traditional rituals. Summarising the issues, one press report noted:

> [The] seizure of tribal cattle for sale to pay collective fines... has gone off quietly, though this punishment touched the African pride on a raw spot... African troops taking part in rounding up the cattle... refused to slaughter any cattle for food. They excused themselves on the ground that ancestral spirits sometimes inhabit the family livestock and they might be killing some-body's grandfather.[19]

The African soldiers were in fact not merely manufacturing excuses. Many genuinely feared upsetting the ancestors. Unlike their white counterparts, African members of the security forces found themselves caught between two forces: the indigenous ancestral world whose influence they could not entirely discount,[20] and their colonial paymaster who de-manded that they denigrate those cultural power bases in exchange for a living wage. The atmosphere was definitely not improved by the authorities' double-edged methods. In competition with the guerrillas for civilian support, they claimed to enjoy the support of the ancestors' representatives, the spirit mediums.[21]

Returning to the matter of cattle-raiding, it gave civilian men the opportunity to avenge the wrongs done to their ancestors and to re-instate their own threatened manhood, but it was also associated with immense risk. Farm guards were armed with guns. Soldiers con-tinually made invasions into the villages looking for illegally acquired meat and other evi-dence such as cattle bones. Soldiers would elicit information from young children, for example, by asking them what they had for supper the previous night. The common an-swer was: 'Sadza [thickened maize meal porridge] with cabbages'. In fact 'cabbages' was the rural people's coded word for the beef derived from cattle stolen from white-owned farms. While serving as a code to mislead the soldiers, the use of the term 'cabbages' also alluded to its abundant supply!

---

19   National Archives of Zimbabwe (NAZ), IDAF Historical Manuscripts, File MS 308/40/3, 'Rhodesian Air Strike Draws Blank', in the Daily Telegraph, 1 March 1973.
20   Lan, Guns and Rain, p.196.
21   Ibid., p. 196; also see Frederikse, p. 130; Terence Ranger, 'The Death of Chaminuka: Spirit Mediums, National-ism and Guerrilla War in Zimbabwe', African Affairs, July 1982, pp. 81, 324; 'Tradition and Travesty: Chiefs and the Administration in Makoni District, Zimbabwe, 1960-1980', in J.D.Y. Peel and T.O. Ranger (eds), Past and Present in Zimbabwe, Manchester University Press, Manchester, 1983.

The ability to mount a successful raiding operation could be celebrated as a demonstration of manhood, though the war-time hunters' welcome on their return was devoid of the pomp that had traditionally surrounded the home-coming of hunting parties in the past. With Rhodesian soldiers often in hot pursuit of returning raiders, their women could not ululate, as they would have done in welcoming the hunters of pre-colonial times.[22]

The propaganda and the realities

By 1973, the eastern half of ZANLA's Tete Province, that is the areas of Centenary, Guruve, Mt Darwin, Bindura, Shamva, Chiweshe and Nyanga in north-eastern Zimbabwe, had become the arena for a severe contest between ZANLA guerrillas and Rhodesian security forces. Both male and female youths were being recruited into ZANLA in increasing numbers. As no significant political work had preceded this exercise, not many people volunteered. In the early 1970s ZANLA continued to press-gang recruits as it did in the 1960s in Zambia. Recruits therefore had no option to decide whether or not to join the guerrillas.[23]

Adopting a universal ploy to get the international community onto their side while alienating the indigenous people from their adversaries, the Rhodesian propaganda accounts exploited incidents of forced recruitment. They featured stories of abuse of women and children by ZANLA guerrillas. One report, for example recounted:

> 3 pregnant women died when force-marched with other captives out into the gruelling terrain of the Zambezi... More than a 100 African women and children have been used by terrorists during attacks as human shields against Security forces... Girls are impressed to become porters, and above all, 'bed-fodder' for the self-styled liberators.[24]

Direct testimonies, often coerced out of people, were also cited to give credence to these claims. In April 1974, for example, one newspaper featured the story of an African woman, Esirina, who was reportedly captured from north-eastern Rhodesia by FRELIMO men in September 1972, before being driven into Mozambique. As the account ran, Esirina's captors had also taken many other villagers to help them drive stolen cattle and carry looted food. The captives were allegedly kept in the bush for months, during which time ten girls were said to have been made 'communal wives', one would suppose 'in communist style'. Bombings by the Portuguese allegedly disrupted the party, causing the guerrillas to flee temporarily. Somehow, Esirina had managed to escape back home with her chil-

---

[22] These paragraphs are based on interviews with civilians in the field.
[23] See David Martin and Phyllis Johnson, *The Struggle for Zimbabwe: The Chimurenga War*, Zimbabwe Publishing House, Harare, 1981, p. 23.
[24] NAZ, IDAF File MS 308/40/3, *Rhodesia Herald*, 26 November 1973.

dren. The District Commissioner was reportedly arranging for her to get a grant from the Terrorist Victims Relief Fund to compensate her for the eye she had lost during the Portuguese bombing raid.[25]

Mass views on military abuses

Most civilian accounts and the testimonies of those who were recruited in the early 1970s, however, are at variance with the authorities' view. Thus Mildred Dengu from the Bindura area reflected on a Rhodesian military operation conducted against her village, as punishment to parents for allowing their children to join and work with ZANLA:

> Our village, the whole Dengu village was burnt down to the ground. Some people had managed to get some clothing items out before their huts were set alight. The soldiers took the clothes and threw them back into the fire to burn. You just remained with what you were putting on and nothing else.... They burnt down the whole village, from where it starts, near the school right up to where it ends. They only left the teachers' houses and the classrooms.... They even shot cattle.[26]

Many of Staunton's interviewees reiterate testimonies of Rhodesian brutalities. Sosana Marange from Mutumba in the Mt Darwin District, for example, spoke of how, in 1974, Rhodesian soldiers burnt down their whole village as jet planes fired at defenceless civilians from above. She told how she and the other survivors of this onslaught experienced one of the most brutally conducted forced resettlements of the early war period. To the civilians this, rather than the guerrillas' recruitment exercises, seemed like a slave-capturing operation:

> The DC drove in front and the trucks followed. We cried. Even the dogs that were around tried to follow us, barking and whining.... Some of them were even run over by the lorries. When we reached the main road we shouted out to friends and relatives that we were going to be thrown away. Everyone cried.[27]

Civilians began to feel the impact of the military involvement in the region. Although many people in these areas had not yet seen guerrillas, the guerrillas' activities elsewhere had started to bring a lot of hardship even to these yet unvisited communities. The Rhodesian soldiers' reprisals were indiscriminate. Panicking that the security situation in this region was getting out of control, government agents took harsh measures against the civilian

---

[25] NAZ, IDAF File MS 308/40/4, *Sunday Mail*, 21 April 1974.
[26] Interview with Mildred Dengu, Sunningdale, Harare, 14 March 1992.
[27] Staunton, *Mothers of the Revolution*, p.17.

population, for they knew that guerrilla war relied heavily for its success on local communities.

Small is beautiful: reminiscences of ZANLA's infancy

ZANLA fighters, whose total figure was said to range between one thousand and two thousand by 1974, and who already included a women's detachment,[28] were struggling to carve out a political and military base for themselves inside enemy-controlled Rhodesia. At this point, discipline in contacts with civilians and with recruits on the journey to the rear camps was still largely observed. On-the-spot punitive action against offenders kept guerrilla breaches of their operational regulations low. Even the Rhodesian media acknowledged this, though grudgingly:

> Terrorists in the TTLS of north-eastern Zimbabwe are said to have made crude attempts to establish courts ...unconfirmed reports say that some better-disciplined terrorist groups have brought some of their own members before these kangaroo courts for offenses like interfering with tribeswomen.[29]

Civilian accounts reveal no major complaints about the guerrillas at this point. Recruits too spoke well of them. Reflecting on their journey to the rear, Rwirai Nyika (the late Mrs Kahondo) said none of their male recruiters had bothered them at all. She went on to explain:

> Of course once we were at the rear some young men may come up with proposals, but now it was up to you to decide whether you liked him or not.[30]

Although problems were beginning to crop up in the camps pertaining to some senior men's relations with female recruits, such misbehaviour seems to have been restricted to the rear. The limited numbers of fighters in the liberation army at that time also made their control easier.

Law enforcement: fuel for guerrilla propaganda

In regard to the conduct of Rhodesian forces and their agents towards civilians there is overwhelming evidence of their callous 'reprisals' in both north-eastern Zimbabwe and in

---

28 ZANU (PF) Archives, File: Defence Secretariat, Doc.: Manuscript of Interview with Josiah Tongogara, (Secretary For Defence) by Edson Zvogbo (ZANU Information and Publicity Secretary), 16 October. 1978.

29 NAZ File MS 308/40/6, Rhodesia Herald, 27 July 1974.

30 Interview with Mrs Kahondo (Cde Rwiria Nyika – now late), Sunningdale, Harare, 11 March 1992.

the adjacent Tete Province of Mozambique where FRELIMO was operating.[31] Hoping to bully civilians onto their side, the authorities engaged in random shootings, the burning down of whole villages,[32] the killing and confiscation of cattle as punishment for supporting guerrillas, the indiscriminate arrest and torture of civilians. The soldiers themselves were guilty of the offences they charged the 'terrorists' with, that is the violation and conversion into 'bed fodder' of women under interrogation for supporting guerrillas.[33] The self-styled protectors exploited the privileges that went with that duty. It was often pointless to report these abuses as they would never be investigated and, even if there was evidence, the perpetrators' position enabled them to either explain it away or do nothing about it.

Zimbabwean novelists, relying on real life experiences, have graphically reconstructed the situation that obtained in the war zones. One such work is that of Stanley Nyamfukudza, whose vivid account captured the arrival of the war and the way in which those who had guns gradually became the law of the land. Around their bases, which were often near rural service centres, the Rhodesian forces' presence created an atmosphere of terror: 'they frightened away all but the most determined prostitutes'. Nyamfukudza related an incident that may well have actually happened:

> some months back... three black soldiers had been hacked to death by a group of furious villagers when they forced their way into the girls' quarters not far from the business centre. The rest of the soldiers' company had invaded the village, beating, raping and terrorizing in revenge, but it was too close to the mission school and traffic passing through the township for word of it not to get out. Severe punishment against all responsible who had acted without the knowledge of their superiors was promised, and that was the last anyone heard of the matter.[34]

Soldiers could certainly go on a rampage whenever they felt like it, accountable only to themselves. As for their destruction of property and the random killings as they 'pursued terrorists', all was 'legal' under the Law and Order Maintenance Act. But sometimes the civilian casualty figures were so large that the news could not be suppressed. In such cases, the victims would be portrayed as having been caught in the crossfire while running with the terrorists. These activities obviously did not endear the security forces to the masses, but they did provide the guerrillas with the material they needed for their own propaganda campaign.

---

[31] Martin and Johnson, *The Struggle for Zimbabwe*, pp. 4-6.
[32] Interview with Mildred Dengu, Sunningdale, Harare, 14 March 1992; see also Staunton, *Mothers of the Revolution*, p. 17.
[33] NAZ, IDAF File MS 308/40/3, *Rhodesia Herald*, 26 November 1973.
[34] Stanley Nyamfukudza, *The Non-Believer's Journey*, Heinemann, London, 1980, p. 38.

Benevolent gestures: the introduction of 'Protected Villages'

Another development arising from the contest between the security forces and the guerrillas was the creation of 'protected villages' (PVs), by the Rhodesian authorities. According to their propaganda accounts, this was an extension of civilian protection through the creation of 'safe havens' that the terrorists could, in theory, not touch. These protected villages allegedly offered sanctuary from harassment by terrorists. In reality, they were punishment enclosures, and they were mainly designed to cut off guerrillas from their civilian support base. Here the camp guards had an upper hand in the appropriation of the privileges that went with providing protection, as is often the case in times of military and political instability. As PV inmates generally had nothing much of their own after losing most of their belongings in the often brutal resettlement exercises, payments to the guards for the favour of 'protection' often took the form of sexual and domestic services by the womenfolk of the 'protected' populations. As women were the ones traditionally charged with the duty to provide the family with food, they sometimes had to submit to improper proposals by the guards to gain access to, for example, water, or to be allowed to go to their fields or to secure food items from the stores.

As they controlled access to resources, the PV guards enjoyed similar influence among the women in the 'protected' communities as that exercised by the guerrillas who controlled food stocks and determined promotion opportunities in the ZANLA camps. The ZANLA camps will be looked at in greater detail in Chapter 3 and the PVs in Chapter 5.

Recruitment into ZANLA

The subject of recruitment in ZANLA has already been dealt with in Josiah Tungamirai's work which examines the process by which ZANLA built its war machinery.[35] Although he did not differentiate between men and women's experience in this exercise, his discussion is useful in summarising the conditions that favoured the recruitment drive. The same circumstances favouring mass mobilisation also helped ZANLA in the bid to get young people into armed struggle.

Apart from questions of land hunger in the country, Tungamirai also identified other reasons that alienated the indigenous people from the government of the day. These were: poor health provisions and unemployment for Africans, the dire shortage of accommoda-

---

[35] J. Tungamirai, 'Recruitment to ZANLA: Building up a War Machine', in Ngwabi Bhebe and Terence Ranger (eds), *Soldiers in Zimbabwe's Liberation War*, James Currey, London, 1995.

tion in the urban areas, as well as the disruptions of the war, which hit health and educational facilities. The disruption of education left many young people unoccupied, giving them no other option but to find their way out of the country to join the liberation movement.[36]

The methods of recruiting young men and women may have been similar and there may have been many common elements in the factors that drove both sexes into neighbouring countries. These factors, however, translated themselves into different experiences for young men and women – other variants being age, the economic backgrounds of the recruits as well as their level of formal education.

The way women enunciated their stance after recruitment had a lot to do with the background from which they had been taken. If they were young girls, they rarely held any political opinions prior to recruitment and may have ventured out to the war out of curiosity. What older women looked for in the war was largely shaped by the nature of the hardships they had already faced in life, depending on their specific location in their respective societies. Illiterate women, for example, women who came from peasant backgrounds were more likely to have a firmer grasp of the injustices of colonial land policies in comparison to their relatively educated colleagues whose major grievances may have been lack of education and job opportunities. Most of the evidence for this section is derived from interviews carried out with the affected women.

Coercive methods

In his account, Josiah Tungamirai, himself a former ZANLA commander, acknowledged that recruitment in the earlier period was often far from voluntary. Schoolchildren were press-ganged by ZANLA in controversial circumstances. One of the most publicised of such events occurred at St Albert's Mission on 5 July in 1973, when school boys and girls were taken across the Mavuradonha Mountains into Mozambique.[37] For the Rhodesians, this was material their propagandists feasted upon, to slander the whole nationalist movement. A 1973 press report shows how such actions often got ZANLA more than it had bargained for:

> A century after David Livingstone witnessed with horror the depredations of the slave trade in the area, ...there is now a new attempt...to impose a traffic in 'black ivory' – human beings...

---

[36] Ibid., pp.37-40.
[37] Janice McLaughlin, M.M., 'The Catholic Church and the War of Liberation', Ph.D. Thesis, Department of Religious Studies, University of Zimbabwe, 1991, pp. 198 - 211.

It is the young boys and girls who are most eagerly sought after...the new raiders wear terrorist uniform and worship the Little Red Book of Chairman Mao.[38]

While such reports manipulated the fear of communism in the West, no evidence suggests that guerrilla recruiters actually had any Maoist literature on them; and it is inaccurate to portray them as having acted purely for personal gain like the slave raiders. Their position on recruitment was often not negotiable because they felt that everyone had a duty to fight. What they did not have was the time to explain to the young men and women why it was essential to make such sacrifices. The late Rwirai Nyika (Mrs Kahondo) spoke of how in 1973 she was taken from school at Chironga Mission in Mt Darwin, where she had been doing her seventh grade. Responding to a question asking why she had decided to join the armed struggle, she explained:

There was no question of choice then. They said we were going with them. So we had to leave school.[39]

Parental attitudes to recruitment

Some young women joined as part of the contribution their fathers had to make to the nationalist cause when asked to do so by the guerrillas:

My father said no but they said they wanted two girls and one boy... They said whether or not we liked it they were taking us because there was lots of work which needed to be done there.[40]

Parents are never keen to have their children join a war, but it was even more difficult for them to contemplate their daughters signing up. If ZANLA had only asked for three children from the old man, without also specifying that it wanted girls, he would undoubtedly have only considered his sons. A father, who would not send his daughter to school because he feared that she would run off with men (who would not pay him *lobola*), would definitely feel no better at the thought of surrendering his daughter to live with armed strangers in unknown lands.

The recruits' educational background

Unlike her brothers, Mrs Mavende, quoted above, had never been to school. Her father,

---

[38] NAZ File IDAF File MS 308/40/3, *Rhodesia Herald*, 26 November 1973.
[39] Interview with Mrs Kahondo, Sunningdale, Harare, 11 March 1992.
[40] Interview with Mrs Mavende, Dotito, Mt Darwin, 13 May 1992.

like many others in his area, thought that schooling for girls fostered prostitution. In spite of this gender-based exclusion from formal education (or perhaps because of it), when she joined ZANLA she did not see the nature of her commitment as being any different from that of her brothers.

Most of the women interviewed for this study, who joined the war in its early phase from the Mt Darwin area, said they had never been to school. Mai Matuwini, who was taken from Dotito in 1973, explained:

> My father had many cattle. Our standard of living was fairly decent. The only problem regarded our education. Our elders in those days were slightly discriminatory. They thought that if girls went to school they would become prostitutes. They concentrated on boys instead. As for us girls, we were sent to herd cattle... We never saw the door of the classroom.[41]

However, her five brothers did go to school. One even went up to standard six, that is eight years of schooling. This was the minimum requirement before one could be considered for training for the few jobs open to Africans in those days, such as teaching, nursing and police work. Mai Matuwini said that her other brothers' education was only interrupted by the war.

Maggie Chirata, born in 1954 and recruited from Mukosa in the same area, recounted a similar story:

> I never went to school. Mukosa was very backward. They used to think that if girls went to school they would become prostitutes. It is only now that girls are going to school in Mukosa. All women of my age in my home area will tell you the same thing.[42]

In truth, most of her comrades who were taken from Mt Darwin by the guerrillas gave similar explanations for failing to go to school: the education of girls had never been a priority with their parents. This point was reiterated again and again.

The politics of deprivation

If these young women had any political ideology at all when they joined the struggle, their motive was to defeat the enemy and liberate the country. The 'enemy', to most of them, was simply the white man who had imposed foreign rule on their country. They were not thinking of a war against male domination, for to most, that was God-given.

---

[41]   Interview with Mai Matuwini, Dotito, Mt Darwin, 14 May 1992.
[42]   Interview with Maggie Chirata, Bindura, 3 November 1994.

When asked what she understood the war to have been about, an illiterate woman recruited as a young girl during that period said that she had no understanding of any form of oppression prior to her recruitment. Then she went on to explain what she had learnt from the guerrillas after joining them:

> We were told that it was not right that the government forced us to build contours in our fields and to pay taxes on dogs. They said we should be left to manage our own affairs.[43]

She saw these issues as ones concerning both men and women, thereby making a separate struggle for women irrelevant.

Apart from the hardships arising out of the government's attempts to implement land alienation policies, and the infamous 1951 Land Husbandry Act,[44] most of the first recruits from the Mt Darwin area also made references to general national grievances such as limited educational and health facilities and the shortage of jobs for Africans. Such nationalist political views were apparently non-gendered in the way they were articulated, but their impact was translated variously according to who received them.

The fate of *chimbwidos*

From 1972, ZANLA's recruitment drive gained momentum. Young women served ZANLA as *chimbwidos* (the fighters' female, civilian aides) and before long the security forces got to know of their activities. In such cases, many young women were forced to leave with the guerrillas and become ZANLA fighters.

One woman who originally came from Rushinga, but has since settled with her husband in Dotito, described her own experience at the hands of the Rhodesian soldiers.[45] As a teenager, she and other girls had got into trouble in 1974 for taking food and water to the guerrillas. They were taken to Rushinga Camp for interrogation and given the beating of their lives. Her half-brother was also beaten so severely that he permanently lost his hearing. Charges against him arose directly from his position as the village headman, for he was held responsible for authorising support to ZANLA.

After being detained and tortured by soldiers at Rushinga Camp for four days, the young woman said she and two other girls and three boys decided they had suffered enough. When they were released they joined the armed struggle.[46]

---

[43]   Interview with Mrs Mavende, Dotito, Mt Darwin, 13 May 1992.
[44]   Grievances arising out of land alienation have been treated in detail by Terence Ranger and David Lan.
[45]   Interview with Mrs Zurukwa (Mai Justin), Dotito, Mt Darwin, 14 May 1992.
[46]   Ibid.

Sexual violations

Both men and women could be subjected to various forms of punishment other than beatings. Women, however, lived with the additional threat of sexual harassment from their tormentors. The women and girls often paid with their bodies for 'protection' in the PVs.

PVs were not the only places where women could be bothered by sexual predators from among the security forces. Those whose homes remained outside the PVs were called upon to do domestic chores for the soldiers and provide them with feminine comforts when the soldiers retired to their bases with prisoners for interrogation 'rituals'. Such experiences often damaged relations within the women's families and communities because they could not openly discuss these particular war-time demands.

Perhaps for that reason, information about personal relations with the soldiers was not forthcoming in the testimonies gathered for this study.[47] Nevertheless, it is not inaccurate to say that sexual harassment by the soldiers was one of the reasons young women left for the liberation struggle, with the aim of returning to avenge the wrongs done to them. Young men also took the sexual violation of their womenfolk as a personal affront to their manhood; this often drove them to get military training and guns so they could come back and reinstate their power.

The horror of 'Reprisal' Operations

Many young people witnessed Rhodesian callousness against their communities. Mildred Dengu, who had been a *chimbwido* and was recruited from the Bindura area, watched her whole village going up in flames as soldiers set out one morning to punish them for assisting ZANLA fighters. The thought of living in the PV with the same soldiers afterwards sickened her.[48] The young girl actually begged the guerrillas to take her with them.

In many instances, young people dreamt of a glorious life in the guerrillas' rear base camps. Mildred Dengu had heard from ZANLA fighters that life in Mozambique was very comfortable and exciting, since that country had just gained its independence from Portu-

[47] These can be found in novels on the war, where they can pass as fiction. See C. M. Matsikiti, *Makara Asionani*, Longman, Harare, 1985; L.P. Mlambo, 'Maokizirari', in Zimbabwe Literature Bureau (compiler), *Hondo YeChimurenga: Nyaya Dzehondo*, Mambo Press, Gweru, 1984, pp. 177-84. The author knew some girls who were raped by soldiers in her home area in present-day Masvingo Province, but the war only came to that area in 1977. The women are married now and would be very disturbed if they learnt that someone still remembered what had happened to them.

[48] Interview with Mildred Dengu, Sunningdale, Harare, 14 March 1992.

guese rule in 1975. On her arrival at a ZANLA rear base in Mozambique that year, she was shocked to find a pole stretching across the entrance where she had expected to see a grand-looking metal gate![49]

The pressures of war and the search for options

With the war disrupting and closing down schools, young people joined their village folk as *mujibhas* and *chimbwidos*, subjecting themselves to all the dangers these positions entailed. Those with relatives in town joined the urban-bound refugee trek, where young women risked succumbing to prostitution to earn a living. Eventually, many such young people would leave for the neighbouring countries, with most hoping to use the liberation movements as a stepping stone to educational opportunities. Sifikile Masotcha was one of the few relatively educated women who joined the war in the early seventies. She and her friend had dropped out of their third year of secondary schooling due to lack of school fees. They left from Salisbury and went to Zambia through Botswana because they had heard about study opportunities in Zambia. Such women subsequently demanded educational opportunities similar to those which some male fighters enjoyed abroad. Later she worked in ZANU's Department of Education as a teacher at Matenje Base.[50]

Schools and pre-war political awareness

Some of the young people joining the liberation movements had been politicised when the authorities jailed their parents, most often the bread-winner. Margaret Dongo, whose family had lived in Salisbury, recalled her father being detained in 1967.[51] She said it was painful to watch her mother struggling alone to make ends meet by selling vegetables. When Dongo was studying at Triashill School she had met the Tangwena children whose families were being expelled from Kaerezi in the Eastern Highlands. She recalled that 'the language that they were speaking was all political'.[52] Later when she was in form two at Gazaland Secondary School in Chipinge, she left with two other girls from the school and crossed the Zimbabwe-Mozambique border to join ZANLA.

As these accounts show, schools were major politicisation arenas in those days. Teedzai Mabhindauko from Chipinge said her teacher had been instrumental in her decision to

---

[49] Ibid.
[50] Interview with Sifikile Masotcha, Kambuzuma, Harare, 20 April 1992.
[51] Interview with Margaret Dongo, Parliament Building, Harare, 10 March 1992.
[52] Margaret Dongo interview in *Social Change and Development*, Vol. 38-39, January 1996.

join the war.[53] He used to explain the political situation to them and he would tune to Radio Mozambique during classes to enable them to listen to ZANU's political broadcasts. That whole class eventually crossed over to Mozambique. She described the fervent feelings invoked by the broadcasts: 'You would feel, let me go and get trained, get my gun too and return home to fight.' She even forgot her shoes in the school playground as she sneaked away with a friend.

Precious Takawira was living with her aunt who was a nurse at the hospital at Old Mutare Mission near the present-day city of Mutare on the eastern border with Mozambique. They were learning every day that boarders from the mission's school (where Precious was in form one as a day pupil), were leaving in large numbers. Finally her aunt's domestic helper said they should go too. Precious said she asked her: 'Go and do what?' She was told: 'To go and liberate the country'.[54] She said she was persuaded and the two of them left in 1975.

Flights from failed marriages and forced relationships

For many young women who learnt about the war, participating in it was sometimes a way to put their lives together after some personal misfortune. Farai Dhlamini, born in 1956, said she had heard of the war back in 1969 from her friend Theresa, who came from Mt Darwin. Theresa, who was living with an uncle in Farai's home area in Chipinge, had told her that some men were secretly taking people out to Zambia and East Africa. Farai said that the prevailing attitude then was: 'It's their war, those who started it. Let them sort out their mess alone.'[55]

Later, after Theresa had apparently returned to Mt Darwin, Farai tried to find out her whereabouts from Theresa's sister, but the younger girl would just look very sad without giving satisfactory explanations.[56] After persistent enquiry, Farai learnt that Theresa had gone to the war.

Later, after Farai had had a baby and failed to marry, she left her job as a general worker at Chisumbanje Irrigation Scheme and went to the war too. By 1975 when she left, the guerrillas were actively recruiting in her area; many other young people were leaving with the comrades who had started teaching them politics. Her brother and two cousins, a boy

53   Interview with Teedzai Mabhindauko, Sunningdale, Harare, 12 March 1992.
54   Interview with Precious Takawira, Sunningdale, Harare, 14 March 1992.
55   Interview with Farai Dhlamini, Sunningdale, Harare, 11 March 1992.
56   Ibid.

and girl, left too, just ahead of Farai. As her mother was taking care of her baby, Farai managed to sneak away quietly, in spite of her uncle's efforts to prevent her from leaving.[57]

Maggie Chirata from Mukosa in Mt Darwin had been married briefly to a teacher, but he had abandoned her following the sudden death of their baby in inexplicable circumstances.[58] When the comrades came to their area, she worked as a *chimbwido* and later she left with them. Clearly, she viewed joining the war as a way of patching up the pieces of her life. Never having been to school at all, she was happy to be doing something at last.[59]

Irene Mahamba in *Woman in Struggle*, provides other crucial reasons why young women may have decided to leave their homes and follow the comrades to their rear base camps. The war sometimes provided young women with an opportunity to escape from difficult family circumstances. Young women or girls may have been running away from undesirable husbands or from furious parents (after getting pregnant); young men also sometimes used the war to escape from the responsibilities of fatherhood, after making a girl pregnant. Some girls followed their men to the war, arriving in the training camps pregnant.

Youthful adventures

As news of the war became common knowledge, many young people, including children, left home in search of adventure. Mary Mucheka, who later regretted her decision to go, ascribed her departure and that of others, to 'a bad wind' or 'a bad spirit'.[60] When it blew in her direction, she went with it in curiosity, 'just to go and see what it was all about'.[61] She was fourteen years old when she ran away from home. She now sees the war as an unfortunate experience in which young people were duped or coaxed to participate.[62]

Muchaneta Mabhunu was only in grade three when her sister left to join up. She heard the comrades preaching about the need to eradicate oppression and thought they might want her too.[63] Her mother, who had just had twins and needed her help with the new babies, ran after her to stop her from leaving, but she could not keep up with the young girl's pace. She was fortunate in being able to join up with a group of guerrillas in the area

57 Ibid.
58 Interview with Maggie Chirata, Bindura, 3 November 1994.
59 Ibid.
60 Interview with Mary Mucheka, Sunningdale, Harare, 11 March 1992.
61 Ibid.
62 Ibid.
63 Interview with Muchaneta Mabhunu, Sunningdale, Harare, 12 March 1992.

who took her with them to Mozambique. Muchaneta arrived there in late 1976, soon after Nyadzonya had been bombed.[64]

Conclusion

The above evidence is mainly derived from the period 1972 to the ZIPA era in 1976. However, the women who joined in the last three years of the war, 1977 to 1979, also gave the same reasons for joining. One of the main differences was that by the latter part of the war, coercive recruitment had been stopped and the camps had become so full that the leaders started telling people to remain at home and contribute from there. Nevertheless, the young people continued to leave for the armed struggle right up to the end, because no one had anticipated a cease-fire in December 1979. Another difference from the mid-1970s was that as the war progressed, relatively educated people began joining up, in contrast to the earlier period where illiteracy rates had been high. Towards the end, however, educational levels began falling again as the recruits became younger and younger.

The situation that developed in the later phase of the war was unlike that in the early 1970s, when the guerrillas entered north-eastern Zimbabwe. In the early period, the guerrillas had not yet created civilian support committees and their access to local services had to be directed to the local leadership, that is to men. Everything else would flow from there, with the various tasks that needed to be done being delegated to the relevant functionaries within the communities and within individual households. To a large extent, the pre-war domestic power relations and patterns of labour division were still maintained.

Right from the beginning, gender, among other factors, was a major reference point in spelling out civilian roles in the nationalist war. The resulting process did not deviate from pre-existing divisions of labour. If anything, the deliberate effort to spell out or clarify what women's obligations were to the nationalist struggle (as opposed to men's) actually removed the possibilities for any overlap. The old divisions were preserved and reinforced.

The patriarchal notion of men as protectors and women as the protected was effectively exploited too in shaping gender roles and experiences in the unfolding guerrilla war, and these social arrangements were generally acceptable to both men and women. Images from young women's accounts of men escorting them when they carried food to the guerrillas' hiding places amply demonstrate this relationship.

---

[64] Ibid.

As for the women's relations with the security forces, the creation and reinforcement of similar notions was one of the main themes running through propaganda accounts. Women were allegedly being raided and violated by ZANLA, and the district commissioners made public shows of their concern by making paternalistic gestures to people like Esirina, whose case was cited earlier.

ZANLA used male labour in road sabotage operations during the nights and the Rhodesians used them to restore roads to usability during the day. This use of male labour reflects a strong adherence to previous patterns of labour division where men did the work requiring strength. In pre-colonial times, men had chopped down trees and dug up the tree roots to clear land for cultivation. In colonial times, men provided the labour for road construction works.

There is little evidence to suggest that any attempts were made to tackle gender-determined roles. What stood out as a new development was that women were recruited to join the guerrilla forces, bringing them into the traditionally male field of soldiering. This undeniably improved women's perception of their worth in society. In both civilian and guerrilla women's accounts, they do not subordinate their contribution to that of men.

Claims that women's mobilisation indicated that a process of re-evaluating women's importance was in progress[65] should be viewed against the fact that men's roles were being re-assessed too. Academics ought to note that, for both sexes, pre-war roles had to be updated to meet war-time demands. In the operational zones themselves, the guerrillas' proclamations regarding the importance of women's roles had the effect of distorting many people's vision of what was actually happening. When slogans were proclaimed: 'forward with the cooking stick', cooking was projected as a powerful role that would ensure the enemy's demise and consequently bring about nationalist victory. For some women, this raised hopes that future power relations would be altered to reflect women's previously undervalued contribution. In patriarchal circles, a different message was derived from this same slogan: women had to stick to their traditional roles as mothers who provided food and in so doing rejuvenated and sustained the nation.

While the Rhodesian authorities' punishments could in many respects be described as indiscriminate, the rationalisation for them was not entirely blind to the different roles different sexes performed in supporting the guerrillas. For example, a young girl and her

---

65   See Ruth Weiss, *The Women of Zimbabwe*, Kesho Publications, London, 1986 and A.K.H. Weinrich, *Women and Racial Discrimination in Rhodesia*, UNESCO, 1979.

friends were punished for cooking and carrying food to the guerrillas, while a male relation received his penance specifically for authorising such service as the village head.

ZANLA's recruitment initially specified that they wanted men. Later, they were explicitly asking that women should join. This was in response to the fact that certain military jobs were traditionally viewed as female functions.

Women more than anybody else in their communities had a better grasp of the worst impact of the regime's policies upon Africans. One's sex was a crucial factor in determining the specifics of how one's life was impacted upon by the general deprivation characterising African life in Rhodesia. Of course generational and class differences also mattered.

Gender was a major reference point when parents budgeted limited resources, as they calculated the potential returns likely to be gained from educating their children. Though not necessarily the main objective, the exclusion of girls from formal education, in turn, helped to keep the gender-based disparities unchallenged. With very little education in comparison to men, women were less likely to get formal employment or to move out of their immediate surroundings. Thus they had little chance of gaining insight into alternative societal organisation. Their isolation denied them the motivation to challenge the circumstances that sharpened their deprivation as Africans, in comparison to their men.

CHAPTER THREE

Women Who Joined Up: Experiences in ZANLA's Rear Base Camps

Introduction

The last chapter discussed the background of the recruits of the early 1970s in order to assess their capacity to constitute revolutionary material for ZANLA once they had joined it. This one will explore those women's experiences within the military organ. It will interrogate ZANU's ideology as it was mediated to the guerrillas within Mozambique and explore how far it mirrored the leadership's gender rhetoric. It will look at the structures of the party and examine the rear base camps to see what role women played in them. In assessing how women fitted into the organisational structure of the party and the army, this chapter will look at the ZANLA Women's Detachment and assess its role, particularly in the transportation of war material. It will also examine the Department of Women's Affairs that ZANU created towards the end of the war. Matters of sexuality and marriage will receive special attention, with the discussion focusing on problems afflicting attempts to revolutionise and standardise marriage for the cadres, as well as highlighting the incidence of women's sexual abuse in the camps.

The chapter focuses on ZANLA from the early 70s, the time when it gained access to bases in FRELIMO's liberated zones in Tete Province in colonial Mozambique, up to the time when the warring parties in the Rhodesian crisis agreed to a cease-fire in 1979. While ZANLA cadres conducting reconnaissance on Rhodesia had relied on FRELIMO's liberated zones for transit bases in Mozambique since 1970,[1] in 1975 ZANU moved its headquarters and its whole war machinery from Zambia to newly independent Mozambique following the collapse of Portuguese colonial rule.

For most of the period covered in this chapter, ZANU's Central Committee oversaw the conduct of the war while the ZANLA High Command directed it. However that structure collapsed temporarily in the mid-1970s. These were generally troubled years for the organisation, culminating in the death of the Party Chairman Herbert Chitepo who was assassinated in March 1975. Suspecting an internal plot, the Zambian government descended on the ZANU and ZANLA leaders whom they arrested and detained until September 1976. In the absence of the leadership, junior officers who had remained outside formed a military union with ZIPRA to continue the war under the name, Zimbabwe People's Army (ZIPA).[2] However, ZIPA was shortlived. Once the old leadership returned, they crushed the Marxist-oriented cadres accusing them of plotting rebellion, the so-called Vashandi Revolt of 1976-77[3]. ZIPA's potential will be assessed to see how substantially it differed from ZANLA, especially in relation to gender issues.

Prospects for an ideology of women's liberation and prospects for a revolutionary war

One way to measure ZANLA's attempts to formulate an ideology of liberation for women is to take stock of the literature compiled for general political ideological development. In general, excerpts from the Chinese Communist leader Mao Tse Tung's writings and those of the neo-Marxist Vladimir Lenin formed the major part of the Political Commissariat's collection of materials for ZANU's lectures. However, the Party did not use them as its points of reference regarding policy on women, until the Xai Xai conference, which occurred only a few months before the warring parties declared a cease-fire in December 1979. Although the *Zimbabwe News* had displayed pictures of 'liberated' women fighters and accompanied them with impressive politically correct captions, there was nothing else of substance. In fact, no reference at all was made to gender inequality in the Political Commissariat's whole collection of lecture material.

---

[1]   David Martin and Phyllis Johnson, *The Struggle for Zimbabwe: The Chimurenga War*, Zimbabwe Publishing House, Harare, 1981, p. 18.
[2]   For a detailed account on ZIPA see, David B. Moore, 'The Zimbabwean People's Army: Strategic Innovation or More of the Same?', in Ngwabi Bhebe and T.O. Ranger (eds) *Soldiers in Zimbabwe's Liberation War*, Vol. 1, James Currey, London with University of Zimbabwe Publications, Harare, 1995.
[3]   *Vashandi*: Shona word for 'workers'. Used in reference to ZIPA's Marxist orientation.

The substance of political education in the camps was quite different from the rhetoric fed to outsiders by ZANU's élitist Information and Publicity Department, the producers of *Zimbabwe News*. Educational factors help to explain why women fighters did not challenge ZANU's claims and demand that matters of female emancipation be taken up in political teaching in the camps. Of primary significance was the low education level of the early recruits who came to constitute ZANLA's principal revolutionary material, with the majority being totally illiterate. Dolphyne points out how this factor can never be over-emphasised in determining women's ability to confront gender-based discrimination:

> Only education can foster in women an analytical and critical mind that would make them question the religious, cultural and physiological bases of their supposed inferiority. Only education can give women knowledge that would expose the fallacies behind the cultural practices.[4]

Faced with limited challenge in this regard, ZANLA's ideological orientation remained within the confining limits of nationalism. The obsession with articulating a universal nationalist position within the organisation stifled debate on other political views. Any issues not immediately identifiable with the conventional struggle (as defined by the nationalist leadership) were viewed as divisive in the camps and were met with repression. When the few better educated fighters made attempts to raise rank-and-file issues, carrying their analyses beyond nationalist parochialism by addressing class differences, ZANU's leaders panicked and acted to convey a clear message to the rest of the fighters: anyone who took the concept of revolutionary war too seriously risked official ostracism and, consequently, their political demise.

It is imperative that the obstacles to a gender revolution be viewed in the wider context of ideological bankruptcy within the organisation, a vice most noticeable when considering the experience of the ZIPA period. It cannot be disputed that their era introduced thought-provoking debate on issues of social inequality amongst the fighters, especially following the establishment of Wampoa College in 1976 (later named Chitepo) to provide the fighters with an education in revolutionary ideology.[5] As rank-and-file issues arose, disparities along sex lines became apparent too to the more analytical cadres.

However, according to the women themselves, even ZIPA's term did not herald much change in the actual substance of women's lives. As for their duties and representation in the leadership structures, Teurai Ropa explained in an interview in 1988:

---

[4] Florence Abena Dolphyne, *The Emancipation of Women: an African Perspective*, Ghana Universities Press, Accra, 1991, p. 56.
[5] Moore, pp. 82-83.

Though women were not physically integrated in the structure of ZIPA, we (were) involved in ferrying war materials to the battle front where we also recruited more girls to join the struggle.[6]

Perhaps ZIPA shared the ZANLA leadership's illusion that all inequalities would fall away once the more apparent inequality resulting from colonial capitalism was removed. However, with an ideological programme in place, ZIPA's term distinguishes itself as a very hopeful stage in Zimbabwe's war – albeit a brief period.

After crushing ZIPA, the leadership did not revisit the issue of political ideology again until 1979, this time in response to widespread disciplinary problems at the front. The first meeting of the Party Ideology Development Committee met in Chimoio, Mozambique, on 12 March 1979.[7] Here Robert Mugabe conceded that there was very little ideological awareness, even amongst the leadership themselves.[8] He spoke of plans to reconsider opening Chitepo Ideological College to start giving cadres proper orientation to avoid problems in the future.

A research team was tasked to make preliminary investigations to help re-launch political programmes. The team recorded a general reluctance by the forces to participate in political discussions in the camps.[9] Reflecting the fears sown by the harsh treatment meted out to those who had participated in political programmes before, respondents voiced concerns like: 'deep political education will cause me to revolt'.[10] Intimidation by security personnel had almost paralysed ZANLA's operational system by compartmentalising its departments. The respondents deemed politics the exclusive concern of political commissars, just as logistical matters were the concern of those in the Logistics Department, they argued. They also said they had not yet heard from the Party (leaders) if they could resume political education since the 1976-77 Vashandi Revolt.[11] The results of the intimidatory measures of the re-organisation period were all too clear.

Another factor militating against a women-focused gender revolution was the number of women's representatives and their hierarchical or organisational location in ZANLA.

---

[6]   Joyce 'Teurai Ropa' Mujuru, 'Women in the Struggle', *Zimbabwe News*, Vol. 19. No. 12. December, 1988, p. 42.
[7]   Ibid. Doc: 'Report of the First Meeting of the Party Ideology Development Committee', President's Office, Chimoio, 12 March 1979.
[8]   Ibid.
[9]   ZANU (PF) Archives, File: Political Commissariat, Doc: 'Circular to the High Command and General Staff Members'. Although the document is undated, it is clear that it was compiled in 1979 because it speaks of the need to appropriately explain to people the real nature of the internal settlement that had seen Muzorewa coming to power. Muzorewa won elections in April and became Prime Minister in June 1979.
[10] Ibid.
[11] Ibid.

Mugabe explained at Xai Xai in 1979 that Sheba Tavarwisa, the Deputy Secretary for Education, was the only woman in the High Command (HC). The HC was ZANLA's highest level of command and it had 28 members. (See Appendix.) Tavarwisa also sat in the Central Committee (CC) from 1977, together with Teurai Ropa, the Secretary for Women's Affairs. The CC had 33 posts in all, including a vacant one for the Deputy Secretary for Women's Affairs. (See Appendix.) This post remained vacant up to the 1979 Women's Congress, the time when the Department of Women's Affairs was actually formally constituted. Prior to that congress, Teurai Ropa worked with the men, occasionally picking up a few women as temporary office-bearers in her department. It is important to view this against ZANLA's total female component.

Throughout the war the statistics provided by ZANLA's officials on the strength of their forces varied considerably. Thus the total number of all forces in 1973 was said to be between one thousand and two thousand.[12] The women's unit at that time, quoted in enemy sources, was about one hundred women.[13] By 1978 ZANLA claimed its total forces were 40 000, and one-fourth of that figure, that is 10 000, were said to be women.[14] By 1979, ZANLA claimed a female component of one-third of the total forces,[15] but the total force aggregate at that time is not clear. However, what is evident is that women were grossly under-represented as their number in decision-making organs did not correspond with their total number in ZANLA. It is essential to bear this in mind in seeking to understand the extent to which women were integrated into the liberation army.

Women's integration in the early 1970s

Once full-scale war developed in the early 70s, ZANLA soon grasped the fact that it needed the masses and it needed women. An assessment of the military commanders' perspectives in the earlier days of the war reveals the premises upon which ZANLA started recruiting women from within Zimbabwe in the 1970s. Speaking of the limited impact of the military attempts made prior to the 1970s, Tongogara related the problems the operations mounted from Zambia faced:

[12] ZANU (PF) Archives, File: Defence Secretariat, Doc: Manuscript of Interview with Josiah Magama Tongogara (Secretary for Defence), by Edson Zvobgo (ZANU Information and Publicity Secretary), 16 October 1978.

[13] National Archives of Zimbabwe (NAZ), File: IDAF, Guerrillas, MS 308/40/5, articles: 'Bases for War on Rhodesia Reported' and 'Women's Detachment of up to 100 is being Trained' in *Sunday Telegraph* , 2 March 1974.

[14] ZANU (PF) Archives, File: Defence Secretariat, Doc: Manuscript of Interview with Josiah Magama Tongogara (Secretary for Defence), 16 October 1978.

[15] This figure was provided by Naomi Nhiwatiwa in her report of the May 1979 ZANU Women's Congress. See Norma J. Kriger, *Zimbabwe's Guerrilla War: Peasant Voices*, Cambridge University Press, Cambridge, 1992, p. 191.

Political education had not gone deep into the masses and also... the geographical barrier – the Zambezi – made it very impossible for us to have a continuous flow of supply... particularly weapons, food and other things. The people would go and get engaged for a week and then exhaust all the ammunition... they are carrying on their backs and... when the battle continues you run away because you have no weapons.[16]

Thus strategies had to be revised, with lessons taken from FRELIMO. Among the new lessons ZANLA grasped was the fact that women could be useful as carriers of war materials to help solve the problem of supply shortages at the front. Thus by 1972 ZANLA had started recruiting women from inside Zimbabwe to meet that need. It is not a coincidence that this year also marked the beginning of more significant military operations into Rhodesia from the north-east. Of course, the use of FRELIMO bases in Mozambique helped a lot, but ZANLA explicitly acknowledged that women played a crucial role in making this new offensive a success:

when we started the struggle in the north-east we had to walk over 180 kilometres and no roads, no cars and all tons and tons of material we pushed into the country to start the war, were carried by women on their heads.[17]

As the organisation had in those days only a limited number of men, the recruitment of women to transport war materials enabled ZANLA to release those men for the traditionally more manly duties of engaging the enemy at the battlefront. The ZANLA leadership also intended to use women to help resolve its recruitment problems within Zimbabwe. Mayor Urimbo, a member of the High Command, explained to his colleagues in 1972 the use to which female recruits would be put:

A woman's work is to mobilise the masses, carrying war materials, carring [sic] for children, carrying specific weapons to the front. They are used for preparing food and feeding comrades.[18]

Later in 1988, Teurai Ropa also reflected on women's importance to the recruitment exercises in those early days:

I think the mobilizing factor was the word that there was a woman [my emphasis] moving armed and engaging in military operations in Mount Darwin... Men felt belittled by a woman joining the war – so they flocked in thousands because to them it was a challenge... parents' morale was also boosted.[19]

---

[16] Ibid.

[17] ZANU (PF) Archives, File: Defence Secretariat, Doc: Manuscript of Interview with Josiah Magama Tongogara, 16 October 1978.

[18] ZANU (PF) Archives, File: HC Minutes, Doc.: 'Meeting of High Command', 22 August 1972.

[19] Joyce 'Teurai Ropa' Mujuru, 'Women in the Struggle', in *Zimbabwe News*, Vol. 19, No. 12, December 1988, p. 43.

Yet even Ropa did not 'join in the war' at this stage primarily as a fighter. Women only started being deployed to field operations in 1978. Mt Darwin, where she was deployed at this early stage, includes the zone bordering Mozambique to which women would come to deliver arms to the men. As she was one of the first few lucky women to receive training on her arrival in 1974, [20] she was able to return fire when ambushed by the enemy.

Such isolated experiences, slightly spiced by ZANLA, did stimulate civilian support for the war, and guerrilla propaganda fired the imaginations of the later crop of recruits from the mid-70s, especially with its anecdotes of women wielding guns and breaking all the rules of the book. It is essential now to view the initial experiences of those who joined earlier, mostly from north-eastern Zimbabwe.

Early 1970s recruits: women of their times

Researchers often discover that their initial assumptions may fail to apply to cases encountered in the field. When this happens, the honourable thing to do is acknowledge the differences and avoid imposing subjective ideas. In the early stages of my research, I naively asked one female former combatant what they had been taught in the war about male and female equality. I remember the unimpressed, if not contemptuous, look on her face as she responded: 'What equality? You mean in sharing food or clothes?'[21] Clearly she did not see the relevance of my analysis and she spoke for a good number of her comrades. This incident served to remind me not to assume that every woman who went to join the liberation struggle wanted to confront gender-based discrimination.

Lacking the benefit of formal education, the female recruit of the early 1970s did not seek to confront gender-based differences, and she did not perceive her struggle as having any additional gender dimension. Most of the young women in the earlier phase of recruitment came from rural Mt Darwin, from peasant farming backgrounds. Most of those interviewed for this study said they had never been to school, explaining that the education of girls had never been a priority with their parents.

The earlier recruits had no objective to challenge male domination or the gender-based division of labour. With their background, most unquestioningly accepted the duties laid down for them as carriers, nursing aides and cooks. Zvobgo spoke of the early recruits as

---

[20]   Interview with Teurai Ropa (Joyce Mujuru), Bindura, 2 November 1994.
[21]   Interview with Mrs Nhanga, Dotito, Mt Darwin, 14 May 1992.

'custom bound'. And it would be wrong to assume that it was only male attitudes that helped to preserve and reinforce these 'customs'. Women were equally conservative. They operated within a framework in which they did not object to male patronage. Molly Chipadza, a former fighter, now employed in the civil service, clarified that point: 'No one then had got to a stage where one would question such things.'[22]

When Teurai Ropa joined the struggle in 1973, with nine years of schooling behind her, she was one of the few women from her area who had received some formal education. However, even this would not have made her views regarding the political scope of women's participation in the struggle much different from that of her colleagues. Although she was later appointed Secretary for Women's Affairs and sat in the Central Committee, her function there conformed to the role envisaged for women when ZANU drafted its constitution in 1964. Ropa's role was to ensure the smooth running of women's supportive duties to the war effort.

In their political perspective, the nationalists expressed equality in interesting terminology. One of their main arguments was that the colonialists oppressed and harassed both African men and women equally. Many women articulated their oppression from that perspective right up to the end of the war. A 1979 document emphasised that position:

> As we buried our sisters and brothers at Chimoio, Tembwe, Nyadzonya and other places, we cried. We cried because we saw more concretely the equality of human beings – men and women – being buried in common graves. Their bones lie huddled together now and forever. It is this pure unity and equality that sustains us and upon which a revolutionary Zimbabwe must be built.[23]

On the basis of equality or similar subjection to suffering, women felt it was fair not to seek special treatment. The men did not promise them that either. The women were not cushioned from the harshness of guerrilla war. They were not to lose sight of the fact that they were in a male world – a rough, and masculine world. In that sense, 'manly' or masculine characteristics were demanded of them if they were to survive in the armed struggle. Yet, in practice, this requirement was just meant to enable them to perform those functions socially defined as 'feminine'. In the circumstances, these were not soft or light duties. All the same, the women were happy to do whatever they could, to contribute to the liberation of their country. Circumstances often forced them to overdo things, however, some-

---

22   Interview with Molly Chipadza, Mt Darwin, 15 May 1992.
23   ZANU (PF) Archives, File: Department of Women's Affairs, Doc: 'ZANU Women's Affairs (League)', undated but presumed to be early 1979, as it mentions plans to host a seminar 'later in the year' in May 1979.

times to the detriment of their own health.[24] The force driving them was their burning desire to convince their male colleagues and society at large that they were 'man enough' to assume even 'more masculine' national duties, such as directly engaging the enemy at the front. What follows is a more detailed analysis of the functions the women performed in the earlier period.

Basic duty: feeding men at the front

Tongogara's account describes how women covered distances of over 180 kilometres on foot with loads of ammunition and other supplies to hand over to their male comrades at the front. By 1974, a Women's Detachment had been created specifically for this purpose, although internal sources do not give the exact date of its inception or its numerical strength.[25]

The women who became members of this detachment spoke of how they were often allocated carrier duties soon after arrival. Mrs Kahondo, who was taken from Chironga Mission in Mt Darwin at the end of 1973, said she started carrying war materials from Chifombo in Zambia in 1974, before she had got any training:

We just started carrying materials. There were some who were already training and when they finished, they came to relieve us, so we could go training too... It's us who opened Takawira Sector in Mutoko... I finally did my training too in 1974 but on completion we were arrested by the Zambians before I had been assigned what to do.[26]

While most of the women who were taken into ZANLA in the earlier period were engaged in carrier duties at one time or another, men also performed such duties.[27] Men with military training often accompanied the women on their journeys. However, when they got to the border areas, the women would retrace their footsteps to the rear bases whilst the men proceeded deeper into Rhodesia, to perform 'more masculine' operations at the battlefront. At the rear, the women would pick up yet more supplies, and in the

---

[24] Interview with Mrs Kahondo (Comrade Rwirai Nyika), Sunningdale, Harare, 11 March 1992. During the war, she developed a heart problem she believed was due to the heavy loads they had had to carry over long distances. The author learnt of Rwirai Nyika's death in 1994. She reportedly collapsed to her death, which possibly resulted from her heart complaint. Findings from the fieldwork also revealed that some former fighters had failed to have children after the war or they had only one child and had not been able to conceive afterwards. While there is need to carry out comparative research on ordinary Zimbabwean women before conclusions can be made on fertility trends for ex-combatants, researches from other wars, including the First and Second World Wars, have shown that the conditions affected some women's reproductive health negatively.

[25] ZANU (PF) Archives, File: Defence Secretariat, Doc: Manuscript of Interview with Josiah Magama Tongogara (Secretary for Defence) by Edson Zvobgo (ZANU Information and Publicity Secretary), 16 October 1978.

[26] Interview with Mrs Kahondo (Comrade Rwirai Nyika), Sunningdale, Harare, 11 March 1992.

[27] Interview with Mrs Mavende, Dotito, Mt. Darwin, 13 May 1992.

company of new groups of trained men going inside Rhodesia to fight, they would journey once more to the border. The process would be repeated over and over again with hardly any time to rest.

Every carrier understood the basic rule that there is no front without the rear. No one complained because they knew the answer only too well:

> Whatever you are carrying, no matter how heavy, remember that is the thing that is going to liberate your father and mother back home. That is the thing that will liberate Zimbabwe.[28]

The women required no further motivation. Many longed for the day when they would be allowed to cross the border into Zimbabwe for direct encounters with the enemy.

Safer in the rear base camps?

The border, marking the boundaries of the two countries, was also the official demarcation of the 'safer' and 'hot' zones of the armed struggle. This did not always hold, however, as encounters with Portuguese forces (before the end of Portugal's colonial adventure in Africa in 1974) and Rhodesian bombing missions into Mozambique (after 1976) demonstrated. Like those at the front, those in rear base camps also have horrid experiences to relate. Precious Takawira, a survivor from the Rhodesian raid of Nyadzonya Camp in Mozambique on 9 August in 1976, recounted painfully the nightmare of the massacre in which hundreds of her comrades perished:

> One only survived because God or the ancestors wished it. I for example went before a firing squad. What happened is, after they had finished firing they drove their trucks over those who still seemed alive. They then asked those who were still alive to give themselves up. I was among those who gave themselves up... We were arranged in three rows. Those in the first row were all shot and killed. Some girls were selected and taken into huts which were later set ablaze. We were surprised when they later told us to stand up and go. We did not move... We did not know where they wanted us to go. Hesitantly, we finally rose and started moving away expecting to hear shots the moment we turned our backs. But they only scolded us, calling us terrorists' wives... Many of us had broken limbs, so we did not go far. We went a short distance and sat on the banks of the Nyadzonya River. Then we heard their vehicles leaving.[29]

These things happened in the so-called safer rear bases. They could happen to nurses and their patients in the bush hospitals or to teachers and their pupils, or mothers and their

---

28 Interview with Mrs Nhanga, Dotito, Mt Darwin, 14 May 1992.
29 Interview with Precious Takawira, Sunningdale, Harare, 14 March 1992.

children in the refugee camps. Rhodesian raids into neighbouring countries killed many people in both ZANLA and ZIPRA. Rosemary Mathe, a former ZIPRA fighter, told the *Sunday News* in 1981 of the disastrous results of Rhodesian attacks. From a contingent of 2 000 women soldiers based at a camp in Solwezi, Zambia:

> the raids took their toll so that when peace finally came... there were only a little over 1000 of us left.[30]

Largely restricted to the rear bases, women were often caught up in these raids. This was especially so in ZIPRA whose policy throughout the war was that only men went to the front.

ZANLA women are said to have first complained of discriminatory practices in 1973. They demanded that as transporters of war materials, they receive military training too. They wanted to be able to defend themselves in the event of enemy attacks.[31] Although, in theory, the leadership adopted a policy to give women the same training as men, their tendency was always to first choose men for training programmes. Many female recruits, who never got the chance to train, returned from the war as 'refugees'.[32]

Responses to revolutionary initiatives for change

After the ZANLA High Command or the 'Old Guard' was released from detention in September 1976, they began to reorganise the party in 1977. As part of the reorganisation, women were asked to sort out what were seen as 'their problems'. The high point of this development was the inclusion in that year of Teurai Ropa, a female member of the General Staff, into the Central Committee as Secretary for Women's Affairs. This was an attempt to silence an unsettling voice rising from within a new group of women in the camps and should not be mistaken for an attempt by the leadership to put female emancipation on the organisation's agenda. The reorganisation took place at a time when the returned leadership was battling to contain the radical ideas that had started circulating in their absence.

Over the years, a new breed of women had found its way into the camps. A significant number of them had received a fair amount of formal education before joining. One or two even had degrees. These women were not content with just being told they were equal with men, particularly when no corresponding deeds matched the rhetoric. Although

[30] *Sunday News*, 31 May 1981.
[31] Ruth Weiss, *The Women of Zimbabwe*, Kesho Publications, London, 1986, p. 80.
[32] See Interview with Casiah Matiashe, in Pia Ehrenpreis, *From Rhodesia Back to Zimbabwe: All My Hopes Were to Go Home One Day: Refugee Stories*, UNHCR and SIDA, 1983, p. 23.

ZIPA had not set up structures to look specifically into women's issues, it had introduced serious discourse on social inequality. The educated women had participated in these debates. ZANU and ZANLA's double standards regarding the treatment of women were criticised. This new group, some of them former pupils of Wampoa college, became a nuisance for the re-installed ZANLA leadership which now fell under Robert Mugabe's presidency.

ZIPA's political project may have been overly ambitious in some respects. The political ideas it contained may have needed to be more finely tuned to fit the Zimbabwean context, as the High Command explained, when they crushed the programme. However, nothing quite justifies the decision to entirely do away with political lessons, as happened when the re-instated leadership regained control of the military organs in 1977.

The unbridled ones

The psychological impact of the collapse of Portuguese power in 1974, followed by the attainment of independence for Mozambique in 1975, led many young men and women with significant levels of formal education to leave Rhodesia for the armed struggle. When, in 1975, ZANLA moved to Mozambique from Zambia, it became relatively easier for recruits to join in larger numbers. Political problems in Rhodesia were mounting after the failure of negotiations of the détente in the middle of the decade.

Among the new wave of recruits were high school leavers. One account related the departure of 200 pupils from Mt Selinda School, both boys and girls.[33] Others had been teachers and nurses. Given their educational background, they were later to become a useful resource in ZANLA's rear base schools and hospitals. They gave political instruction to recruits as members of the Political Commissar's department and served as military instructors in the training department. Others became clerical or secretarial staff in ZANLA's various administrative departments. Some of them rose in rank and reached General Staff level. Further than that, they did not have much room to manoeuvre, and this was to constitute a contentious issue between the female and the male leadership throughout the war.

Unlike their predecessors, many of whom were still hoping to get promotion through serving as carriers with the Women's Detachment, these later recruits were not necessarily all wanting to go to the front, especially when they knew that their basic function would be

---

[33] See interview with Cassiah Matiashe (Comrade Jeans) in Ehrenpreis, Pia, *From Rhodesia back to Zimbabwe: All My Hopes Were to Go Home one Day: Refugee Stories*, UNHCR and SIDA, 1983, p. 21.

to deliver war materials to the men.[34] They challenged this tradition in ZANLA. As Zvobgo's comments intimated, they did not see the rationale behind giving women the same military training as men when they were being prevented from engaging in cross-border operations. They also had serious problems with the emphasis on 'combat' roles as the main criteria for promotion in ZANLA. They argued that women would never achieve promotion since they were systematically excluded from the roles that were accorded priority in ZANLA. A former combatant, Lieutenant Colonel Gertrude Mutasa of the Zimbabwe National Army, reflected in 1993 that by the time of the 1979 ZANU Congress, the women's anger was boiling over.[35] The mood at the congress became explosive, as many women demanded that the rhetoric of gender equality be matched with deeds.[36]

What bothered some of them was that they were saluting men who had never been to the front but had been promoted entirely on the basis of their pre-war qualifications and other professional service to the struggle. They asked why the same treatment could not be accorded them.

Nor would they accept the entire blame for falling pregnant. They expected men to face up to their responsibilities. Julia Zvobgo, a former executive member of the Department of Women's Affairs said she noticed that there was serious dissent amongst women over the fact that motherhood automatically disqualified them from service in the armed struggle in a way that fatherhood did not prejudice men.[37] They even wanted parental duties to be equally shared between men and women.[38] If men were not willing to play their part in this, it was logical that women should be provided with contraceptives. Women amongst this group had no qualms about using contraceptives, if they could find them. They were departing from the nationalist line by taking that position; and, in doing so, they were rejecting the role of reproduction and nurturing that the nationalist patriarchs deemed an essential female obligation.

These women, together with the men who shared their youthful effervescence and their educational background, had expectations that the liberation struggle would provide them with space to reason rather than cripple these skills. One ex-combatant remarked in reference to one of her former comrades, Freedom Nyamubaya:

---

[34] In an informal discussion with the author, Air Chief Marshall Josiah Tungamirai, a former ZANLA Political Commissar, said the later group of recruits who mainly came from schools in Manicaland made a lot of noise but they did not have the stamina to do the kind of work that the earlier group from Mt Darwin had done. He asked: 'Have you ever heard of bald women? Those women from Mt Darwin became bald, like men, because they carried loads and loads of materials on their heads. Those were really tough women.'

[35] Informal conversation with Lt. Col. Gertrude Mutasa, 18 March 1993.

[36] Ibid.

[37] Interview with Julia Zvobgo, Harare, 10 January 1995.

[38] Ibid.

She was very intelligent, so intelligent that some people who did not understand her ended up saying that she was a mental case. Of course it did not help when she turned to marijuana in despair. As for me, I understood clearly how one could end up like that. It was the frustration that her talents were going to waste.[39]

As revealed in her collection of poetry[40] published after the war, Freedom Nyamubaya is indeed a woman with remarkable talent. Her insight and comprehension of gender relations during and after the struggle is remarkable. It is not surprising that she was branded mad by some people. It was a pretext used to ignore true revolutionaries.

ZANLA deliberately deprived such women a formal platform in order to neutralise their voices. Lacking prominence in leadership circles, the women achieved notoriety because their activities featured as problems and reactionary tendencies in official discourse in the camps. They were under constant surveillance by members of the Department of Security and Intelligence, which was dominated by the earlier recruits who had very little or no formal education at all.[41] Although their message to the leadership was clear, it was deliberately underplayed in policy-formulation in the camps.

To channel this new discourse into a structure that did not challenge the very basis upon which the nationalist movement rested, a safety valve had to be opened. This was largely the background to, first, the appointment of Teurai Ropa into the Central Committee as Secretary for Women's Affairs in 1977, and later, the expansion of her unit to become the Department of Women's Affairs in 1978. However, the formal executive membership of the department was only chosen in May 1979.[42]

---

[39] Interview with former combatant Chipo Moyo (not her real name), 5 February 1994, London.

[40] Freedom Nyamubaya, *On the Road Again: Poems from the Liberation Struggle*, Zimbabwe Publishing House, Harare, 1986

[41] The Security and Intelligence Department was dominated by those recruited in the early seventies who came from north-eastern Zimbabwe. These were largely illiterate and did not need much persuasion to dispense severe punishment (for very minor offenses or alleged offenses) to their educated comrades who had joined the war from other parts of the country later. The author attended a female war veterans meeting held during Easter 1992, at Stodart Hall, Mbare. A visibly impoverished ex-combatant, Winnie Kambamura (war name: Zvakaoma), rose to complain about her frustration with their post-war marginalisation. Many of her former comrades murmured to one another, shaking their heads in disbelief, commenting with obvious glee that it could not really be the war-time Zvakaoma they were looking at. She had 'ruled and terrorised' them so much during her stint in security service that they 'had never thought Zimbabwe would treat her like that'. The harshness with which the 'Mt. Darwin clique' dealt with suspected subversive elements was also reiterated in an informal conversation with Captain Sanyanga of the Zimbabwe National Army who joined the war from Manicaland after completing O-Levels. He said they seemed to think it was 'their' war more than anybody else's and they told educated people that their educational qualifications were irrelevant to the war.

[42] The selection of the department's leadership was one of the main purposes of the ZANU Women's Seminar. See Robert Mugabe, 'The Role and History of the Zimbabwean Women in the National Struggle' in *Women's Liberation in the Zimbabwean Revolution: Materials from the ZANU Women's Seminar Xai Xai*, ZANU, San Francisco, 1979, p. 7.

The Department of Women's Affairs

Although the leaders of the new department were amongst those with a fair amount of formal education, there is one unsettling feature about their composition. Teurai Ropa, the wife of the ZANLA Operations Commander Rex Nhongo, was appointed the departmental head. Her deputy, Sally Mugabe, was the wife of Robert Mugabe, the President of ZANU. Julia Zvobgo, the wife of Edson Zvobgo, the Party's Publicity Secretary, became the department's Secretary for Administration.

Probably these women qualified for their new positions: Teurai Ropa had been leader of the women since her appointment to the Central Committee in 1977; Julia Zvobgo had a Masters degree; Sally Mugabe had been a school teacher. But Julia Zvobgo had arrived rather late onto the scene from the United States, and the same could be said of Sally Mugabe. Thus speculation about their husbands' influence regarding their appointment could not be ignored. This might partly explain why they sometimes found themselves ignored by the people they sought to represent.

Given the ZANLA leadership's unwillingness to establish substantive representation for women, these appointments were only made in 1979. By then a number of educated women had joined ZANLA and the leadership had a fairly large pool from which to choose. Thus, the ZANLA leadership did not need risk accusations that the factor of male connections had come into play.

A 'club' for the commanders' wives?

As it turned out the organisation was never able to shake off the image of being a club for the commanders' wives. How seriously could they be expected to confront problems that could be blamed directly on the leadership who were their husbands or their husbands' friends and colleagues? In that sense, they formed a separate category from those educated women who had no male connections at the top of ZANLA's hierarchy.

When asked to comment on the department's activities, one female ex-fighter, Muchaneta Mabhunu, first said she had never heard about it. When I tried to refresh her memory by explaining that Teurai Ropa had led the department, she ridiculed the whole thing: 'Oh that one! It was for Chimoio people'.[43] As Chimoio was ZANLA's headquarters, Muchaneta's insinuation cannot be missed.

---

[43]   Interview with Comrade Muchaneta Mabhunu, Sunningdale, Harare, 12 March 1992.

Some of the departmental leadership's passive response to and sometimes active support of, discriminatory practices against women contradicted what they stood for in theory. Some members actively promoted negative tendencies and practices amongst men by blaming fellow women for pregnancies. The department's resistance to contraception is a case in point.

Although most criticisms of the department are reserved for the post-war period a lot could still be said about the plan of action, which had taken shape from 1977, and been enthusiastically adopted in 1978 as part of the process of re-organising the Party.

When Teurai Ropa started sitting in the Central Committee as Secretary for Women's Affairs, her position must have been unenviable given the ambiguous nature of her job. On the one hand she had to work towards fulfilling nationalist demands to sort out 'feminine problems'. The Party needed convincing that women were worth retaining in the military. As evidence, the male leadership wanted women to put a halt to pregnancies. As a veteran, Ropa was expected to make new female recruits aware of the Party line on sexuality. On the other hand, she had to identify with women, especially the educated ones, who had since joined ZANLA ranks. They wanted practical solutions to female marginalisation rather than rhetoric.

Implementing the two-pronged strategy

In her position as Secretary for Women's Affairs, Teurai Ropa had to juxtapose herself between the traditionalists and the innovators. She had experience based on her early recruitment to ZANLA and she had the benefit of some formal education (well above basic literacy) but she was not as well educated as the later recruits. With a foot in both camps, the leadership considered her the best compromise.

One cannot really be persuaded to see Teurai Ropa's inclusion in the Central Committee as a move towards addressing gender differences, especially when the new Secretary for Women's Affairs worked almost entirely with men. The minutes of a meeting she held with the officers of Osibisa Camp in Mozambique in December 1978 drew attention to the arrangements she had made when she went on maternity leave in June that same year:

I left my department with Comrade Mayor Urimbo and Comrade Mayor left it to Comrade Rex Nhongo who was to work with Comrades George, Dominic, etc.... After holding a meeting with the Executive Committee then came out with the point that 6 months for my maternity leave was too much since Comrade Mayor could not hold two posts at one goal [sic].[44]

The clear inference is that no woman could be trusted to act in Teurai Ropa's absence. Far from being a step towards women's integration into ZANU's decision-making organs, Teurai Ropa's appointment seems merely to have been ornamental.

As Chapter One revealed, on her journeys abroad, she articulated women's problems in a way that always impressed her audiences. She was ZANLA's show-piece, a product of the revolution. She was uncompromising. In fact, to external audiences, she represented the group of women that ZANLA sought to silence inside the camps. As proof of women's full participation in the struggle, they were reportedly found in its every sphere. Towards the end of the war, the official propaganda claimed that ZANLA women had already started running schools in liberated areas inside Zimbabwe,[45] a claim, which the research for this study could not substantiate.[46] Whether such schools ever existed is another matter, but outsiders took the claims as evidence of ZANLA's commitment to giving women the opportunity to liberate themselves (both as women and as Zimbabwean nationalists) through the barrel of the gun. ZANLA had passed the acid test and as a progressive movement it deserved international donor support. Indeed ZANLA did deserve credit in some respects but not in this particular.

Once back in the ZANLA camps, Teurai and her aides could be relied upon to remind fellow women of their obligation to preserve their 'culture'. This in essence meant the reinforcement of patriarchy. This she did well too. Her main targets for this campaign were the female inmates of refugee camps and places like Osibisa. To them she mourned over the threats to traditional 'culture'. According to the nationalist argument, young girls in the camps needed someone to take the place of their aunts; it was because they lacked traditional guidance that they were becoming pregnant. The idle women were supposed to be filling that gap instead of lamenting their neglect by the Party.

The Party is trying always to promote women so that we move together with men like a team of oxen. But the disease with us is we don't put much effort to our duties. You women, you are not doing your duties. Maybe you don't know them but there is the major one of teaching these

---

[44] ZANU (PF) Archives, File: Department of Women's Affairs, Doc.: 'Meeting of Secretary for Women's Affairs With Osibisa Officers', 3 December 1978.

[45] Ibid., Meeting with Swiss delegates, 1979.

[46] Colonel E. Munemo, who worked in the research unit of ZANU's Department of Education during the war, told the author in an informal discussion that no schools had been run by the fighters in the liberated zones during the war.

girls our culture… You don't just seek refugee [sic] here but you came to learn so that you will teach other women who didn't get the chance.[47]

'Revolutionary' roles for women and attendant problems

Teurai Ropa's male aides in this campaign often complemented her efforts by dispensing advice to the women on what they could do to free themselves, instead of complaining about their poor prospects for marriage. Mayor Urimbo advised:

It's high time to free yourselves from capetalist [sic] oppression and man's oppression. There are many things for you to do e.g. knitting, cooking and ironing. Teach those who do not know… You must try your level best to plough many fields… Self reliance is what we want.[48]

There was nothing obviously revolutionary about Urimbo's suggestion.

Teurai Ropa herself made no secret of her view of ZANLA women as an auxiliary or back-up force. She appealed to their supposed nurturing instincts:

Since we can't go home [to the front] we have a lot of duties to do here. We came here to help keep the well-being of boys, washing their clothes, cleaning their houses and treat them when they are sick. We also have the duty of carrying material for the boys.[49]

In the same instance, she reminded the women performing those duties not to think of themselves as special. She said she had detected an arrogance in nurses. The tension within the various groups of women came out clearly as Teurai Ropa set out to cut nurses down to size:

They are making themselves superior than others… They are making themselves qualified nurses instead of medical assistants. So from now onwards stop whatever you do. You are not qualified nurses and should work as nurses of the people… Some of you were very poor but now ZANU has given you everything and fed you, then you try to make yourself superior.[50]

Not surprisingly, Teurai Ropa did not endear herself or her department to many women. Since they could not openly tell her to leave them alone, their cool response to her campaign conveyed the message:

[47] ZANU (PF) Archives, File: Defence Secretariat, Women's Affairs, Doc: 'Women's League Meeting', Doeroi Camp, 28 December 1977.
[48] ZANU (PF) Archives, Doc: 'Minutes of Rally held at Osibisa [sic] Camp', 12 November 1977.
[49] Ibid., File: Defence Department, MMZ Province, 1976-1979, Doc: 'Meeting with Female Comrades (Chaired By Cde Sheba Tavarwisa and Cde Teurai Ropa)', Battalliao Central Camp, 25 April 1977.
[50] Ibid.

Yesterday we visited some of you… but it wasn't very pleasing. Some of you did give us cold shoulders.[51]

The women – the intended beneficiaries of projects initiated by the Department of Women's Affairs – treated these initiatives with a contempt similar to that with which they were viewed by the leadership. Many women saw no point in acquiring skills for which obviously nobody had any respect:

Coming to take us from the camps to sew! We thought we were going somewhere abroad either to China, Romania or somewhere… to be pilots or some kind of qualifications.[52]

It was probably unrealistic that everybody expected to be sent abroad. However, it is understandable why this was so. Those who travelled enjoyed a special privilege when they returned: people listened to them.[53] In view of this, the department approached the Party for scholarships to send women abroad, but their fields of specialisation remained the same: sewing, housewifery and home economics.[54] These skills, it was argued, would make them self-sufficient, a pre-condition for emancipation.[55] The fact that these roles remained conservative and traditional was lost to the supposedly revolutionary ZANLA leadership.

The legacy of missionary education and memories of tradition

The performance of the Department of Women's Affairs bore strong resemblance to the 'civilising mission' of the nuns and missionary wives back home. Perhaps that should not be too surprising, as the influence of missionary teachings remained strong in relation to many other aspects of camp life. The nationalist leaders were traditionalist patriarchs, but their contact with Christian missionary education had reinforced their desire to patronise women. Furthermore their education had emphasised the idea of women as 'housewives'. Thus there was a concerted, almost arrogant, drive to domesticate women, as analysis of their syllabus reveals. Moreover the department's ability to balance its roles is astonishing. It could organise women into lessons on housewifery in line with the official plan, while simultaneously marvelling at how much things had changed for these same women:

---

[51] ZANU (PF) Archives, File: Defence Secretariat, Women's Affairs, Doc: 'Women's League Meeting', Doeroi Camp, 28 December 1977.
[52] ZANU (PF) Archives, File: Department of Women's Affairs, Doc: 'Departmental Meeting', Matola, 24 September 1979.
[53] Ibid.
[54] Ibid.
[55] Ibid.

Before the armed struggle started the work of women was to wash, cook, bear children and toil in the fields.[56]

Mugabe's dream of seeing them removed from their 'stupefying house and kitchen environment', as he proclaimed at Xai Xai, was only realised in that women now cooked and looked after their own children in the mobile homes of the ZANLA camps; and that women were given lessons in 'animal husbandry'.[57] Thus the Department of Women's Affairs was caught in a web which it could not disentangle itself and its leadership did not have the will to redefine the roles that women performed traditionally or had assumed under colonialism.

Evaluations of women's roles

Josiah Tongogara's account informed us that women only started fighting with guns in 1978. He justified this position by saying the duties the women had been performing were equally important to the struggle:

> *actual fighting does not mean on the trigger… every major target we have ever attacked, we have had women included, carrying material, cooking food, carrying lots and lots of things… A few of them have even returned fire previously but now we have drawn a programme whereby women actually go in the same fashion like a man – we cannot isolate the women now, they have got to do the actual fighting, perhaps some will prove to be good.*[58]

Clearly Tongogara was still unsure about women's capacity 'to man' the front. He was ambiguous in his views about the roles women had been performing. At first he said that 'actual fighting does not mean on the trigger', but in the same instance he went on to talk of the new programme that ZANLA had adopted in 1978 that would allow women now to do 'actual fighting'.

Within the context of Tongogara's contradictory statement and Teurai Ropa's derogatory comments to nurses, the official evaluation of the contribution to the armed struggle made by the women fighters is clear. The very few women appointed to decision-making positions during and after the war reflected this negative viewpoint.

---

[56] ZANU (PF) Archives, File: Defence Secretariat, Women's Affairs, Doc: 'Georgina Machel Day Contributions'.
[57] ZANU (PF) Archives, File: Department of Women's Affairs, Doc: 'Report for the Year Ending 31 December, 1978'.
[58] ZANU (PF) Archives, File: Defence Secretariat, Doc: 'Manuscript of Interview with Josiah Magama Tongogara', 16 October 1978.

1978: a turning point or more of the same?

Regarding women's ability to go to the front, the timing of the apparent change of attitude should not be forgotten. By then, operational commanders were reporting that they had created liberated zones – areas where enemy operations had been neutralised. They also reported that civilians had been freed from the enemy's 'protected villages' and that most of these people were living with the fighters in the liberated zones. Such reports raised new questions for women in the camps by 1978:

> If the evacuated masses from the so-called protected villages who have no military conscious-ness can stay in the bushes why can't we soldiers go and stay with them and win their support for our Party?[59]

The ZANLA leadership saw logic in this suggestion. Their original definition of the 'hot' and 'safe' zones were changing with the circumstances and so too were their delineations of male and female zones of operation. They needed women to move arms to those new areas where ZANLA was contemplating setting up bases. This, rather than Zvobgo's claims that ZANLA had ideologically matured, was the main premise upon which the leadership acceded to the demand made by women to be allowed to go to the front, as Chapter Four will show. Otherwise it was content to have women providing 'a home away from home' for the male forces. However, home-making and war-time unions bred serious problems for all involved.

Sexuality in the camps

While 'women's problems' started surfacing at the end of 1974, while ZANLA was still in Zambia, policy to deal with these issues was only formulated a long time after the reloca-tion to Mozambique.

Sexual abuse of women was one of the major allegations levelled against the ZANLA leadership in what came to be known as the Nhari-Badza rebellion of 1974.[60] In a petition to Zambian authorities, the rebels accused Tongogara, the ZANLA's Chief of Defence, of impregnating a girl and arranging for her to have an abortion to save his reputation. An-other high-ranking commander was also alleged to have impregnated another girl and then

---

[59] ZANU (PF) Archives, File: Department of Women's Affairs, Doc: 'Report for the Year Ending 31 December, 1978'.

[60] Patrick Nhari and Dakarai Badza, junior officers in ZANLA, led an abortive coup against their High Command in Zambia, accusing its members of various forms of corruption, including squandering Party funds on women and liquor whilst ignoring the needs of the forces at the front.

to have denied responsibility.[61] The authors of the document were junior officers in ZANLA, and they complained that girls who came from the operational zones to the rear ostensibly to transport war materials and assist as medical personnel, ended up performing other duties:

> for reasons best known to the leadership, these female comrades have been transformed into nannies and house-girls and they are compelled to satisfy the animal lusts of our High Command leadership.[62]

The High Command discounted the allegations as fabrications but the matter requires more serious interrogation.[63]

ZANLA's initial sexual code

Initially the Party forbade both sexual relations and marriage in the camps and in the operational field. David Lan notes that Shona hunters from earlier times had observed prohibitions on sex and that similar traditional restrictions seem to have applied to warriors as well.[64] It is possible that the Party's initial code of conduct for its fighters was informed by such beliefs. Yet, liberation struggles elsewhere had sometimes applied a similar code of conduct in relation to sex. Barbara Jancar wrote of Yugoslavia's liberation struggle between 1941 and 1945:

> A partisan strict moral code governed daily living. Sexual relations were severely discouraged among the common soldiers... but... young people frequently succeeded in avoiding the strict eyes of the partisan command, even though they knew that swift punishment would follow if discovered.[65]

ZANU's attempts to impose sexual restraints on its forces probably derived as much from socialist puritanism as from African tradition. War has always been conceptualised as a male activity and women who take part in it must be as like men as possible. Yet two

---

61 ZANU (PF) Archives, File: ZIPA Affairs, Doc: 'Statement of Fact for the Attention of Major Mulopa', 12 January 1975.

62 Ibid.

63 Ken Flower, the former head of Rhodesian Intelligence Services, later endorsed the ZANU HC's assertion that the rebels were enemy agents who fabricated the accusations. See Ken Flower, *Serving Secretly: An Intelligence Chief on Record: Rhodesia into Zimbabwe, 1964 - 1981*, John Murray Publishers Ltd., London, 1987. However, we cannot judge Flower's credibility on this matter, given that he continued to serve as Intelligence Chief under the Mugabe government. For a man whose career had involved engaging in disinformation campaigns on behalf of government, one can never be too sure when to take him for his word.

64 David Lan, *Guns and Rain: Guerrillas and Spirit Mediums in Zimbabwe*, James Currey, London, 1985, p. 159.

65 Barbara Jancar, 'Women Soldiers in Yugoslavia's National Liberation Struggle, 1941-1945', in Eva Isaksson (ed.), *Women and the Military System: Proceedings of a Symposium Arranged by the International Peace Bureau and Peace Union of Finland*, Harvester-Wheatsheaf, New York, 1988, p. 55.

factors form a constant reminder of the impossibility of them to be exactly like men – pregnancy, which will be discussed in this chapter, and menstruation which will be considered in the next.

The pressures for change

ZANLA later changed its code on sexual relationships and marriage as more and more recruits arrived, fleeing from the deteriorating political situation in Rhodesia. With the ZANU leadership in Zambian jails on allegations of assassinating their own Party leader, Herbert Chitepo, there were no training programmes in place to absorb the recruits throughout 1975. The camps were full of young people with no where else to go. ZIPA, the interim union of ZANLA and ZIPRA, had no resources to organise anything until the beginning of 1976. The result was prolonged idleness and a deterioration of morale and discipline. Consequently, a lot of girls fell pregnant.[66] While sexual activities and pregnancies had occurred before, the halt in fighting or 'détente', as it came to be known, exacerbated the problem. So, as the war progressed, a new and more realistic approach to sexuality and the issue of marriages was called for.

New degrees of freedom in ZANLA's rear base camps

The environment and the camp set-ups provided opportunities for active sexual interaction. Although each camp had a predominant function, there was much overlap, and the distinction between 'military' and 'refugee' camps was sometimes not clear. Each camp had separate male and female barracks, rudimentary pole and dagga structures with thatched roofs. Commanders had individual huts or 'postos', as they were called. Each camp had a communal kitchen where everybody was supposed to assemble for meals.

As the male and female living quarters were in close proximity, and as boys and girls often went out on their own to gather firewood, or poles and thatch for use in construction, there was nothing to prevent sexual relations between them, even though Party laws forbade it. The fiction literature of the war gives extensive accounts of these romances. Shimmer Chinodya's main character in *Harvest of Thorns*, Pasi Nemasellout, mused over his sexual encounter with a female comrade in one of the rear bases:

---

[66] For this background, see ZANU (PF) Archives, File: Commissariat Department, Doc: 'On Marriage', 16 August 1978.

a girl who wore denims... who cut her hair short like a boy and whose fingers were stone-stiff from hauling crates of ammo.[67]

Clearly, the image of the girl was extremely 'unfeminine'. Pasi Nemasellout was surprised by her lack of inhibition as she said afterwards, 'Thank you, I needed it'. He 'had never thought a woman could say that'. Although the incident depicted a revolution in sexual attitudes, Chinodya draws the reader's attention to the ambivalence or uncertainty characterising such relationships:

You didn't want to think she had done it to somebody else before... You had heard girl comrades didn't do it, that doing it would suck the fire out of their guns... now she had done it to you... but you had left her... would she have your child... would she carry the child in a strap together with her bazooka... Or did she know how not to have? [68]

Many young people probably viewed their being out of reach of the social sanctions of family life as an opportunity to experiment with sex, and others used it to relieve the stresses of camp life. Some of these relationships matured into something more meaningful. Because they were free from most of the social pressures that bore upon similar relationships back home, they held a special significance for the young people involved. Memories of them inspired novels like Irene Mahamba's *Woman in Struggle*, the story of a young girl who ran away from a forced marriage in Rhodesia, to discover her true love in a ZANLA camp in Mozambique after joining the armed struggle.[69]

For some people the war dragged on longer than they had initially thought it would, thereby denying them the chance to settle down, marry and have children. This was a problem especially for the more mature women whose potential as prospective wives was deteriorating as the years went by. For such people, sexual relations might have been a calculated strategy to secure marriage partners.

The power factor

Apart from these voluntary liaisons were those resulting from relations of power as the 1974 rebels revealed. Senior officers could easily manipulate their privileged positions of being the controllers and distributors of scarce basic supplies. They could exploit their position as decision-makers, as the ones who appointed people for various tasks in the

---

[67] Shimmer Chinodya, *Harvest of Thorns*, Heinemann, Oxford, 1989, p.218.
[68] Ibid.
[69] Irene 'Ropa Rinopfuka' Mahamba, *Woman in Struggle*, Zimfep, Harare, 1986.

struggle. ZANLA put measures in place to check such tendencies, but they were often ineffective. Women themselves continually complained:

> We have a problem with high-ranking comrades. They force girls to have affairs with them and some of them end up with ten wives. Afterwards they leave the mothers to look for a girl without a child to marry.[70]

Initiations of the female recruit

Complaints were continually made against officers who took advantage of new recruits by exploiting their ignorance of the Party's official policy on sexual relations. Newly arriving girls were popular with the men who thought the new girls were still free from the sexually transmitted diseases that afflicted the camps.[71] Also, the new arrivals were still in good shape compared with those who had been in the camps for a long time and were afflicted with skin diseases. Skin-lightening creams were fashionable those days and, as the toning effect of these creams had not yet worn off, the new arrivals were especially appealing to the men.[72] One female recruit recounted her initiation into ZANLA:

> Comrade Ngondo Iyahlaba came to our barrack, it was already time to sleep... he led me to his barrack... he told me to sit down and wait to be sent as he had told me before. I asked him why he wanted me. He only told me to wait. It was hot and I took off my jersey... He took it and put it in his wardrobe. I tried to run away, but he gripped my skipper [T-shirt] and tore it... Also at Katumba base... Comrade Dhliwayo wanted to rape me and I ran away... All the days, Comrades Gwatakwata and Muchena gave us positions to sleep... all the male comrades I was given to sleep with tried to rape me but... I ran away [73]

Female recruits were clearly vulnerable to the exploits of disgraceful seniors. However, it is necessary to explain the circumstances under which a young girl was given male comrades 'to sleep with'. It was a common practice in ZANLA, and more so in the transit camps, that males and females sometimes shared the same sleeping quarters. Male comrades would form a cordon around the girls, purportedly to protect them from enemy attacks. Sometimes the nights passed without any event but, as we hear in the young woman's testimony, the arrangement could also lead to problems.

---

[70] ZANU (PF) Archives, File: Defence Secretariat: Women's Affairs, Doc: 'Minutes of Meeting of Female Comrades', no date.
[71] ZANU (PF) Archives, File: CC, HC & GS Minutes, Doc: 'Security and Intelligence Department: Minutes of Meeting with Tembwe Camp Administration', 5 January 1978.
[72] Interview with female ex-combatant Precious Takawira, Sunningdale, Harare, 12 March 1992.
[73] ZANU (PF) Archives, File: HC Minutes, Doc: Minutes of 'Meeting of Recruits with Comrade Gava, Batalhao', Tete, 22 August 1977.

Inherent prejudices and social diseases

When problems arose, women often took the blame. Most men regarded sexually trans-mitted diseases, for example, as 'women's diseases'. Typically, an officer receiving a com-plaint of sexual abuse would accuse the female recruit of being morally loose and of spreading venereal diseases in the camps.[74] Venereal diseases were almost always women's diseases. In one High Command meeting, for example, Mpunzarima (a member of the HC) alerted his colleagues to the problem at one of their smaller bases:

> there are five female comrades suffering from venereal diseases and then ten male comrades also suffering from this.[75]

Either Mpunzarima did not see anything unusual in the way he presented his statistics – that is, focusing on the smaller before he considered the larger figure, or he deliberately wanted to emphasise the seriousness of the presence of 'infectious' women and the danger they posed to 'innocent' men. Either way, the case reveals male attitudes towards such social diseases. During World War II, posters distributed with pictures of beautiful women ran captions like:

> SHE MAY LOOK CLEAN – BUT… pick ups, 'good time' girls… spread syphilis and gonor-rhoea.[76]

Women seem always to be the corrupting factor, and the men their helpless victims. The ZANLA leadership's attitude should be seen in this context.

Nationalist politics and views on sexual services

Calls by vocal women for senior officers to be exemplary in their actions were often ig-nored. Some were reported to use force, including beatings, to get young girls to sleep with them.[77] Some former combatants spoke of how commanders would target girls for punish-ment because they turned down their overtures[78] and how, in some instances, senior women in charge of the female barracks collaborated with their male counterparts to 'hand over' young girls to them overnight. One of them remembered a certain senior woman remark-

74 Ibid.
75 Ibid., Doc: 'Minutes of Meeting of Chimurenga High Command', Commando Base, 20 October 1978.
76 Quoted in Claudia Gacia-Moreno, 'AIDS: Women are not just transmitters', in T. Wallace with C. March, Chang-ing Perceptions: Writings on Gender and Development, Oxfam, Oxford, 1991, p. 92.
77 ZANU (PF) Archives, File: Defence Secretariat HQ: Women's Affairs, Doc: 'Proposals on Marriages' by Osibisa Officers, no date.
78 Interview with Teedzai Mabhindauko, Sunningdale, Harare, 12 March 1992.

ing to the young girls under her charge: *'Uri kutofamba zvako. Mhanya. Uri kudiwa nashefu'*. (You dare to walk? Run. The *chef* wants to see you.)[79] This informant went on to describe how a male commander could take a girl for the night to his post. If he liked her, he would call her again the following night; if he did not like her, he would go on to try a new girl. An informant told Ruth Weiss that some male commanders seemed to think that, by virtue of their positions, they were entitled to such services from women.[80]

The other problem exposing women to sexual exploitation was the scarcity of basics in the camps. Many succumbed to the temptation to align themselves to high-ranking men to get special favours in the distribution of things like food and toiletries. Some men exploited this to their advantage and would actually warn recruits on arrival of the hunger in the camps. They would then 'advise' them that the way to survive was to 'behave well' towards them (the officers).[81] In this way, some men ended up with several girlfriends.

Female commanders' exploits

A few female officers evidently emulated the practice of their male colleagues and took new arrivals to have sex with them, although this does not seem to have been a widespread occurrence. In any case, not many women were in high positions. Teurai Ropa, the Secretary for Women's Affairs, strongly condemned the practice:

> These boys have now lost respect for you and they scold you in front of the comrades you command. Even my own dignity is at stake because of your actions. [82]

Whilst the boys who had been abused by the female officers could publicly denounce them and make fools out of them, girls who had received similar treatment from senior men could not do the same. Although the senior women were the ones who had made advances to the boys, the boys seemed to interpret this to be symbolic of their 'conquest' of the senior women. The women were often too embarrassed by the revelations to act against the young boys. Thus, the boys could publicly denounce the women without fear of victimisation. Sometimes they even went further. In one case, schoolboys beat their female instructors who were bathing in the river, causing one to flee back to the base in her underclothes only. When the camp administrators looked at the case, one of them charged that

---

[79] Interview with female ex-combatant Chipo Moyo (not her real name), London, 5 February 1994.

[80] Ruth Weiss, *The Women of Zimbabwe*, Kesho Publications, London, 1986. See also the interview with Prudence Uriri, pp. 74-75, in *Women of Resilience*, Zimbabwe Women Writers, Harare, 2000

[81] Interview with Precious Takawira, 12 March 1992; interview with Julia Zvobgo, 10 January 1995.

[82] ZANU (PF) Archives, File: Defence Secretariat HQ, Women's Affairs, Doc: Minutes of 'Meeting with Female Officers and Trained Female Comrades', Toronga Camp, Chibawawa, 22 October 1977.

the youths involved 'had ultra-democracy' and that this would remain a problem espe-cially, 'if the female instructors continue to fall in love with the big youths'.[83]

From this it appears that the women had traded their power and dignity for sex. Men, however, could lose their dignity when they preyed on young girls but still retain the power to control those under them. This reveals how power shaped sexual relationships and, in turn, how one's sexual activities could sometimes influence the amount of their power.

Refugee women and girls

In pursuing the nature of these relationships further, ZANU's refugee camps call for special attention. These camps largely accommodated people who, for various reasons, fell out-side of ZANLA's military programmes. Some were young boys and girls considered imma-ture for military training and for whom schools had been set up in the camps. The adult population included villagers from the north-eastern border areas who had moved into Mozambique after falling out with the Smith regime. The few, trained people included school teachers and the representatives of ZANLA's administrative departments.

Given the proximity to Mozambican civilian settlements, some refugees had set up their own small villages amongst Mozambican civilians and were practising subsistence farming. For that reason, interaction with the locals was close and FRELIMO, the ruling party in Mozambique, kept a strong presence in the camps as advisors to the Zimbabwean refugees. This whole arrangement caused antagonism between the Zimbabweans and their hosts. Right up to the end of the war ZANLA and FRELIMO vied for control. Zimbabwean women and girls were often the subject of these disputes.

Although FRELIMO often chastised ZANLA over the sexual abuse of women, the Mozambicans' relations with their female guests were not impressive. In one case, a mar-ried woman alleged that a civilian Mozambican man, Katsoke, had pressured her into a sexual relationship after curing her of an illness.[84] Katsoke later volunteered to look after her in the absence of her husband who was fighting at the front. On one occasion he gave her a little money (one dollar) with which she bought some soap. Then she fell pregnant. Katsoke advised her to allow her husband to discover the pregnancy and then divorce her, promising that he himself would then marry her. But when Mushonga, her husband, found

---

[83]   ZANU (PF) Archives, File: Education and Culture Department, Doc: 'Meeting Base', 9 June 1979.
[84]   Ibid., Doc: Meeting, Mabvudzi Base, 3 October 1979. As evidence that socialisation with Mozambican civilians could get quite close, the treatment had involved a ceremony in which beer was brewed to heal the patient.

out, he did not give Katsoke such an opportunity. He decided instead to keep his wife and to sort out the matter of her infidelity later with his family and hers on returning to Zimbabwe.[85]

FRELIMO apparently became aware of the case but, as in many similar instances of interference with Zimbabwean refugee women and girls,[86] ignored the matter. ZANLA had no authority over Katsoke, and without FRELIMO's co-operation there was nothing they could do with him.

Zimbabwean women refugees' experiences in Mozambique were not much different from those of women in similar circumstances in host countries the world over. Often they had to pay for their physical and material needs and those of their families with their bodies. Schoolgirls sought relief from the hunger and strife of the camps by co-habiting with FRELIMO officials and elderly civilian men in the nearby villages. For fear of upsetting relations with their hosts, ZANLA officials could not openly confront Mozambican officials over such matters. In any case, they too often had to defend themselves against FRELIMO's accusations that they were sexually abusing their own women within ZANU and ZANLA. Previous studies of Zimbabwean women in the war have generally remained silent on this issue.

Mounting problems and evasive solutions

Different factors shaped sexual relationships and men and women reacted to the problems emanating from them differently. Although a document from the Department of Women's Affairs outlined lessons on contraception, interviews with Teurai Ropa and Julia Zvobgo, both of whom held significant posts during the war, maintained that no contraceptive means were made available to women except the advice to abstain from sex. Margaret Dongo, who worked as a medical assistant, was surprised that I had even thought of it:

> My dear, to whom could we have gone with such a request? They would have asked us what exactly our purpose in Mozambique was.[87]

Julia Zvobgo reiterated the same position, adding that it also did not feel right especially with so many people dying at home. Teurai Ropa said they tried to make use of traditional herbs with the help of elderly women in the camps, but they did not succeed because they

---

[85] Ibid.
[86] The Education and Culture reports contain massive evidence of young schoolgirls deserting the refugee camps to go and live with elderly Mozambican civilian men and FRELIMO 'camaradas'.
[87] Interview with Margaret Dongo, Harare, 10 March 1992.

had to do it secretly, fearing objections from men. She said that the continual bombing of the camps made men anxious to have children to carry their name through, just in case they died in the war.[88]

Not all women wished to use contraceptives, but given the hardship of camp life, many would have appreciated the advantages of being able to control their reproduction. In fact, some of the women, especially the few who could get out of the camps, arranged to have birth control devices, intra-uterine loops, inserted secretly; if discovered, they were punished and ordered to have them removed. A High Command meeting ruled in one case:

> they should be sent to Maputo to have the loops removed by the doctors who inserted them. The loops could have been removed here in Chimoio but we do not want problems with FRELIMO.[89]

Thus fear of punishment and the general lack of opportunities by most women to get out of the camps meant that the usage and effectiveness of this birth-control method was limited. Consequently, many women and girls fell pregnant. One is left to wonder to whom the lessons the Department of Women's Affairs outlined on modern methods of family planning were delivered. Some women attempted abortion and others succeeded, but this was also punishable. For example, the minutes of the meeting cited above, indicate that some women were once detained at Chimoio's Operational Base for having had an abortion. Sociologist Rudo Gaidzanwa puts abortion into perspective by pointing out how women's actions in crisis situations make fallacious some notions about gender. She noted that women's supposed 'natural' mothering instincts 'do not manifest themselves naturally'.[90] In other words, one needs resources to perform this mothering function. Clearly this wisdom evaded the ZANLA leadership.

Increased cases of pregnancy eventually led to the Party revising its policy relating to sex and marriage. The Political Commissariat Department issued a policy document on the matter in 1978. (See Appendix.) However, drafting policies is one matter; applying them is another. The regulations were difficult to understand, let alone to implement.

---

[88]   Interview with Teurai Ropa (Joyce Mujuru), Bindura, 2 November 1994.
[89]   ZANU (PF) Archives, File: HC Minutes, Doc: 'Minutes of High Command Meeting', Operational Base, Chimoio, 21 May 1979.
[90]   Rudo Gaidzanwa, 'Bourgeois Theories of Gender and Feminism' in Ruth Meena (ed.), *Gender in Southern Africa: Conceptual and Theoretical Issues*, SAPES Books, Harare, 1992, p. 120.

Regulating sexual relationships and war-style marriages in the camps

In formulating regulations relating to marriage in the camps, the ZANLA leadership's decisions were informed by three main factors: first, they were concerned with political and military efficiency; second, they were anxious to respect the customs of their people; and third, they were influenced by colonial marriage laws and by Christian teachings on marriage and morality.

Many of the regulations were dictated by conditions in the camps and were laid down in order to provide those running the camps with a guide to dealing with the problems confronting them. Thus, ZANLA legislated against love based on material gain (Regulation 5), since such relationships created serious tensions in the camps. Moreover, as a military organisation, ZANLA had to insist that marital concerns did not override military ones; hence the regulations demanding a period of service in the army before marriage, and specifying the conditions under which couples could meet as husband and wife. (Regulations 20, 21 and 22.)

Other regulations reflected ZANU's formal revolutionary principles. Thus under Regulation 1 no man could have more than one wife; and Regulation 2 forbade love affairs with married people or with someone else's girlfriend or boyfriend. Regulation 4 threatened punishment to any man who persistently wooed another man's girl-friend. Regulation 24 laid down that 'Marriage is final, no man shall divorce his war-time wife even after independence'. Though they were obviously influenced by Christian teaching, the main thrust of these regulations was to set up an equal marriage relationship between men and women, in accordance with ZANU's proclaimed commitment to gender equality.

In practice, however, even those regulations differentiated on grounds of gender. Only men were prohibited from taking more than one wife – it was not conceivable to the drafters that a woman might seek to take more than one husband. Punishment was specifically laid down for men who tried to seduce other men's girlfriends, because it was assumed that men took the initiative. Even Regulation 24 – 'Marriage is final' – was directed at men rather than women. In the real, unpretentious Shona people's world, unclouded by the rhetoric of the so-called revolution, a man divorces his wife – in the first instance, because he marries her and not the other way round. Men 'marry' and women 'get married' in recognition of the fact that the man pays the brideprice to the woman's family. These assumptions continued to regulate men's perspectives of male-female power relations in war-time marriages in the camps, even in the absence of brideprice payments.

Many of the regulations reflected traditional 'customs'. Regulation 9, which made marriage obligatory in cases of pregnancy, conformed to the practice of the Zimbabwean rural areas both in pre-colonial and colonial times. Regulation 8, which forbade sexual intercourse before marriage, reflected Christian and patriarchal concerns with virginity. The leadership did not want problems with parents back home. Regulation 14 legislated against incest and clearly stated that this rule was determined by 'customs'.

Two main ambiguities arose from these regulations. One was that they were more or less unenforceable in the world of the camps. The other was that even a formal commitment to the values of patriarchy, undermined the revolutionary principles of gender equality.

Finally, colonial law and Christian teachings were clearly influential. Regulation 15, forbidding people with certain defects or diseases to marry, appears to have been lifted from the colonial code, and in fact refers to those 'regarded by medical science as rendering a person unfit for marriage'. Traditionally, those with physical or mental problems could still marry, and even those who were impotent could rely on their brothers or sisters to act on their behalf. But these ideas had been undermined by Christianity with its concerns for marital fidelity. Regulation 17, which prohibited abortion was also probably influenced by Christian teaching. Provision for the issue of marriage certificates under Regulations 18 and 19 clearly reflected bureaucratic and ecclesiastical practice.

Over and above the practical problems relating to enforcement was the incoherence and internal contradictions of a code derived from so many different influences: spirit mediums were accommodated in special areas of the camps and spoke for custom; the presence of priests and nuns reminded the leadership of its Christian education; and Marxian political education and interaction with FRELIMO generated a would-be revolutionary ideology.

The questions put to men and women applying to marry bring out the difficulties with which the leadership sought to grapple. Personal details had to be thoroughly recorded, so that couples could be traced after the war. Investigations had to be made to see if all necessary requirements for marriage had been met. Brideprice was also mentioned in the questionnaire, reminding those about to marry that theories about dispensing with it were just theories, and also implying that the war-time marriage lacked significance until traditional social obligations had been fulfilled. Inquiry had to be made into the existence of spouses back home, which would render such marriages polygamous and unrevolutionary.

These difficulties, together with the contradiction apparent between many of the regulations themselves, made implementation of the code difficult, if not impossible. (Thus Regulations 10, 11, 12, 13 and 25 appear to justify contravention of Regulation 9.) Certainly the code and implementation did not amount to any sort of revolution in the direction of gender equality. *De facto* inequality was most apparent in the case of pregnancy.

The regulation compelling men to marry the women they made pregnant was difficult to enforce because men often denied responsibility. Some men accepted responsibility for the pregnancies but not for the women, or wanted the women but not the pregnancy. Others accused their former lovers of being witches; still others rejected the women for being diseased. Many women only discovered that they were pregnant after having lost contact with the man responsible; sometimes women did not know who was responsible; and if they had been seduced or raped by a senior man they were afraid to name him. Some men ended up having several women naming them as fathers of their unborn children, yet regulations permitted only one spouse. Men even boasted that registering marriages with the Political Commissariat Department did not bother them as it did not prevent them from getting new girlfriends, and that anyway, they had not paid even a coin for the women who claimed to be married to them!

The boundaries of party interference in marital matters

An incident at the headquarters of the Commissariat Department demonstrated some of the main problems in a classical style. One Comrade Dhliwayo beat his two wives over a case of money that had gone missing in the hut they shared. He then banished them to Osibisa camp, telling them not to return without the missing money. The camp administrator tried to stop him but he declared that 'not even the president of the party could intervene' as this was entirely his 'private affair'.[91]

As the case shows, the Party often discovered that boundaries were drawn for it regarding the extent to which it could intervene in disputes between spouses. Dhliwayo's self-declaration as the sole judge over the matter with his wives also demonstrates how the absence of brideprice did not necessarily deter men from assuming that they had the right to exercise their traditional authority in marital unions. Also, it was only when Dhliwayo was tried for violence and disrespect of the Party President that the issue of his polygamous marriage arose. It transpires that the Party had sanctioned his marriage to only one of the

---

[91] ZANU (PF) Archives, File: Commissariat Matters, Doc: 'Comrade Dhliwayo's Case', Commissariat Department HQ, 26 July 1978.

women he was living with and yet, up to that point, everyone had turned a blind eye to the triple union. His case, of course, was not an isolated one. Dhliwayo also chose Osibisa camp as the place where he abandoned his unwanted wives. A look at the nature of this camp will soon show why.

Osibisa Camp: home to war-time mothers

By 1977 the situation in the camps had become critical. The enemy was conducting cross-border raids into neighbouring countries to destroy guerrilla bases. At this time, ZANU took a step that was later to make some women feel terribly alienated. They created a camp isolated from the rest of the camps in Mozambique, to keep expectant and nursing mothers. Osibisa, which is the name by which the camp curiously came to be known, immediately spelt problems for the women, who were obviously not satisfied with the explanation that it was for safety reasons that such arrangements had been made. The camp increasingly came to be seen as a punitive measure. Women complained bitterly:

> Sending mothers to Ossibissa is not good. Jobs should be found for them rather than just neglect them.[92]

For most women assigned to the camp, Osibisa spelt the end of their revolutionary careers. Once committed to it, it was very difficult to get out. The women there were automatically cut off from what was happening outside, and an atmosphere of uncertainty prevailed in the camp. The view of it as a condemnation camp was strengthened by the continual insults thrown at its occupants; women and girls were threatened that if they did not control their lusts, they would end up in Osibisa. Freedom Nyamubaya, an ex-combatant, vividly portrayed life in Osibisa camp in one of her poems, 'Osibisa'. It provides an insight into the atmosphere prevailing in the camp:

> A place of mental torture
> Where women and children were dumped
> Cut off from life
> A mental prison for mothers in war.
> Mentally disconnected, but physically involved...
>
> When it wrecks the human mind
> It destroys the person in them
> Sweeping away the love in them

---

[92] Ibid.; see also 'Minutes of the General Staff Meeting', 29 June 1977, ZANLA H.Q., Chimoio.

Corroding the confidence in them
Leaving only empty and vicious bodies.

I saw them battering each other
Jumping at each other's throats
Witch-hunting and rumour-mongering
Boiling jealous and burning hatred.
Osibisa, a hot camp of frustration...

Unknown by the world at large,
Forgotten by their male comrades
Who made them pregnant[93]

Many things kept tempers boiling in Osibisa. One former combatant gave an example of some of the situations that irreparably soured relations between the women, yet they still had to live in the same place:

> You are sitting there pregnant and wondering if your man is going to live up to his promise to the Party to keep you as his wife. Another pregnant woman comes too and you learn that the same man is responsible. If he was high-ranking, he could visit often on business, and he would talk to the other woman, entirely ignoring you. When the babies are born, he could bring presents for his favourite woman's child. Your own baby may even be sick. How do you think you feel towards him and towards the other woman?[94]

Thus, while life was generally difficult for the mothers, it was even more difficult for the unloved ones, or for those who would receive the news that the father of their child had died in the operational zones. They toiled alone, wondering all the time if their suffering would end. One former inmate of Osibisa said it was difficult to imagine at all that one day the war would be over and they could once more live like normal people.[95]

For those who had toyed with ideas of women's emancipation and concepts of equality between the sexes, everything lost meaning, and they found themselves seeking something more tangible in their frustration. They found themselves re-tracing their footsteps and embracing once more the traditional concepts of womanhood, if they had ever discarded them at all.

One way women could traditionally achieve respectable status was by having many children. These women had children but no respect, because the children had generally

---

93   Freedom Nyamubaya, 'Osibisa', *On the Road Again*, Zimbabwe Publishing House, Harare, 1986, pp.66-67.
94   Interview with Chipo Moyo (not her real name), London, 5 February 1994.
95   Interview with Mai Winnie, Dotito, Mt Darwin, 14 May 1992.

been born in unstable relationships. Thus, they anxiously awaited the end of the war so they could marry and mother their children in traditionally acceptable social circumstances. Such thoughts presented even more problems as they started worrying if the fathers of their children were still alive, or if they still thought of them. If the men who had fathered their children failed to marry them for any reason, would they ever be able to secure husbands in the future?[96]

Because of such feelings of rejection in Osibisa, morale was low among the women. They were bored, and in their search for a meaning to life, in their case a man to assume responsibility over them and their children in the future, they found themselves fighting for the few men they could get hold of, worrying the moralists a lot with their conduct.

No one seemed interested in their plight except to condemn them. They were left to rot there long after their children were grown up and the mothers were ready to resume duties in the armed struggle. Most would have been sent to Osibisa too early in their pregnancy, when they could still have served for a few more months.[97] The women found themselves fighting a second war, but because they had no guidance as to how to fight that war, they took their frustrations and anger out against their womanhood, which they had come to hate, and consequently against one another.

Shaming the mothers

In such circumstances the attitude of their male colleagues was not helpful. The men blamed the women for letting down the revolution and also viewed them as being solely responsible for their present situation. Women or girls found in men's huts or 'postos', as they were called, were arrested and paraded as prostitutes. No one bothered to find out how they had got there. Men were rarely questioned over such issues; the general view was that women had enticed the men into sexual relationships.[98] Those who complained of sexual abuse were often treated as having asked for it:

> If one leaves her barrack, goes to the guarding post to sleep there, then she is a goat in a lion's den.[99]

---

96 ZANU (PF) Archives, File: Defence Secretariat, Women's Affairs, Doc: 'Problems confronting our female comrades in the camps', no date.
97 ZANU (PF) Archives, File: Minutes of High Command and General Staff Meetings, Doc: 'Minutes of Women's League Meeting', 27 July 1978.
98 ZANU (PF) Archives, File: Defence Secretariat, Women's Affairs, Doc: 'Proposals on Marriages', no date.
99 ZANU (PF) Archives, File: Defence Department, MMZ Province, Local Meetings, Doc: 'Rally held at Tembwe Base 1', 17 January 1977.

Instead of investigating cases, the complainants were lambasted:

You are not real ZANU members! You are public prostitutes and I am going to take pictures of you and send them to the masses of Zimbabwe to see. You did not come here to bear children. Some of you are trained sell-outs.[100]

For the mothers at Osibisa, continual taunting characterised their days:

Maybe some of you wanted to test if you can have children. This should definitely cease. We want to hear reports that you are doing work. You should have gardens to cultivate vegetables for your children.[101]

Even some of their female comrades who had children but were in better positions projected the same age-old prejudices. They were not sympathetic: 'You should be doing more than just bearing children!'[102]

Mayor Urimbo, a member of the High Command who accompanied Teurai Ropa on several occasions during her visits to different camps to see women, chastised the inmates of Nehanda Base, over their failure to emulate the heroine after which their camp had been named: 'Nehanda died a virgin but you are doing the opposite'. The factual correctness of the statement aside, his agenda was clear: he meant to shame the mothers. The campaign succeeded in many respects, as women often did not reveal that they were mothers: 'Abroad they ask about women's duties in the revolution but we do not tell them that we have children'.[103]

The represented and the representatives: fragile sisterhood bonds

Once more it is essential to bring the Department of Women's Affairs under the spotlight. Contrary to its proclaimed role as the organ tasked with addressing such problems, from an early period it started displaying features reminiscent of the Women's Federation of the Communist Party of China.[104] Instead of being a vehicle for change to improve women's position, it became a mere transmission belt for Party policy.

---

[100] ZANU (PF) Archives, File: Minutes of High Command and General Staff Meetings, Doc: 'Minutes of Meeting of Recruits with High Command Member', Batalhao, Tete, 22 September 1977.

[101] ZANU (PF) Archives, J. Tongogara in File: HC, CC & GS Minutes, Doc: 'Minutes of Officers Meeting', Pungwe 3, 12 October 1978.

[102] ZANU (PF) Archives, File: Defence Secretariat: Women's Affairs, Doc: 'Minutes of meeting of Female Comrades', no date.

[103] ZANU (PF) Archives, Doc: Officers Meeting, Osibisa, 18 November 1978.

[104] John Schrecker, *The Chinese Revolution in Historical Perspective*, Contributions to the Study of World History, No. 19, Greenwood Press, New York, 1991, pp. 162-69.

Ordinary ZANLA women found it difficult to see the executive members of the Department of Women's Affairs separately from their husbands. Julia Zvobgo, for example, said that advising fellow women to be careful in their relations with senior men, could easily be construed as a purely personal agenda. It could, for instance, easily be said that women in her position merely wanted to ensure that there would be no competition for their husbands' attentions.[105] Their marriage ties also meant that not many women brought their problems to the senior members of the Department of Women's Affairs.

The department concentrated on teaching young girls about culture, entertaining illusions that this would cut down on licentious relations and pregnancies.[106] Reflecting the contradictory attitudes of the male leadership, some of its members chided fellow women for having babies. By passively accepting patriarchal resistance to contraceptives, these women were part of the nationalist conspiracy to exploit female reproduction. Their reluctance to request contraceptives from outside organisations points to their collusion with men to exploit their own sex. They were allowing the men to use women when it suited them, to promote the nationalist cause through producing baby nationalists. One woman explained that they were urged to bear children, 'to replace those being killed by the enemy back home'.[107] They said it was an honourable national duty that only women could fulfil. They were, however, also chastised when they did so.

Security was officially advanced as the reason for the creation of Osibisa, but there are two other possible explanations: the Party was ashamed of the mothers and decided to hide them far from the view of external visitors; or, it was a manifestation of the superstitious belief that the presence of pregnant women could expose ZANLA camps to danger. Lan learnt from one guerrilla's account:

Even at the time of the elections we did not want to see a pregnant woman. If a pregnant woman came to one of our camps, sure that camp will be destroyed.[108]

Although the reasons for confining the mothers to Osibisa varied, their needs seem to have been given low priority. Julia Zvobgo explained that the women felt strongly that they were being deliberately denied their basic needs as a punishment. But she also thought that this perception may have arisen out of their ignorance of what provisions were like in other camps, especially as they were so isolated from everyone else.[109] Many dreamt of

[105] Interview with Julia Zvobgo, Harare, 10 January 1995.
[106] ZANU (PF) Archives, File: Defence Secretariat, Women's Affairs, Doc: Minutes of 'Women's League Meeting', Doeroi Camp, 28 December 1977.
[107] Interview with Mai Fambai, Dotito, Mt Darwin, May 1992.
[108] Lan, *Guns and Rain*, p.159.
[109] Interview with Julia Zvobgo, Harare, 10 January 1995.

receiving training which would allow them to engage with the enemy at the battlefront, but the leadership soon categorised them as refugees. they had become a nuisance with nothing to offer to the struggle but new mouths to feed. One former combatant explained that it was unfair for people to look down on those who returned from the war as refugees, because camp life held a lot of obstacles to frustrate women's intended careers as revolutionary fighters.[110]

Few in the predominantly male leadership of the war stopped to think that women did not just fall pregnant on their own and that their babies had male fathers. Generally, the opinion was that women were careless, which is why they fell pregnant, and so they could not be counted on to assume important responsibilities. Thus, women found themselves being denied responsible positions. The few women who managed to show their real worth discharged their duties well, but those in influential positions, the majority of whom were men, deliberately looked elsewhere when it came to weighing up women's performances as soldiers and organisers. They were not interested in knowing why the rest of the women were not playing their full role in the war.

Perhaps Mozambique was not the best place for positive change in this sphere to occur. The Organisation of Mozambican Women, who the ZANU Women's League in many respects looked up to for inspiration and guidance, had been caught up in the 'cultural snare' and had become an organ to help perpetuate patriarchy. It also became FRELIMO's propaganda vehicle.[111] So its relations with ZANU women could not have helped much.

The women found their struggles severely crippled by whether or not they had relationships with leading men. Women could be divided into those with senior male associations and those without. The former could be further divided into wives, mistresses and casual sex providers. These differences partially consumed the energy of the women's forces and helped to keep them divided.

The few who tried to transcend these divisions and directed their energies at challenging the dominance of powerful men, men who controlled both material and human resources in the camps, risked being accused of retrogressive behaviour and lack of patriotism. As with most liberation movements, the general argument was that female exploitation, including sexual exploitation, would no longer be a problem once the colonial capitalists had been removed.

---

[110] Interview with Precious Takawira, Sunningdale, Harare, 14 March 1992.
[111] See Stephanie Urdang, *And Still They Dance: Women, War and the Struggle for Change in Mozambique*, Earthscan Publications Ltd., London, 1989.

Yet for the women and the young girls who joined the war, questions of sexuality and marital relationships in ZANLA camps often decided their fate. Such matters also formed some of the main issues that informed the discourse on gender relations during and after the war. War-time sexual and marital experiences have significantly determined the way women perceive themselves and the way society regards them, boosting or undermining their confidence in themselves as women. So often, society has critically viewed this aspect of their lives and judged them on it.

The extent of this scrutiny came out clearly at the time of cease-fire in 1979. As the refugees were being repatriated from Mozambique into Zimbabwe and as the fighters were being ferried from the operational zones to their various places of assembly, their buses sometimes stopped as they passed through the countryside, bidding farewell to the civilians who had worked with them through the war. One woman, for example, remarked to another:

> Did you see the passengers in that other bus. They were all full girls, unspoilt. They seem to have known better what they went to Mozambique for. It's such a break from those others with lots of children.[112]

Civilians wanted to see female soldiers returning as 'full' girls, in other words, as virgins whose sole pre-occupation during the war was firing guns at the enemy. When the women who had 'got themselves spoilt' arrived, their civilian supporters felt let down after all the sacrifices the rural people had made for the guerrillas.

General understanding of the predicaments that women experienced in Mozambique needs more research. Documents from the Department of Women's Affairs, the Political Commissariat and the Education and Culture Department reveal the complexity of women's sexual involvement and the nature of war-time marriages.

Women encountered numerous problems in the camps, many of which were imposed on them because of their sexuality. But this is not to say that all women became helpless victims of their male colleagues' wantonness. In spite of all the difficulties, some relationships held firm against those trying times. There are women who have no regrets or bitterness about relations with their male comrades. For the majority, however, the war left scars that may take a long time to heal.

---

[112] This is the author's personal recollection. She was 14 years old and living in Masvingo Province (then Victoria Province) at the time of cease-fire in 1979.

Conclusion

Camp life afforded some women the opportunity to experiment with their sexuality in a way they had never done before. Many others found themselves having to use their bodies to survive the harsh camp conditions and still more found themselves exposed to wanton sexual abuse by their seniors. They were expected to provide men with sex to relieve the stresses of military life, justified as their own contribution to the struggle. At the same time, they were castigated for doing so and labelled prostitutes. Whatever the situation, the majority of women found their room for manoeuvre severely limited by the absence of contraception. The marriage institution failed to provide most women with any security, especially in the absence of the traditional cementing factors, that is, family involvement and bridewealth. Many women ended up performing the function of motherhood under what turned out to be an unscathed or unrevolutionised patriarchal system. Most significantly, ordinary women's sexuality became a much more public concern at this time, as its control had shifted from the sphere of the family to the wider arena of nationalist politics and the military.

Up to this day, the women do not easily provide information on their troubled relations with their male comrades during the struggle. Algerian former fighter and feminist activist Helie-Lucas's observations from her country's liberation struggle shed some light on this reluctance. She commented with much bitterness about the unavoidable mistakes she and her comrades made:

> What makes me angry... is not the mere fact of confining women in their place, but the brainwashing which did not allow us... to even think in terms of questioning the women's place. And what makes me even more angry is to witness the replication of this situation in various places in the world where national liberation struggles are still taking place. We still witness women covering the misbehaviour of their fellow men and hiding in the name of national solidarity and identity, crimes which will continue after the official liberation.[113]

The women who claim to have been equally treated by male comrades in the Zimbabwean struggle have a right to speak for themselves, but the possibility that some fear being accused of selling out on the nationalist cause cannot be ignored. Perhaps that is why some interviewees in this study would only share their war-time experiences on condition of anonymity. As it clearly emerges, nationalist movements have a remarkable silencing mechanism.

---

[113] Marie-Aimée Helie-Lucas, 'Women in the Algerian Liberation Struggle', in T. Wallace with C. March (eds), *Changing Perceptions: Writings on Gender and Development*, Oxfam, Oxford, 1991, pp. 57-58.

The views of those still nursing illusions that they were men's equals in the camps can also be seen in a context in which it was unprecedented for women to be recruited to take part in an armed struggle. However, this chapter reveals all too clearly what actually happened to the majority of these women.

For those contemplating serious revolution, the intimidatory practices of the organisation only added to the other practical problems with which they had to contend. It was difficult for them to visualise a normal future while visions of the present were so warped and the current circumstances so far from normal. Little time and energy were available to invest in formulating an ideal order for a future when one had to worry about how to pull through the present. The social and economic dislocations caused by what was essentially a forced migration into neighbouring countries made the struggle for survival the major preoccupation for the majority of potential revolutionaries.

In the end, women were useful in the various mechanical aspects of the war, but their presence in the camps did not alter pre-existing gender divisions. When the leadership felt their patriarchal-based authority was coming under attack, they denied the would-be revolutionaries a platform and also manipulated social and economic differences amongst the women. These differences manifested themselves in many ways. The largely illiterate recruits of the early 1970s were suspicious of the relatively better-educated recruits who came in the second half of the decade. The former were beginning to nurse hopes that they had displayed enough muscle as carriers to warrant official recognition as 'combatants' and earn promotion. They were unsettled by the new arrivals' contention that the whole notion of 'combat roles' needed reviewing. There were also differences between women with powerful connections in the leadership and those without. These contrasts paralysed women's organisational capacity.

CHAPTER FOUR

ZANLA Women at the Front

Introduction

Prior to 1978, the liberation forces operating in the ZANLA operational zones were mostly male. For the most part the females remained in the rear base camps. However, in 1978, ZANLA claimed to have taken steps to improve the situation and by the end of the war in 1979 it had, at least in theory, given women opportunities to explore their full potential as revolutionary fighters. Yet, as has already been noted, there are still myths to be dispelled regarding these reforms and their timing. Given all the biases regarding the selection of 'combat fighters', and considering all the prejudices surrounding the matter of female sexuality, how much transformation could really be expected to occur? Could ZANLA really overcome age-old, deep-seated prejudices? Did it really make a genuine effort to bridge the gender gap by offering the same military opportunities to women as to men?

The timing of the proclaimed change of attitude towards women's participation in so-called 'combat' or 'frontal' duties in 1978 is closely linked to the creation of 'liberated' zones inside Rhodesia. Only after ZANLA had created 'safe havens' or 'feminised' spaces in some areas within the former 'hot zones', did it consider the idea of women engaging in cross-border operations.

Apart from defining these 'feminised' spaces, did ZANLA really revolutionise duty allocation? Did men and women really fight as equals in the field, as ZANLA claimed? Did ZANLA's supposed appreciation of women's capacities translate into promoting women to decision-making positions in the upper echelons of the organisation i.e. the High Command and the Central Committee?

Following ZIPA's initiatives, ZANLA had managed to divide Rhodesia (see map p. ix) into three operational provinces which derived their names from the Mozambican administrative provinces through which the former could be accessed for military operations: Tete in the north, Gaza in the south, and Manica sandwiched between the two. ZANLA's operations essentially covered the entire eastern half of the country and a sizeable chunk of the south-west. The liberation army claimed to have formed liberated areas in each of the three operational provinces, but its firmest claims lay in Tete Province. For that reason, the evidence for this discussion comes mostly from there.

ZANLA had its own nomenclature for classifying its operational zones. Contested areas were those in which enemy operations were still intensive and its administrative organs still operational. This description actually applied to most of ZANLA's operational areas right up to the end of the war. One such area, Wedza, in ZANLA's Manica Province, was dubbed 'Vietnam', a term reportedly alluding to the continuous sounds of gunfire as the guerrillas and Rhodesian agents exchanged fire.[1]

Liberated areas were zones where the enemy's operations and administrative structures had almost come to a standstill. These were virtually no-go areas for the Rhodesian ground troops. The guerrillas made access impossible by placing land mines and digging deep trenches across the roads. The Rhodesians could not conduct foot patrols either, because the civilian security network would alert ZANLA of their presence and the guerrillas would set up an ambush. The enemy could only hit such areas through air-raids. The guerrillas claimed greatest autonomy in the liberated areas, even setting up village committees:

> The committee leadership give permits to those requiring to move to other areas... our youth who are always on patrol look into movements done by enemy agents after which they are caught and killed.[2]

ZANLA also formed strongholds in areas inside Zimbabwe where colonial administrative structures had been weak. In such areas the guerrillas did not find it too difficult to scare away the few whites who served as functionaries of the colonial administration. Drawing

---

[1] ZANU (PF) Archives, File: Defence Operations, Document: 'Report On Manica Province Front (December 1978 - May 1979)', 28 July 1979.

[2] ZANU (PF) Archives, File: Operations MMZ (Tete Province), Doc: 'MMZ Province Annual Military Report for the Whole Province' (for 1977), 2 January 1978.

a picture of the state of affairs in such liberated zones, operational commanders in Buhera noted:

Some kids of at least 7 years will tell you that they have never seen a white man in their life time… so there is little of military work against the enemy. …As a result our forces are engaged in the training of militia, local nurses and *mujibhas*.[3]

Besides the liberated and the contested areas, ZANLA also designated certain areas as semi-liberated, because the enemy was losing its hold but still conducting ground operations. Because the enemy's intelligence network was not yet broken, the guerrillas had to be clandestine in their dealings with civilians. These areas could contain pockets of liberated terrain, but for as long as surrounding areas remained unstable the guerrillas could not completely trust the village committees. Most of the areas ZANLA described as liberated probably could be more accurately classified as semi-liberated.

In its operational reports, ZANLA did not provide the overall numbers of forces deployed in the field. These figures would have been useful in determining to what extent ZANLA addressed the gender imbalance in its forces inside Zimbabwe in the last two years of the war. As it is the information on male-to-female percentages is limited.

Nevertheless, a few available figures for ZANLA's Tete Province give a general picture of its position. In Takawira and Chitepo Sectors in the north-east, where male and female figures can be compared, ZANLA's supposed drive towards 'demasculinising' its forces at the front was rather weak. For the period March to July 1979, the proportion of women fighters deployed in the area was around eight percent (8%). Thus, on average, ZANLA deployed one woman for every twelve men. Yet, Chapter 3 showed the female component of ZANLA as one-third of the total forces by 1979.

The figures show gross under-representation of women in the operational sectors of Tete Province. Considering that field reports contain no evidence of guerrilla women's involvement outside the zone designated as liberated, the picture is indeed discouraging.[4]

---

3   ZANU (PF) Archives, File: Defence Operations, Doc: 'Report on Manica Province Front (for December 1978 - May 1979)', compiled on 28 July 1979.

4   ZANLA's reports covering the contested zones in the interior of Rhodesia make no reference to the presence of female guerrillas. Neither do civilian recollections of the war as reflected in fiction. All civilian-guerrilla encounters captured are with male guerrillas. Most Zimbabweans got their first opportunity to meet female freedom fighters at the time of the cease-fire. However, there was a general awareness that ZANLA had female fighters because, apart from getting news of their activities elsewhere towards the end of the war, most people knew women or girls who had left to join the guerrilla army.

Gendering 'frontal' spaces

The percentage of women was always low, even in the few areas they were allowed to operate. The pattern of their deployment also remained inconsistent. An operational report for Tete commented:

> Forces in the province are now composed of male and female comrades though the female comrades don't always stay in the field. The Women's Detachment usually concentrates on the transportation of materials to the border and right into the fore-front.[5]

Moreover, whenever there was the slightest indication that the enemy's offensive in an area was gaining momentum, ZANLA responded by withdrawing women to its rear bases inside Mozambique. One incident, reported for the southern operational province of Gaza, aptly summarises ZANLA's stance on female units whenever unstable winds blew through areas initially categorised as calm:

> The enemy has attacked 3 strategic places… there is still the threat of further attacks. F.P.L.M. has ruled that female comrades are not to proceed into the area until the situation is clear. They should be sent back to Xai Xai for their own security, the security of the bridge (across the Limpopo)… and the avoiding of likely confusion between F.P.L.M. and ourselves should anything happen to the bridge while they are there.[6]

The area had become a hot zone, and in the male commanders' view the situation called for real men – for what may be described as a total remasculinisation of the forces operating in the area. Women were automatically cleared from this male space, so ZANLA men could reclaim it from the enemy.

As in the camps, patronising behaviour on the part of sister, or rather, brother organisations, often blocked any meaningful gender revolution within ZANLA, even at the front. The influence of the ruling party in Mozambique, FRELIMO, and its armed wing, FPLM, reinforced the ZANLA commanders' distrust of women combatants' capacities in the operational zones. FRELIMO's patriarchal leadership could openly practise sexism as the need to impress foreign donors had decreased for them as they had attained independence in Mozambique. Not surprisingly, the Rhodesian security forces also viewed the female guerrillas with contempt. On learning that ZANLA was now deploying women in cross-border operations, Rhodesian patrol units were issued with instructions to 'catch the

---

5   ZANU (PF) Archives, File: Operations MMZ (Tete Province), Document: 'MMZ Province, Provincial General Report Covering 1/1/79-31/5/79'.
6   ZANU (PF) Archives, File: Southern Province (Gaza), Sector 4 Operational Reports. Document: 'Special Report On The Bombing Raid on Gaza Province, (Gaza Operations)', 2 December 1978.

women alive and put them in sacks'.[7] The practicality of the operation aside, such threats did worry the guerrilla commanders and drastic measures were taken to prevent them being carried out – they withdrew the women fighters and replaced them with men.

ZANLA commanders were far from convinced that women could face the enemy in battle at the front in the same way as men. They held a deep-seated distrust of women's shooting abilities or competence with guns. This distrust even extended to those women who had received the same training as men. As in the camps, women in the operational zones remained in spaces carved out for them by the men. In particular, there is no evidence suggesting that those areas ZANLA categorised as 'contested' ever saw a single woman guerrilla. Those areas seem to have remained entirely as male zones of operation. Women could go only where the male guerrillas had neutralised the enemy's operations, or where the terrain had been 'feminised'. Consequently, the handful of women deployed to the front were more likely to be found in ZANLA's 'rear' detachments, the areas bordering Mozambique and nearest to ZANLA's rear bases. Deeper into Rhodesia, towards what the guerrilla army referred to as the 'middle' and 'advanced' detachments of the operational zones, the pre-1978 position remained almost unaltered. Basically the presence or absence of women combatants in an area measured ZANLA's confidence in those areas it claimed to have liberated.

By 1978, ZANLA had achieved not so much a position of gender equality in the field, but the exclusion of the Rhodesian security ground forces from certain parts of the country. The exclusion of the Rhodesian ground forces extended the guerrillas' zone of influence over those areas, which now resembled the rear bases in Mozambique. As this neutralized zone expanded, ZANLA needed to increasingly move its 'services' organs, and hence women, into the liberated zones.

In the absence of any military or 'manly' engagements against the enemy, ZANLA could set up service structures, as long as they were out of view of the bombers, the main remaining threat. This situation was similar to the security threats anticipated in the rear base camps. ZANLA could also establish armouries in these relatively safe areas, so that its middle and advanced operational zones would have quicker and easier access to reinforcements. For all these functions, the guerrillas needed women.

---

[7]   Interview with Mrs Mazarura Junior (Mai Caro), Dotito, Mt Darwin, 14 May 1992.

The nature of women's 'frontal' service

ZANLA tasked most of the women deployed in its operational zones inside Zimbabwe with carrying war material. The women also nursed the sick and the injured, and they mobilised support for the war. Essentially, their duties did not differ much from what women did in the camps at the rear. Thus, field operational reports mostly referred to women fighters as being important in transporting war material, in providing nursing services, or politicising the masses in the areas where ZANLA was establishing itself.

Transportation of war materials

The ZANLA Command viewed the Women's Detachment with much apprehension as it went about its operations. Even in the pre-1978 period when the detachment could only go as far as the Zimbabwe-Mozambique border, ZANLA worried about the women and maintained a 'protectionist' policy towards them as the female guerrillas transported war equipment. In spite of the women's record of successful defensive operations against the enemy as the porters went about their duties, field commanders maintained a rather patronising watch over them. Commenting on the women's withdrawal from a border assignment in May 1977, Fox Gava, ZANLA's security and intelligence chief, explained that the action had been taken because the enemy had issued threats to capture them.[8] He told the women that male units were going to control the situation, or in other words 'feminise' the area for the Women's Detachment's operations. Noting that these women had successfully engaged the enemy in battle whilst on the border assignment, Gava thanked them for what he described as 'a historical demonstration'. He promised them that their next assignment would 'probably' allow them to go to Mtoko inside Zimbabwe.[9]

Indeed, in 1978, when enemy operations in the area had been neutralised, members of the Women's Detachment penetrated further into Zimbabwe as promised, into the border districts of Mtoko, Mt Darwin, Nyanga, the Sabi-Limpopo valley, and even deeper into the country into parts of Maranke and Buhera districts. By 1979, field commanders could report:

> Our Women's Detachment comrades are now able to transport material further into the interior detachments giving our fighters the best chance of effectively counter attacking the en-

---

[8] ZANU (PF) Archives, File: Defence Department, MMZ Province, 1976-1978, Local Meetings, Document: 'Meeting Held with Women's Detachment', Battaliao Transit Camp, 25 May 1977.

[9] Ibid.

[10] ZANU (PF) Archives, File: Operations MMZ (Tete Province), Doc: 'Department of Operations: Provincial Military Report for April 1979'.

emy.[10]

The detachment's duties could not be mistaken as they came out quite clearly in most reports. A commander in Tete recorded:

In all sectors there is a women's detachment for material transportation either to the fore-front or the border to facilitate material infiltration into the fore-front.[11]

Whilst keeping to the neutralised zone and remaining in their traditional functions as porters, the women were sometimes distributed amongst male units. This occurred whenever the male commanders considered the climate in the women's areas of operation to be turbulent or not totally 'feminised'.

The problems associated with transporting war equipment were endless. The porters were often poorly armed, which compromised their ability to defend themselves from enemy raids. They were also inadequately clothed for their duties:

The same problem lies to [sic] our female comrades who are transporting war material bare footed. To boost their morale our clothing and footwear supplies from Chimoio should be enlarged. In fact if bags are available we would be very glad if they are supplied to us for the purpose of transporting material to the front.[12]

It was dangerous enough to be caught in an enemy raid while poorly armed, but it was even more dangerous to be both under-armed and overloaded, as the female porters often were. As there were never enough guns for everybody requiring them, the women often had to do without them.

Although the porters had no monopoly on suffering, they were more vulnerable to enemy strategies in the operational zones. Their heavy loads slowed their movements and they spent more time in hostile terrain than did the men's units. The enemy poisoned wells along the guerrillas' routes, forcing them to rely entirely on the water supplies they carried with them. Due to their slower speed, porters spent more time in such regions and often ran out of supplies. A former fighter described the hardship her comrades endured. They operated in Gaza Province in the south, which included the dry Gonarezhou area and their only source of water were a handful of boreholes that had all been poisoned. She explained: 'If one managed to produce any urine at all she would actually have to share it with others.'[13]

---

[11] Ibid., 23 January 1979.
[12] Ibid., Doc: 'MMZ Provincial General Report Covering 1 January 1979 - 31 May 1979'.
[13] Interview with Margaret Dongo, Parliament Building, Harare, 10 March 1992.

The rainy season brought fewer worries about drinking water, but even then the fighters could not be sure because river water could be poisoned. New problems arose when rivers flooded and were extremely hazardous to cross. In one High Command meeting, it was acknowledged that several fighters had drowned whilst trying to cross flooded rivers with war materials.[14] A suggestion was made that rivers be crossed in the dry season, but that had its own problems.

Another important factor relating to women who had joined the struggle, which has not yet received any attention, is that women reported missing their periods during the war.[15] Others seemed to have suffered permanent damage to their reproductive systems due to the endless journeys to the front and the long periods spent in harsh terrain on poor diets or with no food at all. Some have not been able to have children. [16]

Enemy air raids and bombings also made their situation more hazardous. The Rhodesian forces hoped civilians would flee into the interior thus cutting off ZANLA's rear bases from its operational zones and thereby frustrating the efforts of the porters to infiltrate arms and other war materials.[17] Operational reports further related:

> In these isolated areas, the enemy could take an advantage... along our routes with the female comrades. This led to our comrades being ambushed in Nehanda Sector. A unit of 90 - 100 comrades were ambushed with war material, whereby we suffered 8 casualties and a few materials.[18]

From a military operational perspective, the field commanders were probably justified in being apprehensive about the movement of the Women's Detachment and that the porters' gender was immaterial. Yet the nature of the risks involved does not seem to have been the most central consideration in shaping military attitudes. In spite of the risks, porters often went about their duties inadequately armed. Moreover, many of the carriers were still inadequately trained.

ZANLA routinely used untrained personnel to transport war materials until the end of the war. In the border districts, the guerrillas employed dozens of civilian youths as porters

---

[14] ZANU (PF) Archives, File: Minutes HC, Document: 'Minutes of High Command Meeting Held at Operational Farm', Manica, 25 July 1978.

[15] Interview with Precious Takawira, Sunningdale, Harare, 12 March 1992. She thought these problems were due to the lack of salt in their diet, an explanation offered by many of her comrades.

[16] The harsh conditions experienced by women in wars elsewhere have been established to have had serious effects on women's reproductive health and it would be useful to conduct a survey of the problem amongst Zimbabwean ex-combatants.

[17] ZANU (PF) Archives, File: Operations MMZ (Tete Province), Document: 'Provincial Military Report, May - August 1979'.

[18] Ibid.

in the last two years of the war. Reports noted:

> In Nehanda Sector recently a total of 198 boys and girls ran away from the enemy who wanted to collect them to keeps ['protected villages'] and for training. These are now stationed at the base under training helping the female comrades in transporting material to the front being armed with offensive grenades only.[19]

They conducted the so-called training programme in the border bases with limited resources. The training consisted mainly of basic cover tactics and the use of hand grenades. It did not equip the young people at all for the challenges that awaited them. The grenades were more a danger to their bearers than to the enemy. Because FRELIMO disapproved of using youths who had no recognisable military training in transportation duties, ZANLA withheld information about such activities.[20]

The engagement and acceptance of youths as porters, with almost no military training, has significant implications in understanding the importance ZANLA attached to that duty. Despite its importance to women fighters' military curricula vitae, ZANLA only rated porterage as an auxiliary service. It did not count much towards attaining military rank. Yet this is what most female guerrillas, who lay claim to 'frontal' experience, specialised in. Men's potential for military promotion was higher, because ZANLA assigned them what they considered the more crucial roles: ones which on their assessment scale were given more credit. When men transported arms, they were merely 'helping the Women's Detachment'.[21] To all intents and purposes, porterage in ZANLA was a female duty. This view is consistent with the pre-colonial position where women were the main providers of carrier services.

Health matters: the challenges for ZANLA

Nursing was a ticket the female guerrillas also used to cross the border into Zimbabwe. Although these women played a significant role, no evidence suggests that the majority of the guerrilla nurses or medical assistants inside Zimbabwe were women. In the absence of such evidence, the general deployment patterns will be referred to in discussing the number of nurses.

The initial analysis of these last two years of the war revealed many problems underlying the deployment of women guerrillas to the front. Thus, male guerrillas will be assumed

---

19 Ibid.
20 Ibid.
21 ZANU (PF) Archives, File: Operations MMZ (Tete Province), Doc: 'Department of Operations: Provincial Military Report', 23 January 1979.

to outnumber women guerrillas as nurses in the operational zones inside Zimbabwe. However this situation was gradually reversed as mainly female youths trained to join ZANLA's health programmes.[22]

Providing nursing services was part of a wider ZANLA scheme to reorganise civil society in the areas where the guerrilla army had moved. Among other things, the scheme was concerned with organising material and political support for the struggle. ZANLA's Medical Department assumed crucial importance in meeting the health needs of guerrillas and the local civilian communities in areas without hospitals.

Its services became an important factor in guerrilla-civilian interaction. Many health problems in the operational zones could be directly attributed to the activities of the Rhodesian forces, that had closed the existing hospitals. Thus, ZANLA had an opportunity to show itself as a real people's army by addressing the health crises. The enemy's punitive policies against civilians turned out to be a strong political weapon for ZANU and ZANLA. As ZANU's political lectures at the rear made clear: 'It is the people, not weapons, that are a decisive factor in war.' [23]

This was ZANLA's opportunity to give the masses the chance to compare it favourably with the Rhodesian army. Although the liberation army had far from adequate stocks of medicines, and although its victories over disease were quite limited, the masses still appreciated its services.

Reports from the Medical Department documented a serious crisis in the liberated areas. For example, all the sectors of Tete Province, namely Chitepo, Nehanda, Percy Ntini, Chaminuka and Takawira, were in dire need of medical supplies. Takawira Sector was under serious stress with a large civilian population living in caves and bushes in the mountains.[24] Nehanda Sector was also a haven for disease for the same reason: 1 464 'masses' were said to have joined the guerrillas in the bush.[25] In the same sector, disease plagued the Dande Detachment due to food shortages. Fleeing from enemy air raids and bombings in their original settlements people moved to agriculturally unsuitable areas.[26]

---

[22] Ibid., Doc: 'Takawira Sector: General Strategies Conducted in the Sector, January - July 1979'.

[23] ZANU (PF) Archives, File: Commissariat Department, Document: 'ZANU Political Education, People's War, Lesson 3'.

[24] ZANU (PF) Archives, File: Department of Operations, Tete Province, Doc: 'MMZ Province: Medical Department, Operational Report', 28 June 1979.

[25] Ibid, Doc: 'Nehanda Sector, Sectorial MO's Monthly Report, January to March 1979', 16 April 1979.

[26] ZANU Archives, File: Operations MMZ (Tete Province), Doc: 'MMZ Province, Provincial General Report Covering 1 January to 31 May, 1979'.

In Percy Ntini Sector, the war cut off the Red Cross medical supplies on which the area had previously relied. Civilians avoided enemy-administered clinics fearing they would be injected with poisons; the enemy was said to use such extermination methods in areas recognised as guerrilla strongholds.[27]

The numbers of displaced civilians also kept rising as ZANLA fighters were gradually evacuating more and more people from the so-called 'protected villages'. At the close of 1977, for example, guerrillas stormed nine of the ten protected villages in Maramba District in ZANLA's Takawira Sector. Civilians driven into the mountains had neither shelter nor sanitary facilities; they had no food and they had no medicines.[28]

The Rhodesian security agents used chemical warfare, causing many casualties in the ZANLA-controlled areas, especially from 1977 onwards. Apart from reports of poisoned water sources mentioned above, Gaza Province also reported cases of food and clothes poisoning. There were also rumours of enemy attempts to start a cholera epidemic.[29] A medical report for ZANLA's Manica Province noted that government health officials had withdrawn anti-poisons from the hospitals and clinics in areas where poisons were in widespread use.[30] Canned meat brands such as 'Leox', and certain cigarettes were reported to be amongst poisoned consumer items.[31] In addition, people risked contracting diseases from eating beef from cattle the enemy had infected with anthrax.[32]

Given this huge crisis, the field operators constantly pleaded for more health personnel and medicines to be sent to the 'liberated' zones. Even if more nurses came from the rear, the civilian population could not rely entirely on ZANLA personnel. The guerrillas were constantly moving, often before their patients had completed their course of medication. This posed a danger because diseases could only be temporarily suppressed before recurring, often with greater intensity. ZANLA realised that local youth needed training as nursing aides.

Although the majority of ZANLA nurses inside Zimbabwe may initially have been men, guerrillas and the civilians alike viewed nursing as a feminine job. Discourse in both the colonial administration and in ZANLA camps at the rear endorsed the idea that the profes-

---

[27] Ibid.

[28] Ibid., Doc: 'Annual Military Report for the Whole Province', 2 January 1978. (The year covered should be 1977.)

[29] ZANU (PF) Archives, File: Southern Province (Gaza) Sector 4 Operational Reports, Doc: 'Gaza Provincial Mid-year Assessment', 29 August 1977.

[30] ZANU (PF) Archives, File: Operational Reports (Manica), Doc: 'Manica Provincial Operational Report', 6 July 1978.

[31] Ibid.

[32] David Martin, who with Phyllis Johnson co-authored *The Struggle For Zimbabwe: The Chimurenga War* has recently been looking at the extent of the use of chemicals by Rhodesian agents in the Zimbabwean armed struggle.

sion was a female one. Furthermore, women made up the majority of the populations in the liberated areas where ZANLA forces lived. The usefulness of male nurses in such a situation was limited because women felt uncomfortable talking with men about certain ailments, especially reproductive health. Thus, ZANLA targeted civilian women to train as health workers to serve local communities.

Takawira Sector reported that they were teaching medicine to two or three female youths in every base. This way they could help the locals.[33] The International Red Cross, with support from pre-existing local clinics, had set up a clinic in Nyanga.[34] ZANLA trained women before sending them to the Red Cross to be assessed and to receive first-aid certificates.[35] Locally trained women and youths were thus gradually reversing the gender composition of personnel serving under ZANLA's health programmes.

Operational reports also pointed out the need to give civilians lessons on constructing toilets, digging rubbish pits, and about hygiene. Problems in these areas exacerbated the health crises.[36] This was, of course, another sphere in which they expected women to dominate. In a patriarchal structure, the women were supposed to be the keepers of the home. This was also the position taken by the Department of Women's Affairs at the rear (see Chapter 3). If the department had organised itself properly, health education could have been its area of specialisation. However as its training programmes had not even taken shape in the camps, the department had nothing to offer civilians inside Zimbabwe.

Mobilising and politicising the masses

What impact did the presence of women fighters amongst ZANLA forces have in mobilising support for the struggle and in shaping political ideas amongst the people? Teurai Ropa appealed to the leadership to allow women to go into the liberated zones to work with displaced civilians (see Chapter 3). Drawing the commanders' attention to the changing security situation in some parts of Zimbabwe she asked:

> why can't we soldiers go and stay with them [displaced civilians] and win their support for our Party?[37]

33 ZANU (PF) Archives, File: Operations MMZ (Tete Province), Doc: 'Takawira Sector: General Strategies Conducted in the Sector, January - July 1979'.
34 ZANU (PF) Archives, File: MMZ Province, Department of Operations, Medical Department, Doc: 'Medical Operational Report', 19 March 1979.
35 Ibid.
36 ZANU (PF) Archives, File: MMZ Province, Department of Operations, Medical Department, Doc: 'MMZ Province: Operations, Medical Report for January to June 1979'.
37 ZANU (PF) Archives, File: Department of Women's Affairs, Doc: 'Report for the Year Ending 31 December, 1978'.

Ropa persuaded the ZANLA High Command to reconsider its position on women's deployment at the front. Apart from the political points they scored for the army and the Party as carriers and nurses, women were effective in politicising civilians. That they were women *and* soldiers, made ZANLA unusual when seen from the traditional perspective regarding the occupations in which women could or could not engage. This apparent innovation by ZANLA held a special appeal to the masses. It emphasised that the guerrilla army meant business! Field reports recorded the credit the women were earning for ZANLA:

The female comrades have had a very great impact on the masses politically and on our youth militarily. They have encouraged the masses and the youth to work harder and harder.[38]

Mugabe also highlighted the women's work to delegates attending the Xai Xai conference in May 1979:

Let me single out the commissariat work that is taking place in the Operational Areas, especially in the Liberated Zones. We have sent into the country teams of women cadres to carry out in several areas political work amongst our people. They talk to fathers, mothers, boys and girls, and the response has been wonderful all over.[39]

Clearly, they took women's presence in the liberation army as a challenge to everyone to make a contribution. Given the age-old perception of women as delicate beings needing male protection, the presentation of female guerrillas in a tough and traditionally male job, as soldiers, made the work that the masses were being asked to do seem lighter. As women were considered weak, the general feeling must have been that if a woman could do it, then so could anyone else.

The Political Commissariat Department's lectures on revolutionary ideology in the camps did not address gender inequality; and neither did ZANLA's political commissars, (including the women) introduce these issues at the front. In an interview with Teurai Ropa she advanced the official rhetoric on gender policy, testifying to her own emancipation as a woman during the liberation war, I asked her if the guerrilla women had attempted to extend their remarkable experience to fellow women at the front through political teachings. She replied in the negative and said it had been an oversight. She said that the emancipation of women guerrillas had been 'like a honeymoon', and in their excitement they had not realised they were far ahead of everybody else in their thinking.[40]

---

[38] ZANU (PF) Archives, File: Operations MMZ (Tete Province), Doc: 'Department of Operations: Provincial Military Report for April 1979'.

[39] Robert Mugabe, 'The Role and History of the Zimbabwean Women in the National Struggle', in *Women's Liberation in the Zimbabwean Revolution: Materials from the ZANU Women's Seminar, Xai Xai, 21 May 1979*, ZANU, San Francisco, p.17.

[40] Interview with Teurai Ropa (Joyce Mujuru), Bindura, 2 November 1994.

Other women fighters dismissed the idea of female emancipation. Their explanation was because everyone – male and female – was oppressed at that time, there was no need to address gender specific questions. In this respect, civilian education by male and female guerrillas took a similar line.[41] The slogans glorifying the participation of women might appear to suggest otherwise, but the guerrillas were not talking about changing the *status quo*, they were actually appealing to women to support the struggle in their capacities as mothers and as cooks.

At the front, female guerrillas focused on the same issues as male guerrillas. They talked about land, taxes, health provision, the enemy's harassment strategies and, of course, the restoration of indigenous culture. With regard to the latter, the guerrillas had shown the way by restoring the value and dignity of traditional religion. As a policy, ZANLA forces were careful not to antagonise the patriarchal leadership in the areas in which they were operating. That is why the liberation army first sought the co-operation of the spirit mediums, whenever they entered a new area.[42]

Cultural beliefs were among the major obstacles in obliterating gender divisions in the camps. The spirit mediums played a crucial role as the custodians of this culture. As guerrillas moved from the 'safety' of the rear camp to the dangerous operational zones across the border, they became more and more custom-bound in their outlook. The fighters were anxious not to offend the spirits of the land, for in their belief, the spirits' protection was essential for their survival. Women surrendered their guns to colleagues when they had their periods, as the spirit mediums instructed. This was in spite of the leadership's insistence that they should keep their arms all the time.[43]

Those who did not take the spirit mediums seriously would be under pressure to conform, for fear that they would be blamed for endangering everybody else's life. All these experiences diluted revolutionary modernist thinking and, as a result, little of it found its way to the front.

At the rear, the leadership were doing their best to suppress discourse on gender inequality, for this unsettled the patriarchs. An official syllabus for the front, a document produced towards the end of 1979, listed among other things: Party history (the official

[41] Interview with Mrs Mavende, Dotito, Mt Darwin, 13 May 1992; interview with Mai Caro Mazarura, Dotito, Mt Darwin, 14 May 1992.
[42] It has been argued that the mediums benefited more from the guerrillas than the guerrillas did from them. See David Maxwell, 'A Social And Conceptual History of North-East Zimbabwe', 1890-1990, D. Phil. Thesis, University of Oxford, 1995.
[43] Janice McLaughlin, M.M. 'The Catholic Church and the War of Liberation', Ph.D. Thesis, Dept of Religious Studies, University of Zimbabwe, 1991 p. 580.

version), national grievances, and the working system of the village committee leadership. For women's orientation, it listed 'extracts from (the) Women's Seminars.'[44] Before that, ZANLA's official syllabi for the front made no reference to questions of women's emancipation. If the extracts in the late 1979 syllabus did actually come from sections containing thought-provoking material on gender relations, they came rather late to leave any impression on the masses.

Moreover, the presence or absence of women in guerrilla units did not seem to affect the gender composition of the village committees created by the guerrillas. Often these included at least one woman.[45] The main reason for appointing her was to ensure the provision of the guerrillas' material needs such as food and clothing. She was there to help men, to get the needs of 'her children' right. Admittedly, she could sometimes exercise a significant amount of power in her position but that was coincidental.

Women combatants and ZANLA's moral code

ZANLA's code of conduct for its guerrillas at the front included the clause 'Do not take liberties with women', which was later amended at the end to read, 'with men/women'.[46] There were indeed reasonable grounds for the amendment. Several women guerrillas, like their male colleagues, soon dispensed with the official regulations and the spirit mediums' instructions on sexual matters. Once they felt secure in their areas of operation, the fighters' anxiety not to upset the spirits of the land declined. With that went most sexual restraints. Some women's relations with their male comrades, as well as with young civilian men, caused a stir. Some commanders of women's platoons operating in ZANLA's Musikavanhu Sector in Buhera were noted for their exploits in that sphere. The leadership had to recall a couple of women to the rear.[47]

The leadership acted on cases of women 'taking liberties with men' as soon as the news got back to the rear. As one would expect, such news travelled at an incredible speed! Without condoning the behaviour of the women, it is clear that when male guerrillas com-

---

44 ZANU (PF) Archives, File: Operations MMZ (Tete) Province, Document: 'Chaminuka Sector, June - October 1979: Political Programme for the party Leadership Committee and the Masses'.

45 The author's own mother served on one such committee in a contested and an all-male zone of operation, as Organising Secretary. Her duties involved registering the contributions to the village's 'war fund' which was a compulsory requirement for all villages in the war zones. She also ensured that there was always enough food for the guerrillas. When there was a 'pungwe' in the village, she had to work with other women to ensure the gathering of not just enough food for everyone who would come, but clean blankets too for the guerrillas.

46 ZANU (PF) Archives, File: Commissariat Department, Document: 'ZANU Political Education, People's Army Lesson 4: Democracy'.

47 ZANU (PF) Archives, File: HC Minutes, Document: 'H. C. Meeting', Operational Base, Chimoio, 21 May 1979.

mitted similar offences, the commanders dismissed their behaviour with a mere shrug – the men were just being men.

As a rule, ZANLA did not give its fighters contraceptives. The leadership was against the whole idea. In the operational field as a result, some of those sexually active women became pregnant and had to be returned to the rear bases. While the leadership's policy on contraception was largely inexcusable, the incidence of pregnancies amongst female guerrillas in the field served as a handy excuse to prevent women from participating in cross-border operations.

Memories of field experience: the myths and the realities

Some women who participated in cross-border operations refer to that period with much pride and satisfaction. Although service at the front generally remained segregated along gender lines, the women speak of their stint in the field as a time when they experienced equality with men. After so many years of confinement to the rear they had at last got a chance to be 'in the thick of things'.

Women in the predominantly female carriers' units could be commanders and be in charge; one could 'feel like a man'. Successful encounters with the enemy might produce juicy stuff for publication in *Zimbabwe News*, the Party's official organ. The female guerrillas involved would now be counted amongst heroines – or heroes? That made the women feel extremely liberated and – like men. Teurai Ropa's experience provides us with a useful anecdote in that regard:

> One of the helicopters spotted me. Because I had no other alternative, I just pointed my gun at it and fired. I thought I had missed. I saw smoke coming from it and thought it was just the exhaust. A few moments later, I heard a boom! The helicopter crashed... That was at Dotito, near Mt Darwin, and it is the battle that many people have now come to identify with me.[48]

Others were not so lucky, as they got caught up in ambushes and died. In Buhera (A) Detachment of Musikavanhu Sector, in Manica Province, a surprise attack on a unit of female fighters left fifteen of them dead in late 1979.[49] One could be captured too. A former combatant recalled how she ended up in prison, entirely at the enemy's mercy:

---

[48] *Moto*, No. 94, November 1990, p. 7.
[49] ZANU (PF) Archives, File: Manica Province, Operational Reports, Document: 'Operational Report', 1 August 1979.

He asked me: 'If I had not caught you, isn't it you would have killed me? You wanted to kill me, didn't you? Now that I have you here, tell me, what do I do with you?' [50]

The ex-guerrilla would not say what in the end her captor decided to do with her, because talking about it depressed her. She still finds it difficult to cope with the experience of imprisonment and she cannot stand confined spaces. They bring up visions of her prison experience.

Other occurrences in the field should have sounded alarm bells for the fighters that their stints as combatants had not changed their situation much. For instance, women fighters, rather than men, were more readily branded as witches by their own comrades. At worst the fighters could accuse male comrades of possessing invincibility charms. Women found it difficult to clear their names once they had been accused of practising witchcraft. One incident in Chitepo Sector suggests a tendency amongst fighters to regard witchcraft as a female profession.

In this incident, Mabhunu Waroyi Muchapera[51] claimed to be possessed by spirits. In that 'state', he named two female fighters witches, one of them a platoon medical assistant. He said she kept a snake behind the base kitchen. Reportedly, the security man in the group believed the allegations. To confirm them, he invited other base commanders to gather all the female fighters in the unit so the 'spirit medium' could pick out the witches from amongst them.[52]

The exercise would probably have netted several women fighters had the witch hunter not exceeded the terms of his engagement. He accused some sectorial commanders (some of the men who had instituted the witch-hunt!) of corrupt practices. Of course they automatically halted the exercise, and nullified the initial witchcraft findings. The whole drama ended on a sad note: the 'spirit medium' blew himself up with a grenade, purportedly to pre-empt disciplinary action over his conduct.[53] All the same, the field commanders expected the 'spirit medium' to find the witches from amongst the female fighters. ZANLA apparently had not quite successfully 'defeminised' witchcraft, at least not in the minds of its fighters.

---

[50] Interview with Chipo Moyo, (not her real name), 5 February, 1994.
[51] The name literally translates to 'Boers, witches, we will finish you'.
[52] ZANU (PF) Archives, File: Department of Operations, Tete Province, Document: 'MMZ Province, Chitepo Sector: "Report on Mabhunu Waroyi Muchapera" ', 1 October 1979.
[53] ZANU (PF) Archives, File: Department of Operations, Tete Province, Document: 'MMZ Province, Chitepo Sector: "Report on Mabhunu Waroyi Muchapera" ', 1 October 1979.

The same comparisons made about the structure of the military in ZANLA camps could also be made about its structure in the operational zones inside Zimbabwe. They can also be made for other military structures in widely varying cultural and historical contexts. Cynthia Enloe noted:

Militaries depend on the maintenance of a popular presumption that the most rewarded, highest status military activities can go only to the masculinized members of society. When women are used in the military it is only 'for the duration' and in roles defined as 'auxiliary'.[54]

Observing the intimate relationship between 'real men' and the military, she contended that the whole notion would collapse if it were not supported 'by certain myths about what it takes to be a "real woman"'.[55] In ZANLA, such myths were kept alive by the spirit mediums and through the offices of ZANU's Secretary for Women's Affairs. This ensured non-interference with the structure of the military and, hence, the preservation of all other patriarchal institutions and practices that went with it in the 'liberated' zones.

Although militaries confine women to certain roles that are different from those of men, the methods they use to evaluate and reward service are notoriously similar. Parallels can be drawn with armed struggles from as far afield as former Yugoslavia. Barbara Jancar wrote of the Yugoslavian experience:

And while men may have commented over and over again on the partizanka's remarkable courage and self-sacrifice, this recognition of the qualities of the woman fighter did not translate into giving even the most trusted of them a role in the wartime decision nor in the final disposition of victory.[56]

The experiences of the ZANLA Women's Detachment were quite similar in this respect. Throughout the struggle ZANLA extolled the women's roles verbally and in administrative records. Since the end of the war, several 'eulogies' have been delivered in the Detachment's honour. One would expect this appreciation to be expressed in tangible terms: for example, through involving the women in decision-making. However, no significant move was made in that direction during the war, in the transition to peace, or after independence.

---

[54] Cynthia H. Enloe, 'Beyond 'Rambo': Women and the Varieties of Militarized Masculinity', in Eva Isaksson (ed.), *Women and the Military System*, Proceedings of a Symposium Arranged by the International Peace Bureau and Peace Union of Finland, Harvester-Wheatsheaf, New York, 1988, p. 91.
[55] Ibid.
[56] Barbara Jancar, 'Women Soldiers in Yugoslavia's National Liberation Struggle, 1941-1945', in Eva Isaksson (ed.), *Women and the Military System*, p. 63.

Conclusion

In ZANLA's case, the myth of gender equality was apparent throughout the war, and it was clearly reflected in the power structures and patterns of labour division.

The allocation of geographic space and duties at the front remained a gendered process. Women remained in 'feminised' spaces, serving as auxiliaries and as women. Men proceeded to 'tougher' zones, to earn military colours as 'real men', exchanging fire with and laying ambushes against the enemy. Women would only fire guns in self-defence, when they had no other option, as in the legendary example of Teurai Ropa: 'Because I had no other alternative, I just pointed my gun and fired.'

If a woman was lucky, she lived to tell the tale and joined the list of heroes or heroines. If the experience was not so glorious, she sank into obscurity quietly, and like most 'auxiliaries', learnt to cope with the pain of watching 'real soldiers' receiving their medals, their appointment to high-ranking positions. The marginalisation of women in post-war structures mirrored all the vices of the war period.

CHAPTER FIVE

Civilians and Soldiers in ZANLA Operational Zones: From Détente to 1979

Introduction

The assessment of the camps in the previous chapters revealed unsettling power struggles and exploitative tendencies in male and female relations. ZANLA failed to articulate clear ideological principles to regulate the conduct of a revolutionary war and this failure resulted in disciplinary problems. These problems had repercussions in the operational zones, where the fighters came into contact with civilians amid a concerted counter-insurgency operation by the security forces and their agents.

Following Mozambique's independence in 1975, recruitment into the armed struggle occurred at an unprecedented rate. ZANLA immediately relocated its whole war machinery to the newly independent country. As it was now based in a politically friendly environment, the logistics of moving recruits across the border became easier. Zimbabwean nationalism also experienced a psychological boost from Mozambique's success. At the same time, relations among the various nationalist parties became increasingly strained as anticipation of African rule in Zimbabwe rose. Partisan interests led to power struggles within the nationalist movements. The Rhodesian régime and its allies manipulated these divisions further. Underground security agents found many loopholes through which they could infiltrate the nationalists in order to identify their various supporters for extermination and to stir further internal strife. Some of these schemes have been discussed by Henrick Ellert, a former member of the Rhodesian Special Branch, and Ken Flower, the former head of the Rhodesian Central Intelligence Organisation.[1] It is difficult to think of any aspect of civilian life with which the security agents did not interfere. This was the political climate that prevailed when insurgency operations were renewed in the second half of the 1970s.

The changing face of the war since the mid-1970s

When the ZANLA leadership was in prison in Zambia in 1975-76, ZIPA reinstated military training programmes (see Chapter 3). By 1976, fighting was once more in full force, with operations being more effectively conducted from Mozambique, where ZANLA, after moving its camps from Zambia, was based. This meant that ZANLA now had much greater access into areas inside Rhodesia. Zimbabwe and Mozambique share a very long border, which runs across mountain ranges covered with thick vegetation. This provided camouflage for the ZANLA fighters and made the patrolling of the guerrillas' entry and exit points by Rhodesian forces an extremely trying task.

With ZANLA making inroads from Mozambique, the Rhodesian government forces began to lose their hold in the north-east, particularly in ZANLA's Tete Province, where the war had started and where ZANLA would later establish its first 'liberated zones'. In 1976 the ZIPA-led guerrillas managed to open two new zones of operation in Rhodesia, adjacent to Mozambique's Manica and Gaza provinces. These same names were also adopted for the new operational zones (see map on p. ix).

Towards understanding guerrilla indiscipline

Serious developments in the conduct of the war occurred at the front after the interruptions of the mid-1970s. As the war resumed in 1976, it expanded into areas hitherto untouched. Simultaneously, a new wave of guerrilla operations gave rise to concerns about the fighters' conduct in the operational field. Their relations with one another and with the civilian population came increasingly under the spotlight.

Previous works have already addressed some of the problems that arose in that period; Sister Janice McLaughlin suggested that they were due to the adoption of haphazard training techniques by ZANLA's junior commanders during their senior leadership's incarcera-

---

[1] Henrick Ellert 'The Rhodesian Security and Intelligence Community 1960-1980...' in N. Bhebe and T. Ranger, *Soldiers in Zimbabwe's War*, University of Zimbabwe Publications, Harare, 1995, pp. 87-103; Ken Flower, *Serving Secretly: An Intelligence Chief on Record: Rhodesia into Zimbabwe, 1964 - 1981*, Murray, London, 1987.

tion in Zambian prisons.[2] Professor Terence Ranger discovered deep bitterness in Makoni, especially against the *mujibhas*, who were blamed for most guerrilla misconduct.[3] While pointing out that peasants continued to support the principle of war right up to the end, Ranger concedes that in its last two years, complaints against guerrilla misconduct had become so widespread that it could be said that a crisis of guerrilla legitimacy was brewing.[4]

Arguing from yet another perspective, Norma Kriger held that the problems derived from rural people using the guerrillas to settle their own local differences.[5] These observations are all useful and say much about how indiscipline manifested itself. They do not, however, satisfactorily explain the root of the problem.

Ranger's findings in Makoni raise further questions. In the first instance, why did the fighters lose control of the *mujibhas*, and why, in general, did ZANLA find itself harbouring increasing numbers of bandits in its ranks. Kriger's argument raises the question of why the guerrillas were so open to peasant agency and manipulation. The matter is complicated and cannot be adequately addressed without reference to the problem of ideological antipathy in ZANLA's rear base camps.

Ideology in ZANLA and discipline in the field: unexplored connections

Ranger came close to addressing the root of the matter when he drew attention to continual changes at the top of the Party hierarchy.[6] So too did Sister McLaughlin when she linked indiscipline to poor training. However the ZIPA era, to which she apportions blame, was in fact one period during the war when the most committed attempt to address questions of political ideology was made. It is not being suggested here that the ZIPA leaders had necessarily arrived at the right answers. Nevertheless, their attempt to create a political forum held great potential to reduce indiscipline. Yet, the old leadership of ZANU descended heavily on these attempts and crushed them indiscriminately. Furthermore, they did not create anything substantive to fill the ideological void their move created. As the war continued, steps to redress this were taken at a rather leisurely pace, resulting in dete-

2   Janice McLaughlin, M.M., *On the Frontline: Catholic Missions in Zimbabwe's Liberation War*, Baobab Books, Harare, 1996, p. 231; see also pp. 206, 229.
3   T. O. Ranger, *Peasant Consciousness and the Guerrilla War in Zimbabwe: A Comparative Study*, James Currey, London, 1985, p. 292.
4   T. O. Ranger, 'Bandits and Guerrillas: the Case of Zimbabwe', in D. Crummey (ed.), *Banditry Rebellion and Social Protest in Africa*, James Currey, London, 1986, pp. 386-90.
5   Norma Kriger, *Zimbabwe's Guerrilla War: Peasant Voices*, Cambridge University Press, Cambridge, p. 170-211.
6   Ranger, 'Bandits and Guerrillas', pp. 384-85.

riorating discipline among the fighters dispatched to the field.

Although disciplinary problems in the camps may have pre-dated the ZIPA era, up to that point they seem to have been successfully contained, as there were then fewer ZANLA guerrillas to handle. But the mid-1970s saw the rear camps flooded with recruits, most of them merely schoolchildren, much younger and more impressionable than those recruited when the war started. The problems of handling these large numbers were compounded by the confusing political events of the period.

ZIPA's decision to use the détente period to prepare new arrivals ideologically for what awaited them was perhaps the most appropriate thing to do. But following the harassment and disbanding of the ZIPA leadership, ZANLA's Political Commissariat Department worked under the restricting dictates of the Security and Intelligence Department. This department used illiterate people to harass anyone coming up with critical views. Indoctrination re-placed free thinking and most efforts were devoted to weeding out those who had sup-ported the *Vashandi*,[7] reminding the forces who the official leaders of the armed struggle were.[8] Recruits continued to be taught to use guns, but their mentors made inadequate reference to the political context within which they were to operate these weapons.

Many fighters did not know what to do when faced with opposition (real and imagi-nary) in the field. For many, their major point of reference was how their leadership had confronted the in-house problems of 1974 to 1978 by purging the troublemakers.[9]

Without appropriate political training to confront the complexities of the operational zones, the fighters had little ability to put civilian definitions of 'sell-outs' into their proper perspective. Would they be able to understand the differences between the newly opened operational areas and north-eastern Zimbabwe, where people had already seen better behaved freedom fighters in the early 1970s and knew how to distinguish them from en-emy-sponsored impersonators?

The terrain the fighters were moving into was so contested and complicated, and the pressures on them so trying, that it was essential to prepare them for it by inculcating or at least raising debate on the ideological thrust of the armed struggle. These handicaps should not be underestimated as we examine guerrilla-civilian interactions in the face of a callous

---

[7] *Vashandi* is the Shona word for workers. Such a description of ZIPA alluded to their Marxist and Soviet-oriented political leanings.
[8] Almost all the official documents prepared after 1977 bore the slogan: 'Forward With Comrade President Robert Mugabe!' Earlier documents made no such references to the Party President.
[9] Thomas Nhari and Dakarai Badza together with their followers were executed following the late 1974 revolt; some of the ZIPA leadership met with the same fate in 1978.

counter-insurgency campaign by the Rhodesian régime.

Until now, most analysis relating to guerrilla misconduct has been based on observations from outside ZANLA.[10] The nationalist leaders have often not taken lightly to accusations against their forces' conduct. Their response has often been to blame the atrocities on the Rhodesians' counter-insurgency smear campaign, and to brand criticism as emanating from elements 'bent on robbing Zimbabweans of their hard-won independence'.[11]

It is true the Rhodesians' hidden hand was responsible for many gruesome crimes that were unfairly blamed on the nationalist armies. Nor can it be entirely discounted that some critics of ZANLA's conduct may have ulterior motives. ZANLA's own records, however, should clarify some of the confusion by giving a credible internal source to what might be termed 'guerrilla voices'. These voices will help to enhance our understanding of the nature of the problems afflicting civilian-military relations in the late 1970s.

Thus, this section will make extensive use of reports by ZANLA's operational commanders on the state of discipline – or indiscipline – among guerrillas in the field. The very existence of these reports is proof of a conscientious and determined intention to maintain orderly relations between the guerrillas and the people. It is also proof that breaches of discipline by guerrillas were not hidden from the leadership in Mozambique. I do not wish to suggest that the state of affairs revealed in the reports was universal throughout ZANLA's operational areas. Nevertheless, these reports do show widespread tensions between guerrillas and civilians. Many problems arose out of gender issues, more specifically out of relations with local women and girls.

Any attempts to date the issues covered should take the problem of the ZANLA records' periodisation into consideration. (See for remarks on periodisation). Janice McLaughlin and Terence Ranger already differ on this matter; McLaughlin ascribes the disciplinary problems of 1977 to 1978 and Ranger says the problems became more widespread in the last two years of the war, 1978 to 1979.

---

[10] Janice McLaughlin, M. M. had access to the ZANLA Archives and refers to Commissariat and field reports on guerrilla indiscipline. She does not quote them extensively, however.

[11] The producers of the film, *Flame* (on the experiences of female fighters), found themselves confronted with hostility by ex-guerrillas and by ZANU officials for reflecting some of the negative aspects of the war, such as the sexual abuse of women.

Reports from the field: voices of disillusionment

Although this study is mainly about women's experiences, evidence of the various other forms in which indiscipline manifested itself upon civilians helps to put women's experiences into their proper perspective. It also reveals the extent of a problem that many people in post-war Zimbabwe still refuse to address. For this reason, the ZANLA reports ought to be maximally utilised.

They shed light on incidents of indiscipline in all ZANLA's three provinces: Gaza, Manica as well as Tete where ZANLA exercised its greatest autonomy.[12] The reports also contain cases which the High Command deliberated on at the rear after the operational commanders had submitted them from the front. Operational commanders also reported on the nature and responsibilities of civilian support committees and youth organs which they had set up in liberated areas. They also provided information on PVs.

Gaza Province

Uneasiness about the reputation of the nationalist movement and concern to create a better understanding with the people clearly emerges in the reports from Gaza Province. A field officer in Sector Four (covering Matibi, Chifumira, Chitaudze), requested that Ndebele-speaking ZANLA forces be deployed to the area to bridge language barriers with the local people. He called for the deployment of disciplined forces, in his words, fighters whose conduct was 'based on Chairman Mao's eight points of attention'.[13] This was deemed essential to counter ZAPU propagandist claims that ZANU was a Shona party. He said there was need also to demonstrate that there was a difference between ZANLA forces and ZIPRA hooligans whose campaign, as the report summarised, was directed at derailing the nationalist cause and tarnishing ZANLA's image. The ZANLA officer explained the nature of the problems as he compiled his report on 29 December 1978:

> Before the arrival of ZANLA for military operations (in 1976), ZAPU had organized its old members at provincial and Sectorial levels as chairmans (sic) and these are the very people preaching against ZANU.[14]

---

12   In the liberated areas of Tete Province, one would expect ZANLA to have had the greatest opportunity to cultivate a deeper understanding with the civilian population and therefore to be able to exercise a reasonable amount of control over its forces.
13   For the Eight Points of Attention, see Ranger, 'Bandits and Guerrillas', pp. 381-82.
14   ZANU PF Archives, File: Southern Province (Gaza), Doc: 'Sector Four Political Report', Commissariat Department, 29 December 1978.

ZIPRA indiscipline was said to manifest itself in various ways including senseless attacks on propertied civilians, as well as raping women:

> They force the masses to sleep outside while they sleep in the masses' houses with their daughters by force.[15]

If the ZANLA officer thought such indiscipline only existed in ZIPRA ranks, he was wrong. His colleague in Belingwe in nearby Sector 3, had already noted earlier in June of that year (1978) that the Eight Points of Attention were being blatantly ignored, and that the detachments urgently needed to be reinforced by what he termed 'ideologically equipped' forces.[16] Those currently deployed there had sunk irretrievably into drunkenness and were responsible for many unreported cases of pregnancy. The report also criticised random killings:

> The masses are now in a state of confusion... most of them were accused of being in possession of communication radios and arms but out of all those shot no gun or radio was surrendered to prove to the commanders the truth about the accusation.[17]

Another report made similar observations, noting that the disciplinary crisis dated back to the period of command under Rape Mukaradhi whose name means 'rape the Coloureds'. In his era, ZANLA forces had been keeping civilians in their bases right through the night; there was excessive beer-drinking including the intake of 'tobbie', a highly alcoholic spirit; they also smoked dagga and womanised at will.[18] The masses were treated ruthlessly, with the main attacks being directed at rural teachers and businessmen, from whom huge, fixed sums of money were demanded.[19]

Mukaradhi was eventually replaced, but his legacy remained. When another Operations Commander, Hector Muridzo, came into the sector and tried to restore discipline, he fell out immediately with two of his senior colleagues, including the Sectorial Commissar. In addition to this, a local *ambuya* [20] reportedly accused Muridzo of being in possession of magic to protect himself, but she deemed its powers harmful to the rest of his comrades. This severely undermined the new commander's authority at a delicate time. Desperate to enforce his command, he reportedly adopted harsh measures that resulted in a rebellion, finally compelling the provincial commanders to withdraw the warring sectorial command-

---

[15] Ibid.
[16] Ibid., Doc: 'Political Report Covering Sector Three', 25 June 1978.
[17] Ibid.
[18] Ibid., 21 June 1978.
[19] Ibid.
[20] *Ambuya*: the Shona word for grandmother; also used respectfully to address any elderly woman or one with skills associated with old age and wisdom. In this particular case, the *ambuya* was either a magician or a spirit medium. The equivalent male word is *sekuru*.

105

ers to the rear. The stress on civilians, especially young women, inflicted by this whole episode cannot be over-emphasised, as explained in the report (compiled afterwards) that sought to capture the events of this period:

> The forces refused to go for battles as they said they were afraid of Muridzo's magic... beer drinking increased, sleeping with girls in bases was compulsory [my emphasis] as it was said to be a strategy against ZIPRA attacks, taking liberties with women was legal because they were allowed to sleep with their girlfriends in the same blankets, heavy fixed funds were imposed on the masses, each section to its liking... requisitions flocked to businessmen for sweets, biscuits, Castles[21], female clothing, e.g. nickers [sic], petti-coats [sic]... The fighters also started to use skin-lightening creams... Venereal diseases were one of the commonest diseases among the forces. Fierce contradictions emerged... because of women.[22]

Civilian elders were reported to have become very disturbed, wondering what had got into 'their children', but complaints against such behaviour were suicidal. Even Gaza's Provincial Field Operations Commander, Freddie Matanga, found the undisciplined guerrillas difficult to handle. Withdrawing the rebels had been his last attempt to arrest a situation that had got out of hand. The rebels had become daring and had made arrogant assertions. Showing their confusion over the significance of rank in the military and over what, in ideological terms, it meant to belong to a liberation movement, the fighters declared:

> We don't care what a Provincial Commander is. Who is Freddie? Freddie is not ZANU. We are afraid of the Party, not an individual... Muchapera Mabhunu came here... a few days after his return to the rear he rebelled... we are still within the Party, aren't we?[23]

As the fighters had not denounced ZANU and were in their words, 'still within the Party', they were unrepentant:

> We are going to continue with what we have been doing since 1976 when we opened this sector. We came out of many situations with our behaviour.[24]

The report stated that throughout this turbulent period, the fighters had not given any account of their operations to their seniors. By their own admission, they had conducted themselves deplorably since their arrival in 1976. This contradicted a 1978 report, which recorded that since the opening up of the area that had previously been dominated by ZAPU, but had had occasional visits from the Dzakutsaku, Abel Muzorewa's private army, good progress had been made in mobilising the masses. As evidence of their success, the

---

[21] A brand of bottled beer.
[22] ZANU (PF) Archives, File: Southern Province (Gaza), Doc: 'Report: Sector 3', 21 June 1978.
[23] Ibid. Mabhunu Muchapera, a former provincial field officer, had apparently criticised these fighters' conduct already, but for some reason he fell out with the leadership soon after his return to the rear.
[24] Ibid.

June 1978 report claimed that even some ZIPRA forces referred to derogatively as the *machuachua* had come to join ZANLA.[25] They claimed that the situation in Belingwe had started to deteriorate to anarchy in mid-1977.[26]

The discrepancies regarding the date of the onset of the problems might be explained by the rebels' failure to submit any operational reports to their seniors. They had apparently assumed that everything was fine when it was not.

In Gaza's Sector Two (Makonesa, Madyangove, Berejena, Nemauzhe), the disciplinary situation was reported to be generally satisfactory, with the exception of a limited number of cases where the commander was certain 'a few strokes at the back' of the offenders would do the trick.[27] He had already administered such treatment in public to a few fighters for their failure to handle the masses properly. Others had been involved in 'love affairs', one resulting in a pregnancy. Both the fighters and their civilian lovers were beaten following a public trial.[28] Apparently, the transparency shown by the commander in dealing with offenders had paid remarkable dividends in the area with regards to guerrilla-civilian relations.

Manica Province

In some detachments of Musikavanhu Sector (Bikita, Gutu, Basera, Chikwanda and Zimuto) in Manica Province, fighters were reported to have deteriorated into what were described as 'roving rebels', as many of the fighting units had split up.[29] They were also reported to have accumulated lots of charms to protect themselves as they moved into their operational areas, supposedly to ensure their invincibility in contacts with the enemy. These charms, however, introduced mutual suspicion among the guerrillas and their units, thereby contributing to the divisions. The guerrillas were also reported to be drinking and smoking dagga, which gave them false confidence and caused them to patrol the countryside in broad daylight.[30] This had invited enemy attacks resulting in loss of life.

[25] The fact that the Sectorial Commander for Sector 2 is taking note of happenings in Belingwe, (now Mberengwa), which is actually in Sector 3, shows how fluid the boundaries of ZANLA's operational areas were. ZANU (PF) Archives, File: Southern Province (Gaza), Sector 4 Operational Reports, Doc: 'Political Report Covering Part of the Southern Front ... Sector Two', Operations Department, Southern Province, 4 June 1978.
[26] Ibid.
[27] Ibid., Doc:'Sector Two Annual Report - January to September 1978', 14 September 1978.
[28] Ibid.
[29] Ibid., File: Defence Operations, Doc: 'Report on Manica Province (Dec. 1978 - May 1979), 28 July 1979.
[30] Ibid.

There were more incidents of careless behaviour in Nyamombe Detachment of Monomotapa Sector in the same province. The guerrillas were camping in people's homes, reportedly spending long periods there because they had got involved with local girls. Unfortunately, these young women were being captured by the enemy and used to lead security agents to the guerrillas' hide-outs.[31] Rather than review their own reckless conduct, the fighters were said to be searching for sell-outs among the civilians, and under pressure to produce them, even when they did not exist. Thus civilians often pointed fingers at their innocent neighbours to save their own skins.[32]

The use of dagga was further identified as the cause of several guerrilla suicides and shootings.[33] Civilians were said to be terribly confused as they could not distinguish between the freedom fighters and the auxiliaries or pseudo-guerrillas.[34] The Rhodesians do not seem to have needed to conduct a smear operation in this area as ZANLA fighters were effectively ruining their own organisation's reputation.

Still in Manica Province, in Tangwena Sector, which covered the areas of Chisasike, Wedza, Sadza, Chiwetu, Gandanzara and Chiduku, several pregnancies resulted from the guerrillas' sexual exploits.[35] The fighters were reported to have no respect for one another and sometimes quarrelled in front of civilians. They smoked dagga, addressed civilians in vulgar language, and were also reckless with their guns.[36]

The report noted that in this area, the masses' political understanding was far higher than that of the guerrillas, as the former listened to ZANU's political broadcasts on Radio Mozambique.[37] Due to their own embarrassment when the fighters were unable to satisfy the civilians' requests for up-dates on political developments, some of the fighters were said to have started to listen to the broadcasts as well, so that their explanations would not be contradictory. Many would otherwise have tuned in to stations featuring the latest pop music!

---

[31]   Ibid.
[32]   Ibid.
[33]   Ibid.
[34]   The auxiliaries were former ZANLA fighters who had remained faithful to the discarded former President of ZANU, Ndabaningi Sithole. He had also secured new recruits with assistance from the Rhodesian government and the Rhodesians were using them as an underground organ masquerading as ZANLA to identify the latter's supporters. They also committed crimes under the name of ZANLA to discredit Mugabe's followers.
[35]   ZANU (PF) Archives, File: Operational Reports, Manica, Doc: 'Provincial Operational Report', 6 July 1978.
[36]   Ibid.
[37]   Serving as ZANU's propaganda instrument, the broadcasts gave accounts of successful mobilisations, military victories, as well as explaining the Party's position regarding mushrooming nationalist organisations and their negotiations with the Rhodesian government led by Ian Smith.

Desperate to mend relations between the people of ZANLA's Tangwena Sector and the fighters, the provincial commanders exchanged those who were responsible for pregnancies in the area with others from Musikavanhu and Monomotapa Sectors in the same province. Their misdeeds had caused serious antagonism, especially because some of the women they had interfered with were married. One of them was the wife of a man who had once served as a policeman.[38] It seemed that the culprit involved with the former policeman's wife had thought of spiting her husband, to punish him for working on the wrong side.

The local people, however, drew negative inferences from such acts. They construed it to mean that a victorious ZANLA would share out, as booty, the women of the vanquished. Certainly this did not help the Party's image, especially as the government's propaganda spread through leaflets showed, among other 'communist evils', pictures of women weeping after discovering that they had been infected with venereal diseases by ZANLA men.[39]

Tete Province

In Tete Province it is plausible to think that by the late 1970s ZANLA had established a rapport with the local people. They had operated there earlier than anywhere else and they had recruited intensively from there. Nevertheless, even Tete was not spared the degeneration in guerrilla discipline. This was notable in Chaminuka Sector, which covered the areas of Nyahui, Chesa African Purchase Farms, Madziva, Musana, and Mazoe. It was reported:

> The comrades have taken much of trigger happiness forgetting political work. This has put a very great impact on our mass and youth political standing… Gossip… creates tension amongst fighters… Comrades demand too much from the masses e.g. special diet, despite the fact that the masses have been impoverished by the war.[40]

The report lamented the guerrillas' ideological inadequacy, which was said to be most apparent in their preferences for extremely westernised dress. Instead of concentrating on their political improvement, they were said to be pre-occupied with western magazines and novels, as well as listening to pop and rhumba music, all deemed culturally alien.[41] The leadership requested mobile political units to come and re-educate them.

---

[38]   Ibid.
[39]   Julie Frederikse, None but Ourselves: Masses vs. Media in the Making of Zimbabwe, Zimbabwe Publishing House, Harare, 1982, p. 122.
[40]   ZANU (PF) Archives, File: Operations MMZ (Tete Province), Doc: 'MMZ Province, Provincial General Report Covering January - May 1979'.
[41]   Ibid.

Chaminuka Sector's Madziva (A) Detachment was said to have the most dire need of lessons in discipline, especially for the benefit of the *mujibhas* and *chimbwidos*, who were moving around with the misguided guerrillas.[42] The sectorial commander noted critically[43] that these youths, who had been partially trained in military techniques, were being used by the fighters as security shields.[44] When guerrillas used the youth in this way, that is keeping them at their bases[45], they encouraged circumstances that promoted gross misbehaviour and worried the elders a great deal.

A few more complaints came from Takawira Sector where some forces had formulated their own operational regulations based on the advice of self-styled spirit mediums.[46] They were also interfering at will with civilian women and girls. The Provincial Commander had already intervened, treating each of the offenders to 45 cuts.[47]

High Command attempts to enforce discipline

Many instances of indiscipline went unchecked and civilians were at the receiving end of this chaotic nationalist operation that was now responsible for massive social disruption.

The High Command in Mozambique tried a few cases, so that punishments could be administered upon offenders. Most of the cases receiving such attention were those involving a death or deaths amongst the forces themselves as the losses had to be accounted for with ZANLA's Personnel Department at the rear. Assaults against civilians would be recorded by the fighters as disciplinary measures taken against the enemies of the revolution. Sexual offenses against women were difficult to bring to light because the victims could easily be intimidated into silence. A girl who discovered she had become pregnant sometimes had to lie that a *mujibha* was responsible.[48]

Some cases, however, could not be successfully covered up; and guerrillas who genuinely fell in love and wanted to marry the mothers of their children found themselves in

---

[42]   ZANU (PF) Archives, File: Department of Operations, Tete Province, Doc: 'Sectorial Commander's Monthly Report for August-September 1979', MMZ Province, Chaminuka Sector.

[43]   ZANU (PF) Archives, File: Operations MMZ (Tete Province), Doc: 'MMZ Province, Provincial General Report Covering January-May 1979'.

[44]

[45]   The theory was that if the children of local people stayed the night at the guerrilla bases, sell-outs or informers would be less likely to go and tell the Rhodesian Security forces where they were.

[46]   Ibid., Doc: 'Takawira Sector Monthly Report, March - April 1979'.

[47]   Ibid.

[48]   See Juliet Makande's account in Irene Staunton, *Mothers of the Revolution: The War Experiences of Thirty Zimbabwean Women*, James Currey, London, 1990, p. 49.

breach of operational regulations. (See Appendix). This category of cases raised security concerns, apart from the financial considerations that had to be taken into account. Guerrillas who assumed family obligations sowed great discontent amongst local people upon whom the fighters depended for their material needs. Although ZANLA took such practical considerations into account, it was no consolation for those who were left to pick up the pieces.

Among the cases heard on 26 April 1979 was that of Sub Shumba, a field commander in Masvingo Sector in Manica Province. He admitted that he had forced girls into sexual relationships and afterwards he had beaten one of his comrades to death for similar crimes. In justifying his sexual offenses, he said that spirit mediums had told the fighters to sleep with civilian girls to neutralise the effects of clothes poisoning.[49]

Another fighter by the name of Mugaradzakasungwa admitted that he had married a girl at the front after she had become pregnant by him. He had used Party funds to provide for his girlfriend and child. Oblivious to the fact that he had already violated Party regulations on sex and marriage, he had gone on to take turns with his assistant to have sexual relations with yet another local girl. He had also got drunk and harassed civilians.[50]

Still another fighter, Regie Kamba, who had been operating in Buhera, admitted to ill-treating civilian girls and forcing them to submit to sex with him. He also admitted to excessive drinking while at the front. Another guerrilla also pleaded guilty to 'marrying' whilst at the front.[51]

A case heard on 21 May 1979 involved a guerrilla in Buhera, Manica Province. He had thrown a bomb into the hut where his girlfriend and two of his comrades were sleeping; he suspected one of the men to be in love with his woman. The bomb had killed the two guerrillas in the hut and it injured the civilian girl seriously.[52]

These cases represent just a fraction of the guerrilla misdemeanours, which civilians experienced in the last phase of the war, at the hands of some of the people who were supposed to be fighting to liberate them. In view of the guerrillas' behaviour, how much emancipatory potential did their presence in the operational areas carry for civilians in general and for women in particular. The implications of these developments for theories

---

[49] ZANU (PF) Archives, File: Minutes HC & CC, Doc: 'Meeting Held at Operations', Chaminuka HQ of Security and Intelligence, 26 April 1979.

[50] Ibid.

[51] Ibid.

[52] ZANU (PF) Archives, Minutes HC, Doc: 'High Command Meeting', Operational Base, Chimoio, 21 May 1979.

that a gender revolution would take place concurrently with the nationalist struggle will be considered later.

The discussion turns now to state-imposed restrictions on civilian liberties in the rural areas. As ZANLA reports correctly point out, these impositions by the state were brought upon the civilians because of their support for the guerrillas.

Protected Villages

Protected Villages (PVs) were referred to in Chapter 2 but were not closely examined. Mike Kesby, a social geographer, has discussed PVs as terrains of gender contestation, arguing that both the guerrillas' and the security men's involvement with civilian women challenged patriarchy and notions of manhood in a way that had not occurred before.[53] He argues that the temporary nature of these war-time spaces explained why, in spite of apparent evidence that gender relations were reversed in the PVs, the old order was restored as soon as the war ended. Two other researchers also cover the subject of PVs, Eleanor O'Gorman in Chiweshe and Heike Schmidt in Honde Valley.[54]

ZANLA reports noted the existence of five PVs in Gaza Province. These were Chironga, Chibwedziva, Chiteya, Boli and Chipinda.[55] On being driven into these camps, the people had been made to leave behind their food reserves, which had then been burnt. Compounding these food shortages, shops had been closed, and even basics like salt were unavailable. The fighters reported that they were teaching the people to produce homemade salt.[56] This of course was the women's duty as they were the ones who had to produce salted food. Water supplies in the PVs were limited and a rationing system operated. In addition to these problems, there were neither sanitary nor health facilities. Harassment from armed guards was the order of the day.[57]

---

[53] Mike Kesby, 'Arenas for Control, Terrains of Gender Contestation; Guerilla Struggle and Counter-Insurgency Warfare in Zimbabwe 1972-80', ms. 1996.

[54] Heike Schmidt, 'The Social and Economic Impact of Political Violence in Zimbabwe, 1890-1990', D.Phil. thesis, Oxford, 1996. Schmidt's thesis deals with the Honde Valley where the whole population was collected in Protected Villages. She argues that the inhabitants of the PVs developed what she calls a 'keep ethnicity'– a communal identity that allowed them to survive. After the war, when the PVs were opened and most people left them, some women remained on their sites. Residing at an ex-PV, these women were able to pursue lifestyles not condoned by rural society. Eleanor O'Gorman's work, which deals with Chiweshe, has not yet been completed.

[55] ZANU (PF) Archives, File: Southern Province (Gaza), Sector 4 Operational Reports, Doc: 'Political Report Covering Part of the Southern Front ... Sector Two', Operations Department, Southern Province, 4 June 1978.

[56] Ibid., 'The Commissariat Annual Report', Southern Province (Gaza), Commissariat Department, 10 April 1978.

[57] ZANU (PF) Archives, Sector 4 Operational Reports, Doc: 'Political Report Covering Part of the Southern Front ... Sector Two', Operations Department, Southern Province, 4 June 1978.

Apart from the shortages of food, reports of young women being raped by the guards abounded. Concern was expressed over the PVs fostering a culture of loose living amongst the youth, and this was reported to be giving rise to chronic sex-related diseases.[58] Not surprisingly, the affected communities were reported to be very concerned with their living arrangements:

> According to our culture, sister and brother when they are at teenage [sic] they are not allowed to sleep in the same room... Now what hell! The DAs [District Assistants] are worsening matters, father, mother, brother and sister are forced to sleep in one room and sometimes at gun point.[59]

Comparable problems were reported elsewhere. The fighters' remarks on PVs in Gaza Operational Province are closely corroborated by the evidence of an expatriate doctor who attended to such camps in the Chipinge area in ZANLA's Manica Province. Referring to curfew constraints on farming, a predominantly female responsibility, the doctor commented:

> This becomes an immense difficulty when it is necessary for them to walk sometimes, many miles to get to their fields... till their land and get back before the gates close. If they are not back before the gates close they are subject to being shot... we have noted in the area an increase, a rather marked increase in malnutrition among the small children and an increase in communicable diseases.[60]

The doctor also reiterated ZANLA's observations about the problematic social implications for the indigenous people of their new living arrangements:

> These people are not accustomed to living in such close proximity with other people and this... seems to have resulted in the breakdown of morals to some extent among young people... I heard many stories about the young women being threatened by these guards... being forced into love affairs with these men against their will. These were stories. I can say from a medical standpoint there was a very high incidence of venereal disease among the guards, I treated many of them. Whether this is coming from within the protected villages or not, I assume it is... they must be involving themselves in sexual intercourse among the people of the pvs, that is just my assumption of course, my conclusion I should say. Again I will mention this because this is something that concerned... African mothers and fathers, a great deal, a very great deal.[61]

---

[58] ZANU (PF) Archives, File: 'The Commissariat Annual Report', Southern Province (Gaza), Commissariat Department, 10 April 1978.
[59] Ibid.
[60] National Archives of Zimbabwe File MS 589/7/4, 'Testimony of Dr Selwyn Spray', Geneva 452nd and 453rd Meetings, 27 July 1977.
[61] Ibid.

The guerrillas' and the doctor's comments pertaining to the guards' sexual exploits will be analysed further when we examine them against claims about temporary changes in power relations between the sexes and between the generations.

Protected Villages and interactions with guerrillas

In spite of the hardship resulting from the deplorable conditions and the extreme situation of scarcity in the camps, the inmates retained responsibility for the provision of the material needs of ZANLA fighters in those areas. Field reports acknowledged that the PV inmates continued to perform security functions for the guerrillas and that they smuggled food out to them.[62] Rhodesian intelligence reports on Gaza noted that ZANLA had created 'povo camps or secret villages'[63] in areas where most people had been moved into PVs. These camps were reportedly located in Sengwe, Matibi Two and Ndowoyo Communal Lands and it was noted that they were used 'to provide the CTs [communist terrorists] with food, security and other normal social needs.'[64] The secret villages were said to be either spaces cleared underneath bushy areas or clusters of huts accommodating several families who cooked and slept there. Whilst the fighters strictly controlled people's movements from these secret places, they also assigned patrol duties to *mujibhas* who monitored enemy movements.[65]

Those of Irene Staunton's interviewees who had lived in PVs testified that support to the guerrillas continued. One of my informants in this study, Mrs Mazarura from Dotito, also said the fighters would become agitated if they saw no food. She said that in their PV at Chakoma in Dotito, Mt Darwin, the camp guards did not mind if women pounded grain during the nights.[66] Since the grinding mills had all been closed by the soldiers, women had to work at night to ensure they produced enough mealie-meal for their families as well as for the guerrillas. Daytime was saved for vital outdoor activities such as agricultural work, collecting firewood, or making essential social contacts with relatives in neighbouring PVs.

Frustrated that the guerrillas were not starving to death as they had intended, PV authorities would get angry with the inmates, especially with the women who were known to be the crucial factor in these unlawful transactions. They punished them by imposing new

---

[62] ZANU (PF) Archives, File: Department of Operations, Tete Province, Doc: 'Sectorial Commander's Monthly Report For August - September 1979', MMZ Province, Chaminuka Sector.

[63] *Povo*: term adopted by ZANLA from FRELIMO to refer to the people or the masses.

[64] Rhodesian government confidential report, 'ZANLA Modus Operandi: Operation Repulse, RIC ... Fort Victoria', 19 December 1978, p. 6. (Doc. in the private possession of Professor T. Ranger, Oxford).

[65] Ibid.

[66] Discussion with Mrs Mazarura Snr., Dotito Mount Darwin, 13 May 1992.

constraints on their already restricted productive pursuits, such as sometimes denying them exit to go and work on their fields, or reducing, if not totally withholding, domestic water supplies.[67] As restrictions kept increasing for the inmates, the guerrillas saw less and less food coming out of the camps. In the end, they sometimes stormed the camps and drove their inmates out.[68]

'Liberation' from the PVs

ZANLA forces congratulated themselves for mounting several successful operations against the camps and 'liberating' the inmates. They wrote of their operations in Takawira Sector, Tete Province: '[People] in 9 of the 10 PVs in the area were freed when the PVs were destroyed'.[69]

A report about PVs in Gaza said that the despicable living conditions had seen many people taking the initiative to free themselves, and that by 30 April 1978, ZANLA had 'deployed' 40 to 60 families.[70] The families led nomadic lives as the fighters continually moved them to avoid detection.[71]

It is indisputable that while some people, especially the young, left because they could not tolerate the harassment and abuse in the PVs, most people were driven out by ZANLA. However, one former PV inmate, an old woman who had lived in Chiwara Camp in Dotito did not view the ZANLA's gesture in quite the same terms as the fighters. She did not see herself as having been liberated by the operation in any way. Some guerrillas had tactlessly remarked as they drove out the people, 'We cannot be starving outside whilst you are just sitting in here.'[72] She said that they spoke of returning them *kumatongo*, that is to their original homes. However, at the time of their 'liberation', the Rhodesian security forces were escalating their bombing activities in the area. So it is difficult to see how the fighters had hoped to resettle people in their former homes without making them sitting ducks for enemy bombs. Not surprisingly, the proclaimed resettlement exercise was never implemented. People simply ended up roaming the bushes seeking cover from the continual attacks. For someone who endured severe beatings by the soldiers, sustaining a permanent

---

[67] Irene Staunton, *Mothers of the Revolution*, p. 7.
[68] Interview with Ambuya Munhukare Mususa, Dotito, Mt Darwin, 13 May 1992.
[69] ZANU (PF) Archives, File: Operations MMZ (Tete Province), Doc: 'MMZ Province, Annual Military Report for the Whole Province', 2 January 1978.
[70] ZANU (PF) Archives, File: Southern Province (Gaza), Doc: 'The Commissariat Annual Report', Southern Province (Gaza), Commissariat Department, 10 April 1978.
[71] Ibid.
[72] Interview with Ambuya Munhukare Mususa, Dotito, Mt Darwin, 13 May 1992.

hearing impairment, Ambuya Munhukare Mususa's opinion of the whole guerrilla liberation exercise may seem odd, or she may even sound ungrateful: 'Maybe the guerrillas wanted us to go and die with them too in the bush'.[73]

This could not possibly have been ZANLA's motive. However, as mentioned earlier, reports from some commanders chastised others for keeping civilians with them as shields against attack. When Ambuya Mususa and others found themselves under a hail of enemy bombs from which the guerrillas could not protect them, it is not difficult to see why she and others felt as they did. The risk of enemy bombing had always been there: ZANLA reports for the last two years of the war made constant reference to escalating air raids in the areas they had 'liberated'.

If ZANLA had really meant to free the PV inmates, then they could not have done it at a more inappropriate time. No one disputes the appalling conditions in the PVs, but these were nothing in comparison to what the 'liberated' inmates experienced in the mountainous veld. There, the living conditions were even more appalling and there was the added danger of enemy bombs, indiscriminate and merciless. With their military background, the fighters were better placed than the civilians to escape to safety. Although they returned later to see what help they could give to those civilians who had survived the harrowing three months, however, the latter could not help feeling that they were being used as pawns and that the guerrillas were self-centred in their conduct.[74]

Apart from the bombardments, ZANLA acknowledged that liberating the PVs was no easy task. The 'liberated' were forced to live just as if they had returned to the Stone Age: with no shelter, no food, no clothes and no blankets. There were no medicines to treat the large numbers who fell ill, and these, under the circumstances, grew daily.[75] Their conditions were sub-human. ZANLA's reports contained desperate pleas to the rear for help as the situation for the 'liberated' populations deteriorated, and death from malnutrition and under-nourishment occurred at an alarming rate.[76]

Pressure mounted on those who had not yet been 'liberated' and remained in nearby PVs. Now those who lived there had to provide not just for the guerrillas but for the released populations as well. Mrs Mazarura recalled how desperate the situation had be-

---

[73] Ibid.
[74] Ibid.
[75] ZANU (PF) Archives, File: Operations MMZ (Tete Province), Doc: 'MMZ Province: Operations, Medical Report for January - June 1979'.
[76] Ibid.

come, as shown by the urgency of the fighters' and the *mujibhas'* behaviour when they visited the PVs:

> They would just burst into your hut, grab just about anything they could lay their hands on. They would take pots and plates, jerseys, bags, ...even the bag in which you kept the baby's nappies... they just poured out the contents onto the ground.[77]

She laughed resignedly as she reflected on those days, and was evidently relieved that this period was well over. Those 'liberated' to the bushes, the majority being women, children and old men,[78] were unable to produce anything for themselves. Thus even their stint in the PVs could be looked back upon as a golden period, ironic as this may sound.

Civilian organs and liberated zones

The guerrillas set up civilian committees to mobilise human and material resources for the war. The committees were found all over ZANLA's operational areas and they were charged mainly with seeing to the fighters' welfare and solving disputes, as well as giving directives to youth organisations.[79]

The adult organs constituted the village committees, made up of five people. Younger people formed the youth wings, made up of *mujibhas* and *chimbwidos* and some youths acted as porters and nurses. As with guerrilla units, the adult committee members represented the five ZANLA departments found in the operational field inside Zimbabwe.[80]

An operational report from Manica Province spoke of the autonomy of some of these civilian organs in ZANLA's liberated zones:

> Generally most security is being done by the masses, mostly our youth. All the patrols, the checking up of visitors in operational areas, reconnaissances [sic], the follow up of how the enemy patrols is completely [my emphasis] in the hands of youths. Now that we have set committees, ...there is also a security man usually known as a runner... he is underground... This man together with the youths reports any suspected moves to the committee members

---

[77] Discussion with Mrs Mazarura Snr., Dotito Mt Darwin, 13 May 1992.

[78] These were the categories of people who mainly constituted PV dwellers as they could not flee to towns or join the guerrillas. See Heike Schmidt, 'The Social and Economic Impact of Political Violence'.

[79] ZANU (PF) Archives, File: Southern Province (Gaza), Doc: 'Sector Two, Detachment Three, Operations', 17 December 1978.

[80] These were the Departments of Operations; Political Commissariat; Security and Intelligence; Medicine; as well as Logistics and Supplies.

first, then the chairman records and reports to the people's forces – ZANLA... Sell-outs are arrested and executed by the masses. Criminals are disciplined. Hooligans are dealt with.[81]

As this account shows, the security officer was definitely always a man who worked with youth, more often than not with male youth. Women, however, also sat on these committees to help organise the guerrillas' material needs. As one of the main duties of the committees was to organise catering (the provision of food and blankets) for *pungwes* or night meetings, women members were considered essential because they were the traditional food providers.

As a report from Gaza showed, in most ZANLA-controlled areas the guerrillas were already toying with theories about using the committees as the basis for a new civil administration to fill the vacuum being created as colonial institutions disintegrated. It recorded that:

The creating of Party Committees is another victory we scored... They now feel very sure that they are the government of tomorrow.[82]

Regarding the committees' importance in providing food, it was reported that they produced enough because they worked 'collectively', and the report also remarked on the changes in civilian attitudes regarding their war-time roles:

The masses now know that they aren't collaborators or supporters but revolutionary fighters.[83]

As for the youth, their work was physically taxing and the dangers it entailed cannot be over-emphasised. Male youth organised patrols and gave clearance to all movements in the area. They were also responsible for blocking roads to restrict enemy movements.[84] The boys were also useful in assisting their fathers in operations to drive looted herds of cattle from settler farms. The meat was shared out in a way that reportedly showed that the civilians were 'well advanced in their political understanding'.[85]

Once more providing evidence of consistency in maintaining gender divisions in the allocation of war-time duties, the report remarked on girls' efficiency in providing bath water to the guerrillas and sewing and laundering their clothes.[86] The young women were also applauded for their role in ensuring 'that every woman is well dressed culturally and

---

81 ZANU (PF) Archives, File: Defence Operations, Doc: 'Report on Manica Province (Dec 1978- May 1979),' 28 July 1979.
82 ZANU (PF) Archives, File: Southern Province (Gaza), Doc: 'Sector Two, Detachment Three, Operations', 17 December 1978.
83 Ibid.
84 Ibid.
85 Ibid.
86 Ibid.

[does] not act lumpen-wise.'[87] As in the camps, the pressure for women to police each other was relentless. This was to ensure that everybody respected local etiquette.

Committee positions could be influential, and dangerous, especially in contested zones, as Kriger noted in Mutoko.[88] People could be appointed to such positions to get them into trouble with either the security agents, who were always hunting down the guerrillas' key supporters, or with the guerrillas themselves, if the work that needed to be done was not satisfactorily performed.[89]

A critical report compiled by one H. Mutisi in the heavily contested Makoni area warned against over-dependence on youth and civilian committees in dealing with security matters. He argued that as they were not trained for such work, they were bound to make mistakes and get caught in enemy traps, which would be costly in terms of human life and civilian support.[90]

In Madziva in Tete Province questions were raised about the youth's lack of discipline that made some even more feared than the guerrillas themselves.[91] Chapter 4 shows that some youth received quasi-guerrilla training in the border areas towards the end of the war. Armed with grenades, many came to see themselves as liberation fighters. Thus it was not uncommon for the *mujibhas* to call for *pungwes* on their own. They would then dispense what they saw as 'revolutionary justice' to those deemed out of line; and, at the end of the *pungwes* or night meetings, they too could claim their share of feminine comforts from *chimbwidos* and other village girls.

Armed men's contests: exercises of muscle power and women's fate

The fighters' contentious relationships with civilian women and girls at the front mirrored the attitudes and situation in ZANLA's rear camps. As in most military situations, when discipline collapses, the abuse of women is one of its major manifestations. Like those in the rear base camps, civilian women and girls in the war zones found themselves caught in

---

[87]   Ibid.
[88]   Kriger, *Peasant Voices*, p. 200.
[89]   Staunton, *Mothers of the Revolution*, p. 131.
[90]   ZANU (PF) Archives, File: Defence Department, MMZ Province, 1976-1978, Local Meetings, Document: 'MMZ Province, Takawira Sectorial Operational Zone, Observation', by H. Mutisi, 10 August 1977.
[91]   Terence Ranger and Norma Kriger's findings of widespread bitterness against *mujibhas* in Makoni and Mutoko respectively are a reflection of a common feeling in most rural areas. At cease-fire, as people sighed with relief at the end of the war, many also rejoiced at the fall of the *mujibhas* as their guerrilla patrons now moved into the Assembly Points.

a very precarious situation. Force, backed up with guns, shaped their relations with military men.

For women in places like the PVs where basic provisions were scarce, a situation similar to that in the camps obtained: those in control could, and often did, subject women to sexual abuse in exchange for access to scarce consumables. Women could also be the instruments through which male contests were resolved.

Women were also used to relieve male stress, especially those associated with military service. Shimmer Chinodya's fictional account articulates the frustrations and the anger that sometimes overcame the guerrillas as they compared their exposure to danger and to the often harsh weather conditions with the civilians' relative safety and comfort. His main character, Comrade Pasi Nemasellout, lashed out angrily as he reflected upon these contrasts: 'Blast the village girls.... . Safe in huts. Warm. Dry. Running off to towns to live with relatives when things get hot.' [92]

The guerrillas and the soldiers both vented their exasperation with the war on women from whom they demanded the same sexual favours they allegedly provided to men on the 'other' side.

In view of the civilian-military relations in ZANLA's operational areas in rural Zimbabwe, the prospects for a gender revolution under the circumstances prevailing in the last phase of the war can be assessed. Kesby's theories about the PVs provide a useful reference point. The main thrust of his argument about women's contentious relations with the PV guards was that:

> the new disciplinary impositions of the state did not de-stabilise what it was to be a woman in the same way as they undermined what it was to be a man. [93]

Women have been subjects of military disputes in the past, but never before in the history of the country had their bodies been used as a terrain for military and political contestation in this manner. So this, by any standards, was no 'familiar' experience.[94]

Kesby further argued that young women were able to assert their sexuality in a way they had not been able to do before, as their male relations were now unable to contain

---

[92] Shimmer Chinodya, Harvest of Thorns, Heinemann, Oxford, 1989, p. 212.
[93] Mike Kesby, 'Arenas for Control, Terrains of Gender Contestation; Guerrilla Struggle and Counter-Insurgency Warfare in Zimbabwe 1972-80', Journal of Southern African Studies, vol. 22, 1996, p. 561-84.
[94] Ibid.

their wards' decisions to behave 'immorally'.[95] It is difficult to see how a woman could assert her sexuality through the experience of what in most instances were cases of coerced sex or rape. For obvious reasons, Kesby was not too keen to use such terms in his description of women's sexual relations with military men or others who enjoyed military backing, such as the *mujibhas*.[96] He did not delve deep enough into the implications of these experiences for women. Unprotected sexual contacts with guerrillas, camp guards or soldiers often meant pregnancies and venereal diseases. Children born under such circumstances received no support. No treatment for venereal diseases was available and some women and girls sustained permanent damage to their reproductive organs.

To all this, one should add the social stigma, which is evident throughout Kesby's informants' testimonies. It strikes a strange note that the women who were 'liberated' by war-time sexual relations with armed men are so conspicuous. All his informants talked about 'other' women's experiences rather than their own. This may suggest that thoughts of this period provoke feelings of shame rather than pride and triumph or secret musing. This may be the explanation why no women admit to having been involved with camp guards, in spite of the common occurrence of such relationships. The truth is, very few found the experience sexually liberating.

Kesby became trapped in his theory, for it can only be sustained by shifting attention from the women, the direct victims of the camp guards' or guerrillas' sexual exploits, to the male 'owners' of these women or girls.[97] It is true men were humiliated in an unprecedented way. However, being the direct objects of these abuses, women were no less affected.

While acknowledging the helplessness experienced by local men as 'foreign' military men arrived on the scene and appropriated their women and other local resources, we should still be careful not to blindly endorse theories about the war-time erosion of local male authority. First and foremost, the contests for control occurred between different categories of men. Apart from that, war-time notions of what it meant to be in control need to be put in their proper context. Mr Mazarura, who was in a PV in Dotito, offered useful insights into this as he reflected on the guerrillas' nightly visits to the PVs. He said that they would fire a shot into the air to announce their arrival, at which point the guards would disappear into their trenches.

---

[95] Ibid., p. 24.
[96] Ibid., p. 28.
[97] Ibid., p. 26.

We would hold a pungwe *with the boys through the night and they would leave at dawn. At sunrise the guards would peep from their holes to make sure the boys were gone before creeping out to start harassing us, demanding to know how the terrorists had got in. We wanted to ask them that very question themselves. Since they were supposedly guarding us, they should have explained to us how the terrorists got in. But we could not point that out because they had guns.[98]*

This account shows that Mr Mazarura and fellow civilian men were not convinced that the camp guards were in control. The latter's disappearing act into their 'holes' was definitely not perceived as a manly thing to do. During the harassment that followed the guerrillas' visits, as the guards paraded about with their guns, civilian men were probably exchanging furtive smiles, wondering who really the man of the day was. The knowledge that the gun-bearer would be less courageous without his gun kept civilian men's sense of manhood and superiority largely intact through the harassment by the militaries. For women, it was no consolation to know that even 'creeps' could exert upon them any demands they wanted, as long as they carried guns.

None the less, claims regarding the young women's ability to assert their sexuality during this time cannot be totally discounted.[99] However we should also remind ourselves that most of the so-called women were in fact children, young girls hardly past puberty. The war made them women before they were ready, and the majority have neither emotionally nor physically recovered from their traumatic experiences. Although some appeared to have enjoyed the so-called leverage it gave them over their parents or guardians,[100] our analysis should not lose sight of their immaturity at the time.

Many girls, however, made futile attempts to escape this abuse. As women and girls had done in previous crisis situations, some took refuge in marriages of convenience. Juliet Makande's story in *Mothers of the Revolution* underscores the predicaments and the cruelty with which the war thrust young girls into womanhood.[101] Her pain and fatigue as the war continued to exert pressure on *chimbwidos* is plainly expressed: 'I felt it was all too much. I was very tired.'[102] She weighed her options, which were limited under the circumstances, more limited than they had ever been for Zimbabwean women in the past. As a simple village girl, she sought refuge in marriage, but she soon found that what seemed like useful options often turned out to be something else:

---

[98] Discussion with Mr Mazarura, Dotito, Mt Darwin, 13 May 1992.
[99] Ibid., p. 30.
[100] Ibid., p. 31.
[101] Staunton, *Mothers of the Revolution*, p. 49.
[102] Ibid., p. 51.

my only thought was to find a man and get married and get everything over. ... I never thought that if you fell in love with a man, and he made you pregnant, that he would then say he didn't like you.[103]

As academics or feminists, researchers may be keen to build a case for female agency during crises. We need heroines. However, care should be taken not to let this obliterate visions of the truth, no matter how distressing.

During the war, the guerrillas could not be named as fathers, making the possibilities of marriage to them remote. The fighters were not supposed to be sexually involved with civilians, and there was no redress in such matters, apart from meting out physical punishment to the guerrilla involved. This only happened if the case received the attention of his seniors and if they decided to act on it. ZANLA's regulations stipulating that it would not interfere with civilian marriages automatically put marriage with civilians out of the question for guerrillas. The trials and punishment of those fighters who attempted marriage with civilians amply demonstrated this position.

Similar problems affected women when the men were Selous Scouts or soldiers or camp guards. It could be anyone, but the consequences were generally the same: pregnancy, disease, possible damage to their reproductive organs, abandonment and stigmatisation.

The leadership may have hoped to use spirit mediums to protect women from marauding armed men, as David Lan suggests, but in cases like that of Sub Shumba the result could be the opposite. Some self-styled 'spirit mediums' could prescribe extremely unconventional remedies for the guerrillas' physical and psychological ailments, such as telling the fighters to engage in the sexual violation of women to protect themselves.

As Juliet Makande's account demonstrated, war has a widening effect on gender disparities in that it narrows women's options as men take selfish measures to demonstrate their masculinity. Women's prospects to negotiate for concessions in a gendered power structure are substantially lowered in a military situation. In other words, there is less room for female agency than in peaceful times. Military exercises are forums for men to express masculine extremism. As amply demonstrated in the PVs, masculine extremism objectifies women rather than making them equal partners with men. Thus during wars, when militaries are in control, if the gender gap seems to narrow, it does so in spite of, rather than because of, the war.

---

[103] Ibid., p. 56.

Conclusion

By the cease-fire in 1979, the former PV inmates, who were mostly women, literally crept out of the caves and the bushes that had been home to them for almost three months. Those who saw them arriving in the villages cried,[104] not in celebration of the returnees' heroism but because of what these people had gone through and the sheer miracle of their survival. Such were the feelings dominating most reunions at the cease-fire and afterwards.

War-time labour allocation hardly transgressed gender lines in Zimbabwe's rural areas. If anything, the war made women's productive pursuits tougher than they had ever been before. Thus civilian women's main concerns in the rural areas during the war were, in the main, what Molyneux defined as 'practical gender interests' rather than 'strategic gender interests'.[105] There was less talk, if any, about the need to abolish the gender division of labour, or about freedom of choice over child-bearing, than there was about how to keep the family fed and alive in the face of often draconian manoeuvres by the military. Many guerrillas forgot their role as freedom fighters and engaged in gross abuses of their power to secure civilian women's sexual services. When and if the guerrillas took any action to defend women, they reprimanded men who beat their wives. However their major concern was to minimise obstacles to women's agricultural endeavours, upon which the guerrillas themselves depended. That was hardly an attempt to create a revolutionary environment where women could begin to challenge male authority or fancy themselves as men's equals.

Perhaps ZANLA needed to provide role models for civilian women from within its own ranks. One might argue that such figures were indeed presented to civilians, if we refer to the claims cited in Chapter 3 that by 1978 policies in relation to female deployment in the operational zones had been revolutionised. If so, why did this not leave a permanent impression?

---

[104] Interview with Ambuya Munhukare Mususa, Dotito, Mt Darwin, 13 May 1992.
[105] Maxine Molyneux, 'Mobilization without Emancipation? Women's Interests, the State, and Revolution in Nicaragua', in *Feminist Studies*, Vol. 11, No. 2, 1985, p. 233.

CHAPTER SIX

Women in the Transition to Peace and National Independence

Introduction

As the war with guns raged on in the rural areas of Zimbabwe and in neighbouring Mozambique and Zambia, off the battlefield politicians were attempting to negotiate a settlement. Kumbirai Kangai, ZANU's Secretary for Welfare and Transport during the war, recalled how most of these negotiations had ended up being nothing more than 'talks about talks', due to their failure to achieve anything of substance.[1]

Some negotiators did, however, cover ground and make progress. At the end of 1977, Ian Smith the Rhodesian Prime Minister was able to persuade internally based African leaders to commit themselves to some serious negotiations with his government. These leaders were: Abel Muzorewa, the leader of the United African National Congress (UANC); Ndabaningi Sithole, who had been dropped from the ZANU presidency in favour of Robert Mugabe, but still led a small following which retained the name ZANU; and Chief Jeremiah Chirau. The negotiations progressed through 1978, culminating in national elections in April 1979. The elections excluded two of the nationalist parties: Mugabe's ZANU and Nkomo's ZAPU. Of these two groups, Mugabe's forces worked the hardest to cause disruptions and to dissuade people from voting.[2] As far as ZANU was concerned, the

---

[1] Kumbirai M. Kangai, 'Some of the Important Events of the Period 1972-1982', in *Zimbabwe News,* Vol. 19, No. 12, December 1988, p. 46.

[2] See Janice McLaughlin, M.M., 'The Catholic Church and the War of Liberation', Ph.D., Dept of Religious Studies, University of Zimbabwe, June 1991, p. 369. ZANLA deployed many fighters in this period to intensify the war and to demonstrate that they were not part of the negotiations. This is the period when women fighters made their deepest inroads into the country to bring in reinforcements and carry out mobilisation work.

bombs Smith dropped on the guerrilla camps delivered his message. He did not want the camps' inmates to see the 'peace' he was negotiating with their supposed leaders inside Rhodesia.

During the voting, Rhodesian soldiers force-marched people to the polling stations. Often, they found deserted homesteads, as their occupants had made off for the bushes and the mountains, where they remained in hiding for the duration of the elections. For those who could not make themselves scarce, such as those in Protected Villages, the guerrillas had briefed them on what to do. In one of his works, Shona novelist James Mujeyi portrayed a scene at a ballot queue where a disguised Rhodesian soldier engaged in a conversation with a civilian voter. In an attempt to assess the mood of the voters, the soldier remarked how 'pissed off' he was for being dragged to the ballot box. The civilian readily offered useful tips on what to do under the circumstances:

> That should not be a problem at all. You just scratch whatever rubbish you want on the ballot paper, or you can even vote for three parties, then we'll see if they can work out what that means. ... The war will continue.[3]

The guerrillas had taught the voters these kinds of tactics to make the whole exercise futile. But the situation was different in the urban areas where the guerrillas exercised least control. At the end of the election, the authorities declared Abel Muzorewa's UANC the winner in the poorly attended elections. In June 1979, he became the Prime Minister of what was supposedly a new country, Zimbabwe-Rhodesia.

The question of how much support Muzorewa commanded inside Zimbabwe remains a debatable matter. However, the exiled nationalist parties made it clear that they did not recognise his authority at all. Thus, after the election the war intensified and the new government failed to secure international recognition. At the beginning of August, a few months after Muzorewa had assumed his post, the Commonwealth Heads of Government Meeting took place in Lusaka.[4] Using tactical diplomacy the delegates achieved positive results with Margaret Thatcher. To find a lasting solution, Thatcher agreed to organise a conference in London including all the parties concerned in the Zimbabwean crisis.[5]

The negotiations to draw up a constitution for Zimbabwe started at Lancaster House in London on 10 September 1979. After three months the parties involved emerged with

---

3   James Sungano Mujeyi, *Kusaziva Kufa* (Ignorance is Deadly) Longman, in association with The Literature Bureau, Harare, 1987, p. 109.

4   David Martin and Phyllis Johnson, *The Struggle For Zimbabwe: The Chimurenga War*, Zimbabwe Publishing House, Harare, 1981, pp. 314-15.

5   Ibid., pp. 314-15.

what was generally viewed as an agreement. The agreement called for a cease-fire, during which ZANLA and ZIPRA fighters deployed inside Zimbabwe were to gather into designated local Assembly Points (APs), in order for peaceful elections to be conducted. ZANLA and ZIPRA agreed to stop all cross-border incursions from neighbouring countries and the Rhodesian forces agreed to cease attacking these countries.[6] The British Government sent Lord Christopher Soames to Salisbury (now Harare) to act as Governor; he assumed formal control of the country until elections were held and an acceptable government installed.[7]

The return of the 'Boys from the Bush' and the transition to Independence

The ZANU component of the Patriotic Front (PF)[8] attending the London conference was entirely male.[9] The ZANLA leaders who came into Zimbabwe to liaise with the Commonwealth Monitoring Troops to get the fighters into the assembly points were also all male, except for one woman whom a press report named as Linda Tafadzwa.[10] In all ZANLA had 44 commanders, and an equal number representing ZIPRA. Most reports did not refer to any female presence among the newly arrived 88 commanders:

> The ZANLA officers arrived at 6.50 p.m. from Maputo. ... All the men were taken to an undisclosed destination for briefing before being deployed. ... The bus carrying the ZIPRA men was surrounded by ecstatic supporters as it crawled from the airport grounds.[11]

Other reports were clearly anti-PF, with the strongest distrust being expressed against ZANLA, which in turn trusted no one. The events of the three months following the onset of the negotiations in September had happened too fast for the nationalist leaders to have time to explain satisfactorily what was happening. While the leaders made public statements telling the fighters to assemble in the designated places, many received secret instructions to hide their arms and remain in their operational zones. These mixed signals

[6] Zimbabwe Rhodesia Government, *Report of the Constitutional Conference*, Lancaster House, London, September - December. 1979, p. 24.

[7] 'Doc. 1050: Lancaster House Conference: 'Report' and 'Rhodesia Cease-Fire Agreement'', 21 December 1979, in Goswin Baumhogger and others (eds), *The Struggle For Independence: Documents on the Recent Development of Zimbabwe (1975-1980)* Vol. 6, Institute of African Studies, Africa Documentation Center, Hamburg, 1984, pp. 1244-1245.

[8] The idea of a united front (the Patriotic Front) had been forced upon ZANU and ZAPU by the Frontline states and the OAU. In spite of the PF's ailing health since its formation, its membership managed to present a united front at Lancaster and were going to participate in the elections jointly. However, Mugabe pulled out of the partnership soon afterwards and registered his party in the elections as ZANU Patriotic Front (ZANU PF). Nkomo's Party participated as Patriotic Front ZAPU (PF ZAPU).

[9] See list of delegates in Zimbabwe Rhodesia Government, *Report of the Constitutional Conference*, Lancaster House, London, September to December, 1979, p. 4.

[10] National Archives of Zimbabwe (NAZ), IDAF Historical Manuscripts, File MS 308/7/1, 'Thousands Turn Out To Welcome PF Commanders', *Rhodesia Herald*, 27 Dec. 1979.

[11] NAZ, IDAF Historical Manuscripts, File MS 308/7/1, 'PF Guerrillas Get Heroes Welcome', *Rand Daily Mail*, 27 December 1979.

did not reassure the fighters about their leaders' faith in the agreement they had just signed.

Both the Rhodesian and the British press exploited the guerrillas' apprehensions, and their reports contained alarmist theories about an impending crisis:

> the reaction of the 'boys from the bush', as the insurgents are known, is entirely unpredictable. ... Some guerrillas will no doubt heed the cease-fire call and make their way to the assembly areas. But the men are likely to be suspicious, nervous and trigger-happy. The slightest misunderstanding might lead to bloody confrontation. [12]

Exploiting real and manufactured incidents of guerrilla violence and other intimidatory practices, the media maintained a determined campaign to discredit the nationalist fighters to ruin their chances in the elections. The press warned that with the return of 'the boys from the bush', everyone had better watch out. [13] The warnings went:

> Many others have long since forsaken any political allegiance and have come to enjoy the status of regional warlords, killing, plundering and raping at will. [14]

On the other hand, the press portrayed internally based forces as the only hope of neutralising an extremely volatile situation. Thus it campaigned for the continued non-confinement of Rhodesian soldiers and Muzorewa's men, purportedly so they would help maintain order. It identified the most devious guerrillas as those in ZANLA and alleged that they had already started denouncing the agreement. [15]

The accusations of intimidatory practices among ZANLA were not always without substance. Nevertheless, the Rhodesian forces, with backing from Pfumo Revanhu, the personal army of the newly installed Prime Minister Muzorewa and Sithole's forces who masqueraded as ZANLA, were all violating the terms of the cease-fire. They attacked returning guerrillas, [16] and committed other horrific and inhuman acts leaving behind 'evidence' to incriminate ZANLA forces. Observers reported the civilian death toll to be around one thousand per month. [17] Several attacks were made on Church institutions and, as Mugabe

---

[12] NAZ, IDAF Historical Manuscripts, File MS 308/7/1, 'Monitoring Troops In Danger', *Daily Telegraph*, 27 December 1979.

[13] NAZ, IDAF Historical Manuscripts, File MS 308/7/1, ' 'Boys From Bush' Back', *Daily Telegraph*, 27 Dec. 1979.

[14] *Ibid.*

[15] NAZ, IDAF Historical Manuscripts, File MS 308/7/1, 'Monitoring Troops In Danger', *Daily Telegraph*, 27 December 1979.

[16] Zimbabwe National Archives, IDAF Historical Manuscripts, File MS 308/7/1, Text of BBC Report, 29 Dec. 1979.

[17] Munyaradzi Mushonga, 'The Formation, Organisation And Activities of The Catholic Commission for Justice and Peace in Rhodesia with Particular Reference to the Rhodesian War, 1972-1980', BA Hons. Dissertation, University of Zimbabwe, Dept of History., 1990, p. 44.

was portrayed as the anti-Christ, the attackers hoped everyone would assume that he was behind the acts.[18]

ZIPRA also had some violations in its ranks, though its smaller numbers of forces meant that the leadership was better placed to contain their activities. The press was less hostile to ZAPU too, because it hoped that a victorious Nkomo could be compromised, like Abel Muzorewa.

Despite violations of the cease-fire terms by others, Lord Soames' transitional government was always threatening to exercise its disciplinary powers to disqualify ZANLA offenders from the elections.[19] Apart from constant character assassinations, ZANU and ZANLA faced so many obstacles that their leadership could hardly campaign in preparation for the general elections. In the face of this intimidation and hostility, many ZANLA 'boys' readily heeded the secret call to hide their arms, remaining outside the assembly areas. Obviously, their actions were under scrutiny, and Muzorewa's army made a bid to flush them out. Thus ZANU had to use even more cunning strategies to manoeuvre through the hurdles confronting it at that time.

Women and ZANU's electoral campaign

The media focused on 'the boys from the bush' because ZANLA had deployed few women fighters inside Zimbabwe. In addition, the guerrilla leaders who came to help implement the cease-fire exercise were almost all men. By excluding women fighters from the limelight, ZANLA was able to cheat the monitoring system. During the cease-fire ZANLA deployed its women fighters extensively, especially in areas where the men were under pressure to leave for the Assembly Points (APs).

To appeal to a largely female electorate, ZANU calculated that women campaigners would be crucial in its election bid.[20] So, ZANU set out to woo women voters by using its female fighters. Actually, some of ZANLA's best political commissars were women. Some of these female guerrillas, however, had to be in the APs to avoid the embarrassment of

---

[18] Julie Frederikse, *None but Ourselves, Masses vs. Media in the Making of Zimbabwe*, Zimbabwe Publishing House, Harare, 1982, pp. 296-97.

[19] In his identification of problem areas, Soames painted ZANLA-controlled zones as the worst affected. See 'Doc. 1119: 'The intimidation Map', 18 February 1980, in Goswin Baumhogger and others (eds), *The Struggle For Independence: Documents on the Recent Development of Zimbabwe (1975-1980)*, Vol. 7, p. 1346.

[20] ZANU (PF) Archives, File: Women's Affairs Department, Document: 'Meeting with Women Held at Matola Residence', 7 January 1980. Apparently, urban women had been very instrumental in bringing about Muzorewa's victory.

having none at all, especially after ZANLA's many claims that women were fully involved as combatants. Thus ZANU needed to infiltrate more female fighters into the country. Although the cease-fire terms ruled against any movement of trained fighters across the border, ZANLA grossly contravened these rules to infiltrate more female guerrillas into Zimbabwe, as the party sought to meet its political needs.

Under the agreement, trained forces had to remain in the rear bases in neighbouring countries through the elections. Many refugees were also in those same bases. The United Nations planned to repatriate them to Zimbabwe immediately, so the adults among them could participate in the February elections.[21] The ZANLA leadership did not miss the opportunities the repatriation exercise offered. It designed a strategy whereby its trained fighters, mostly women, joined the refugee trek into Zimbabwe. Under these arrangements, ZANLA guerrilla campaigners even made it into the urban areas,[22] in spite of the internal forces' strict surveillance. (Amid much controversy, Lord Soames had delegated monitoring duties to the internal forces.) A former ZIPRA combatant revealed that she and many of her comrades also returned from Zambia under a similar secret ZAPU scheme.[23]

Remarking on the slowness of the official refugee repatriation exercise and the hostile atmosphere created by Rhodesian interrogations at entry points, Stella Makanya wrote later:

> Such a situation left the refugees who were in the neighbouring countries... very impatient. When it became clear that the Rhodesian authorities wanted to frustrate the returnees and interfere with their participation in the forth-coming elections, many decided to take the same initiative they had taken when they fled the country instead of waiting for the official repatriation.[24]

Although the complaints against the authorities were quite justified, some of the refugees who got 'impatient' and repatriated themselves were trained guerrillas entering Zimbabwe on pre-election party missions.

After hiding their arms, women fighters could more easily mingle with the civilian population. Even those who passed through official refugee checkpoints were less likely to be suspected of being trained fighters. They easily subverted the monitoring exercise be-

21 Zimbabwe Rhodesia Government, *Report of The Constitutional Conference*, 1979, p. 24.
22 Interview with Mrs Mazarura Junior (Mai Caro), Dotito, May 1992. She said some remained in Harare after the elections and they had to be followed to be taken to APs.
23 Interview with Helen Moyo (Comrade Ntombiyezwe Nyathi), Sunningdale, Harare, March 1992.
24 Stella T. Makanya, 'The Desire to Return: Effects of Experiences in Exile on Refugees Repatriating to Zimbabwe in the Early 1980s', in Tim Allen & Hubert Morsink (eds), *When Refugees Go Home*, United Nations Research Institute, Geneva; also by James Currey, London, 1994, p. 121.

cause of the universal notions of men as aggressors and women as helpless victims. This patriarchal perception of women also helped the women fighters qualify as refugees in the men's eyes. With ZANU unfairly denied a campaigning platform, the women became a useful tool. ZANU charged them with familiarising its supporters with the election procedures, and with such details as how to identify Mugabe's ZANU PF from Ndabaningi Sithole's ZANU.[25]

Putting the Party before all

In the rear camps, the new officers of the Department of Women's Affairs explained to their comrades the issues currently at stake. Teurai Ropa had a special message for those going to participate in the campaigning exercise: the female fighters had a duty to go and reclaim the souls of those lost to ZANU PF's rivals, Muzorewa, Sithole, Chirau, and Nkomo.[26]

Previously, the inmates of places such as Osibisa Camp had resented being categorised as refugees. When they learnt of the importance of the political contest that was about to occur in Zimbabwe, they assumed titles that they, as trained soldiers, would never have considered before. ZANLA women had not been involved in the Lancaster House negotiations. They had also been excluded from their Party's official representation now working with the Commonwealth Election Supervisors inside Zimbabwe. To get to Zimbabwe, to the crucial arena of the day, the women therefore agreed to assume temporary refugee status. This seemed the only way to cross the border in time to help their Party through the elections, and to get themselves into the political limelight. In any case, the assumption of what was previously a demeaning title was only a temporary measure to cheat the monitoring system.

Almost immediately problems arose for some of the women. Their instructions to leave for Zimbabwe came so unexpectedly that they had no time to arrange for the care of their children.[27] Although they wanted to be involved at this crucial time, they were understandably concerned about their offspring. The Central Committee responded to the issue of child-care by ordering the mothers who could not part with their children to return to the camps and stay with them forever.[28] The leadership apparently needed the

---

[25] Ndabaningi Sithole, the ex-President of the Mozambique-based ZANU, remained with a small following and retained the use of that same name for his party. It was partly to show distinction with Sithole's party that Mugabe's adopted the name ZANU PF in the 1980 elections.

[26] ZANU (PF) Archives, File: Women's Affairs Department, Document: 'Meeting with Women Held at Matola Residence', 7 January 1980.

[27] Ibid.

[28] Ibid.

women fighters' services and support at this time, but they were still unwilling to address the issue of child-care. This was a major obstacle to women's full integration into ZANLA during the war (see Chapter 3).

The women knew that if they failed to give the required services to the party, the men would use it later as an excuse to exclude them. Julia Zvobgo and Teurai Ropa were annoyed that their comrades had raised the matter of child-care with the Central Committee at all. They were also upset that the women had by-passed them as the women's official leaders.[29] Thus the women ended up blaming one another over an issue the Central Committee should have legitimately addressed. In the end, they advised the mothers to arrange with friends for the care of their children.[30]

Despite both the in-house problems and the cease-fire constraints, several groups of women fighters managed to make it to Zimbabwe before the elections. They were going to see ZANU PF through the general elections as campaigners, a role they were to play many more times after the war. Immediately they had to co-ordinate their activities with the civilian organs created during the war, especially with the youth wings.

Pre-electoral partnerships, tactics and promises

From this period onwards the Department of Women's Affairs and the youth wing formed a crucial partnership in ensuring victory for ZANU in all post-war elections. The two organs formed the core of what later become known as the ZANU PF Women's League and the Youth Brigade.

The joint effort of ZANU PF's political commissars and the youth paid dividends. The young *mujibhas'* methods were effective in selling the cock (ZANU PF's election symbol) to the voters. Commenting on the use of the crowing cock as ZANU PF's symbol, Ken Flower, the former Head of Rhodesian Intelligence Services, wrote of ZANU PF campaigners' overwhelming success:

> *in the Shona language there is more sensual connotation and the added symbolism of heralding a new day, a new era. The massive turnout of voters (estimated at over 90 per cent of those eligible to vote) was achieved in part by herding of the voters and a shepherding of the queues*

---

[29] Ibid.
[30] Ibid.

*at polling booths by young men who flapped their elbows up and down to signify a rampant
cock after sexual conquest, much to the amusement of men and women alike.[31]*

These sexist performances, playing out the subjection of the female by the male, were
well received by the intended audience. Not even a decade of guerrilla war, in which the
women had struggled to ward off sexual predators of all sorts, had altered people's thinking. In the patriarchal world to which the rural folk were accustomed, they expected such
virile qualities of those who desired to rule.

ZANU PF took greater care, however, in preparing its election manifesto (which the
largely illiterate rural voter would not need). The written document maintained the myth
of gender equality. This was, perhaps, for the benefit of the haughty women whom ZANLA
had struggled to contain in the camps. Their educated supporters in the towns and, maybe,
foreign sympathisers, also wanted to see all those politically correct clauses included. Some
of the latter had representatives among the newly arrived election observers. During the
war, ZANU and ZANLA had presented themselves as the emancipators of oppressed women,
and now these outsiders were around to see things for themselves. Thus, the manifesto,
released on 25 January 1980, declared among its 'Thirteen Fundamental Rights and
Freedoms':

*Under a ZANU PF Government, women will enjoy equal rights with men in all spheres of
POLITICAL, ECONOMIC, CULTURAL and FAMILY life.[32]*

The manifesto also promised to uphold the right to vote, of 'every citizen who reached
the age of eighteen', including women. The Zimbabwe Constitution drawn at Lancaster
House had already made the same stipulation.[33]

Composition of the government of the victors

A ZANU PF government came into power in April 1980, after performing remarkably well
in the February elections.[34] ZANU PF acknowledged women's contribution to its success,

---

[31] Ken Flower, *Serving Secretly: An Intelligence Chief on Record: Rhodesia into Zimbabwe, 1964 - 1981*, John
     Murray Publishers, London, 1987, p. 269.
[32] 'Doc. 1093: Election Manifesto of ZANU - Patriotic Front', 25 January 1980, in Goswin Baumhogger and others
     (eds), *The Struggle for Independence: Documents on the Recent Development of Zimbabwe (1975-1980)* Vol. 7,
     p. 1310.
[33] Ibid.
[34] ZANU (PF) secured fifty-seven of the eighty parliamentary seats that the African parties contested for. Its former
     Patriotic Front partner, PF ZAPU, secured nineteen seats; three went to Muzorewa's UANC and the last was
     taken up by Sithole's ZANU. Whites voted separately for twenty seats reserved for them under the Lancaster
     House Constitution.

amid declarations that after all the women had done in the war, pushing them back would no longer be possible.

Out of the 57 seats ZANU PF secured in Parliament, women won five.[35] These women, out of a total of 80 candidates were the only women the Party had fielded for the elections. On the PF ZAPU side, three women were among the party's twenty candidates who succeeded in gaining parliamentary seats in the elections. In all, this meant that eight per cent of the 100-seat Parliament was female.

With a majority in the new Parliament, Mugabe had no trouble choosing the members of his Cabinet. Only five posts went to ZAPU men, including one to Joshua Nkomo. Two others went to whites, also male. ZANU had appointed one of these men to Senate to qualify him for the ministerial post. The Party also invited five more men to join the Cabinet through the same route, as they did not have parliamentary seats. In all, the new Prime Minister, Robert Mugabe created 23 senior ministerial posts, and nine others for deputy ministers.[36]

Three of ZANU's five female parliamentarians filled Cabinet posts: Teurai Ropa became the Minister of Youth, Sport and Recreation; Victoria Chitepo, the widow of the former Chairman of ZANU, Herbert Chitepo who was assassinated in 1975, became Deputy Minister in the Education and Culture Ministry; and Naomi Nhiwatiwa became Deputy Minister of Posts and Telecommunications.[37] Mugabe did not appoint any women to the Senate to qualify them for Cabinet posts.

Teurai Ropa later moved from the Ministry of Youth, Sport and Culture in 1981 to head the belatedly created Ministry of Community Development and Women's Affairs (MCDWA). Welcoming this development she explained:

> Prime Minister Mugabe and his government after independence saw the need ... as a result of research done on women during the struggle. The policy of this government concerning women aims at a transformation of women's status so that they can assume their rightful role in society as participants alongside men on the basis of full equality.[38]

---

[35] 'Doc. 1142: Final Results: Elected Candidates', 4 March 1980, in Goswin Baumhogger and others (eds), *The Struggle for Independence: Documents on the Recent Development of Zimbabwe (1975-1980)* Vol. 7, p. 1389.
[36] 'Doc. 1154: Appointment of Prime Minister Mugabe and his Cabinet', 13 March 1980, in Goswin Baumhogger and others (eds), *The Struggle for Independence: Documents on the Recent Development of Zimbabwe (1975-1980)*,Vol. 7, pp. 1412-1413.
[37] Ibid.
[38] *Africa Report*, Vol. 28, No. 2, March-April 1983, p. 18.

Political participation in post-war Zimbabwe

As well as indicating the direction of future developments, the new government reflected the gender composition of war-time organs. Except for a few civilian supporters of ZANU PF and members of the opposition whom Mugabe appointed, those who became ministers in 1980 had held similar-level posts in ZANU's war-time structures in Mozambique. For example, those who had been in ZANU's Central Committee, as Secretary for Education or Health during the war, marched into the new cabinet as the Minister of Education or Health. Because ZANU had largely excluded women from its top administrative structures in the war, it was not surprising that they were almost out of the picture in similar level structures after the war (see Appendix).

Teurai Ropa's first appointment as head of the Ministry of Youth Sport and Recreation seemed contrived, placing her in what the ZANU PF leaders saw as women's area of speciality – minding the children. Also, based on what they saw as the shared experience of women and youth in the refugee schools during the war and the pre-election campaign, ZANU's rationale for defining women's post-war duties becomes clearer. ZANLA women had carried war material with the youth; they had taught them in refugee schools in Mozambique; they had looked after children in places like Osibisa Camp; they had kept 'culture' alive among the young people during the displacement; and their partnership with the youth in the election campaign had been crucial in bringing ZANU PF to power.

ZANU's leaders may have assessed women's functions in the same way as they assessed those of the youth. Before the *Legal Age of Majority Act of 1982*, women, like children, were legal minors. In that respect, they and the youth were dependent on adult men and, therefore, the male leadership could trust them to act with minimum self-interest. In most socialist-oriented countries, moreover, the ruling parties traditionally linked women's and youth organs to generate support.

The newly created Ministry of Women's Affairs and Community Development worked closely with ZANU PF Women's League, and its leaders also doubled as leaders of the League. The latter operated in the same political spaces as the ZANU PF Youth Brigade, so maintaining strong war-time links between the women's organisations and the youth. As new political challenges arose, the Women's League led the youth (their children), some of whom had now grown into young men, in disturbing forms of 'sporting' and 'recreation'.[39]

---

[39] In the 1985 General Elections, in places like St Mary's Township, a very poor location in Chitungwiza, they bulldozed those families who were 'caught on the wrong side' out of their homes, and they also set some of the homes on fire.

For those who had been optimistic that the officially backed organisations would provide influential forums to address gender-based discrimination, the prospects for the future seemed dim. Gradually, disappointed women began to break away. Rather than ex-
pend their energy in party wars they sought to create alternative platforms to address the
disparities. They set themselves up in non-governmental organisations, creating organs
like the Women's Action Group.[40] ZANU PF, however, was not happy with organisations
operating 'out of the orbit of the League'.[41] Announcing that they regarded themselves as
the only legitimate women's voice, the leadership of the ZANU PF Women's League charged:

> The aims of these organisations are not clear to us because originally, these organisations were
> of a charitable and social nature. Lately however we see them delving in political issues. Our
> question is 'on whose behalf?' Their meddling in politics confuses the scene and we do not
> know whether they are now for minority parties.[42]

Teurai Ropa directly castigated one newly formed group, the Women's Task Force,
whose members she described as 'the elite group of women'. She accused the task force of
two things: merely sitting around doing nothing, or when they worked at all, of opposing
the league. She vowed to act 'to stop all this confusion'.[43] Such threats created an atmosphere of intimidation, thereby restricting and curtailing women's organisation outside the
dictates of the Party. The message was clear: unless people wanted to organise around
charities, whose terms of reference excluded meddling in politics, there was no space for
them.

As long as the Party retained control, the scope of women's political activity remained
narrow. The voices of those who had exclusive mandate to talk sounded more and more
parochial. War-time legacies continued to haunt the official women's organs whose political activities hardly ventured further than singing praises for, and denouncing opponents
on behalf of, the Party leadership, the men.

Reflecting on these early developments in an interview in 1995, Julia Zvobgo spoke
bluntly, describing the Women's League (of which she used to be a leading member) as 'a
curse'. She suggested that people should not be appointed to posts they could not handle,
just because they sang the loudest praise of the Party.[44] Her former colleagues would
probably dismiss her as one of the elite women who did not want to co-operate with Party

---

[40] For a comprehensive list, see Voluntary Organisations in Community Enterprise (Voice), Directory of Non-Governmental Organisations, Voice, Harare, 1988, pp. 109-14.
[41] Zimbabwe News, Vol. 16, No. 2, Feb. 1985, p. 16.
[42] Ibid.
[43] Ibid.
[44] Ibid.

programmes, or who entertained separate political agendas.[45] But her opinion reflects widely held views in Zimbabwe regarding the position of the Women's League, as being more useful to ZANU PF's patriarchal leadership than to the movement for women's liberation.

Programmes for women's economic empowerment?

It remained unclear as to who was the main driving force in ZANU (PF) regarding women's affairs: the Women's League or the Department of Women's Affairs. However by February 1985, Teurai Ropa said they had some 2 500 projects running, in 'dress-making, animal husbandry, poultry' and 'bakeries in rural areas'.[46] This was the same old song played in the ZANLA camps, where they had confined women's projects to the domestic sphere. Moreover the projects had serious structural problems and their woes were compounded for most of the period in question by natural disasters.[47]

Poor rains meant poor cash flows to sustain the bakeries or the animal 'husbandry' projects in the rural areas. They also affected the targeted consumers' purchasing capacity. Uniform-making ventures got caught in a vicious circle. Headmasters would place orders with tailors. They needed cash advances from the headmasters to buy the necessary materials. The headmasters had to raise the money from the parents who were also the tailors. Such enterprises formed part of the 2 500 projects in the MCDWA's files in Harare, but they were not viable and could not function.

Other problems arose from the lack of specialised assistance given to the projects. Designed to sustain and benefit women without much education, the projects were doomed from the start because the women were not given education or support. Educated women who could have played an advisory role were, in the main, employed elsewhere. Sometimes educated women were perceived by the Party as belonging to an 'elite group' with, allegedly, a political agenda to ruin ZANU PF. This attitude is unsurprising in view of the Party's history of marginalising educated people during the war, in order to stamp out political criticism in the camps (see Chapter 3.)

---

[45] Julia Zvobgo's husband, Edson Zvobgo's clash with some ZANU PF members during in-house struggles prior to the 1995 General Elections led to allegations that he contemplated replacing Robert Mugabe as the Party President. See *Parade*, April 1994, pp. 6-9.

[46] *Zimbabwe News*, Vol. 16, No. 2, Feb. 1985, p. 14.

[47] For a discussion of the impact of poor rains on the rural people's economic activities in the early eighties see, Michael Bratton, 'Drought, Food And The Social Organisation of Small Farmers in Zimbabwe', in Michael H. Glantz (ed.), *Drought and Hunger in Africa: Denying Famine a Future*, Cambridge University Press, Cambridge, 1988, pp. 227-35.

Even in the higher echelons of the MCDWA, invitations to conferences or workshops to discuss developmental issues went to staunch Party supporters, though their credentials in the subject under discussion may not have been impressive. The selection process, of course, had negative consequences for programmes meant to economically empower women or to give them a certain degree of independence.

Another problem seriously hampering economic projects had to do with the land tenure system in the rural areas, not to mention land deprivation and overcrowding. Without claim to land, women worked on land allocated to their husbands or to other male relatives. Many lost the little income they had earned to such men. In the end, women had no capital for further investment in their projects. Women's relation to land under the current land tenure system remains a contentious issue and requires the government's prompt action.[48]

Other problems arose because the Party leadership had to clear the MCDWA's and the league's projects. For example, in 1983, the Party was restructuring its provincial leadership, which was predominantly male. The league then took the position that it would only support projects in those provinces that had been restructured.[49] This sounded like a warning. People who did not co-operate fully with the Party's restructuring programmes, could find themselves excluded from developmental projects. In addition, the power elites, the men, determined the pace of the restructuring exercise, depending on how well they co-operated with the senior Party officials. If these elites dragged their feet, women's projects suffered. Thus they were punished for matters over which they had little if any control.

Some women complained to the league that anti-Party elements were preventing them from participating in development. Teurai Ropa outlined the allegations:

> They have found out that some employers and administrators turn away Party activists, purely on tribal grounds. Some are generally rude to the workers and make derogatory statements about the Prime Minister which are intolerable.[50]

Such problems had little to do with gender. Nevertheless, the league took the alleged anti-ZANU PF attitudes very seriously and recommended forwarding the allegations to the Central Committee. The atmosphere of intolerance became pervasive. For example Party zealots demanded that women advisors in the economic projects be filtered through the ZANU PF machinery to exclude Muzorewa supporters.[51] Whatever the exact substance of

---

48 See Government of Zimbabwe, *Rukuni Commission: Report of the Commission of Inquiry into Appropriate Agricultural Land Tenure Systems*, 1994.
49 *Zimbabwe News*, Vol. 14, No. 1, Apr. 1983, p. 29.
50 Ibid., p. 30.
51 Ibid.

the claims of exclusion and prejudice, ZANU PF partisan concerns, rather than women's economic empowerment, often pre-occupied the league. Thus it rendered itself useless as an agency meant to improve women's position in relation to men.

Women's sexuality and access to social space

In the years immediately following Independence, stories of mothers dumping their new-born babies abounded in government-controlled newspapers such as *The Herald*. Commenting on this, Rudo Gaidzanwa, a sociologist, said poverty was the major contributory factor.[52] It is not clear whether 'baby dumping' had increased or whether it appeared to have done so as a result of the increased press coverage. If the latter, why was the issue given so much (unsympathetic) attention?

A partial answer may lie in the Party patriarchs' attempt to reinforce certain social values compromised during the war and threatened by the unprecedented influx of people into urban areas from which they had previously been excluded. As they had always seen women as the guardians of culture and custom (the definitions of which are rarely agreed upon), the tone of the newspaper reports reflected general male anxiety over women's freedom. The goverment-controlled press also seems to have orchestrated this campaign to invoke feelings of horror at women's increasingly irresponsible behaviour. In other words, women were being held responsible for what the ZANU PF patriarchs feared was an impending social collapse. At the same time, the government was reluctantly making changes to improve women's legal status. By linking women directly to negative practices (such as baby dumping) the officially controlled press may have been attempting to thwart feminist-oriented initiatives.

Reacting to reports ladling all the blame on women for abandoning their babies, Ruth Chinamano, a ZAPU parliamentarian, introduced a motion to raise debate on the matter.[53] It became apparent in the highly charged discussions that followed that the courts needed to investigate the women's socio-economic background before judges passed harsh sentences. A male parliamentarian, Mr Shields, reminded the house: 'the girl who dumps the baby has already been dumped by some man along the road.'[54] Mr Shields and others recommended rehabilitation of the young women rather than rejection by society. Ruth Chinamano, commenting afterwards, said she had been surprised that no other female

---

[52]   Rudo Gaidzanwa, 'Bourgeois Theories of Gender and Feminism', in Ruth Meena (ed.), *Gender in Southern Africa: Conceptual and Theoretical Issues*, SAPES Trust, Harare, 1992, p. 120.

[53]   *Parliamentary Debates*, Zimbabwe House of Assembly, 6 November 1984, p. 443.

[54]   Ibid., p. 445.

parliamentarians had participated in the discussion.[55] Their reluctance to challenge male opinion apparently reflected their insecure political position. They feared being seen to condone irresponsible behaviour by members of their sex when they were supposed to be grateful for the legal changes the men were making in their favour.[56]

ZANU PF's female parliamentarians appear to have been silenced, because they knew that their male colleagues were determined to find excuses to check women's liberties, in order to offset the impact of the rhetoric regarding gender equality that they had brought back with them from the war. Organs like the Women's League maintained the rhetoric of egalitarian liberation, largely to motivate women to work hard to rebuild the country. However, some league members interpreted the implications of sexual equality in simplistic terms, further antagonising the patriarchs, rather than engaging them in serious debate about male-female power relations. In 1992, a former combatant working in the Department of Women's Affairs, the reduced unit of the former MCDWA, thought the pronouncements by the league's members in the first years of Independence did not really do the Zimbabwean women's movement much favour:

> You do not just wake up one day and say to a man, you are doing the cooking today. It closes debate. Yet this is what some of the women were saying at the rallies, things which they were not even doing in their homes! But some of their audiences obviously took on their suggestions, to our detriment![57]

The misunderstandings arising from these domestic conflicts often led to violence. Some husbands told their wives that the Women's League 'nonsense' should be left at the rallies where it belonged. The men were still the masters of their houses! One of the biggest ironies about these disputes was that the League never intended to challenge patriarchal control. It designed its 'empowerment' projects to reinforce the domestication of women.

The Ministry of Health's family planning programme also led to increased cases of domestic violence and increased patriarchal resistance to any moves intended to give women more autonomy. Resistance to measures that enable women to control their reproduction has always existed. Gaining momentum in the war, it had assumed radical political dimensions.

---

[55] *Parliamentary Debates*, 15 November 1984, p. 796.

[56] This relationship of female politicians' dependence on their male colleagues in government was most apparently demonstrated when, in 1982, the MCDWA organized demonstrations to thank government (of which it was part) for passing the Legal Age of Majority Act. See Gaidzanwa, 'Bourgeois Theories of Gender and Feminism', p. 115.

[57] Interview with Molly Chipadza, Mt Darwin, May 1992.

The thrust of the arguments against contraceptives in the ZANLA camps (see Chapter 3) were the same as those preached in the guerrillas' operational zones. They had received enthusiastic support from traditionalists who enjoyed the backing of activists from religious organisations such as the Roman Catholic Church.[58] Also, urban, working men with wives in the rural areas did not like the idea of their wives using contraceptives. They feared that their women would be free to lead promiscuous lifestyles in their absence. As family planning personnel used forums such as the women's clubs to spread information about contraception, some men stopped their wives from attending these clubs. The work of local playwrights featured on television reflected the confusion and misunderstandings that prevailed in relation to the use of artificial birth-control methods.[59]

A police manoeuvre demonstrated the on-going conflicts, which were about ensuring that women remained under male control. In 1983 the police conducted an infamous 'clean-up operation'.[60] They picked up some men for vagrancy, but they rounded up hundreds of women for moving at night, alleging that they were prostitutes. The police decided that since the women obviously had nothing better to do, they should take them to the Zambezi Valley to engage in agricultural production. They claimed this would not only benefit the women, but also the people of that terribly underdeveloped part of the country.

This was not the first time 'loose women' had been penalised in this way. Rhodesian colonial authorities often raided men's hostels in the urban centres to flush out the women living there and return them to the rural areas. FRELIMO in nearby Mozambique had conducted similar sweeping operations in Maputo, and among its targets were women without husbands and those in common-law marriages.[61]

Fortunately for the women arrested in Zimbabwean towns in 1983, the police exercise received much public criticism, and in the end, the police were forced to release them. Rudo Gaidzanwa observed:

---

[58] For some of the main arguments against colonial family planning programmes see A.K.H. Weinrich, *African Marriage in Zimbabwe and the Impact of Christianity*, Mambo Press, Gweru, 1982, pp. 118-23; for comparative arguments, also see Jacklyn Cock, *Colonels and Cadres, War and Gender in South Africa*, OUP, Oxford, 1991, p. 37.

[59] See Juliet Chikanza, 'Ndaizivei' (Had I Known), in J. Chikanza, *Vakasiiwa Pachena*, Mambo Press, Gweru, 1984.

[60] See Zimbabwe Women's Action Group, 'Operation Clean Up', in Miranda Davies (Compiler), *Third World, Second Sex*, Vol. 2, Zed Books, London, 1987, pp. 226-28; Gaidzanwa, 'Bourgeois Theories Of Gender and Feminism', in Ruth Meena, (ed.), *Gender in Southern Africa: Conceptual and Theoretical Issues*, SAPES Trust, Harare, 1992, p. 115.

[61] Stephanie Urdang, *And Still they Dance, Women, War and the Struggle for Change in Mozambique*, Earthscan Publications, London, 1989, pp. 189-97.

some of the organisations and individuals were against the arresting of women who were 'decent' or 'innocent', that is married or single but not lacking in virtue, but not against those who were not.[62]

This showed the limitations within which the arguments for opening up political and social space for women took place.

Undesirable outcomes: legal reforms for women

The policy makers in the new government held unrevolutionary attitudes in relation to the status of women. This background highlights the political, economic and social atmosphere within which change was supposed to occur.

Essentially, the legal reforms made in relation to women were the unintended outcome of the ruling party leadership's pre-independence rhetoric regarding gender reform. ZANU PF's war-time assertions and the politically correct views it pronounced during the pre-election campaign finally caught up with the Party. Its leaders had raised expectations, both among middle-class women in Zimbabwe and among the external organisations supporting the liberation war. With regard to gender equality, the ZANU PF leaders were reluctant revolutionaries.

During the war, outsiders did not know about the situation prevailing in the camps and the operational zones. Inconsistent practices had largely gone unchallenged. However, with Independence, there was no shortage of assessors prepared to scrutinise the new government's statutes to see how the ruling party fared, at least in terms of legal reforms intended to address sex-based discrimination.[63] Without doubt, Zimbabwe's exposure to global scrutiny had a strong bearing on the pace and content of legislative reform.

Apart from the rhetoric from the guerrilla camps during the war, academics and religious organisations inside Rhodesia had been calling for change in the legal position of African women, especially in relation to so-called Customary Law.[64] Women like Olivia Muchena, a prominent member of the recently dissolved United African National Congress (UANC) government of Abel Muzorewa, had already researched the socio-economic

---

[62]   See Gaidzanwa, 'Bourgeois Theories of Gender and Feminism', p. 120.
[63]   With its relatively well-developed economic infrastructure in comparison to other Southern African countries at the time, Zimbabwe offered a suitable environment for the operations of non-governmental agencies in the region. This brought in a strong foreign presence.
[64]   See Report of the *Commission to Inquire into the Legal Status of African Women*, Church of the Province of Central Africa, Diocese of Mashonaland, 1976.

position of Zimbabwean women. Her findings were available to policy makers.[65] Though largely carried out among elite African women, the findings and recommendations of these pre-Independence enquiries were useful in spelling out fairer laws for women.

The content of the legal reforms

The legal gains women made in the years after Independence are thoroughly dealt with in other works.[66] Thus only the main ones are summarised here. Although most of these laws had the potential to improve women's legal position, non-legal constraints stood in the way of making them work for the majority of women. The social practices outlined earlier as problems in transforming women's lives in post-war Zimbabwe may not have been legally based, but some were so entrenched that they could be said 'to have attained the force of law', as Edson Zvobgo explained in 1983.[67] The conservative assertions of the majority of speakers during parliamentary debates on these matters reflected the general social reluctance with which legislators were accepting the reforms.

Commenting on the social pressure on legislators to retain the dual legal system that applied customary law to vital aspects of African family life (despite its bias against women), Maboreke wrote:

> Most African people have neither completely moved away from the customary way of life, nor have they remained squarely rooted within it. In most cases they have a foot in each world. Very often the modern executive moving sleekly along the streets of the capital city is 'transfigured' into an ancestor-worshipping traditionalist overnight when he/she goes 'home' to the rural area to appease some disgruntled ancestor or avenging spirit believed to be manifest through some misfortune.[68]

During the war the guerrillas were also caught between these two worlds, the cultural world of the sprits, and the modern world of the revolutionaries. Women, regarded as the 'granaries' storing social values, found themselves receiving contradictory instructions when those values were not clearly articulated. The new laws were supposed to better women's

[65] Olivia N. Muchena, A Socio-Economic Overview: Zimbabwean Women, African Training and Research Centre For Women, United Nations Economic Commission for Africa, Addis Ababa, 1982. This is an up-dated version of a 1979 publication bearing the same title.
[66] See Mary Maboreke, 'Women and Law in Post-independence Zimbabwe: Experiences and Lessons', in Suzan Bazilli, (ed.), Putting Women on the Agenda, Ravan Press, Johannesburg, 1991; Julie Stewart, (ed.) Working Papers on Inheritance in Zimbabwe, Women and Law in Southern Africa Research Project, Working Paper No. 5, Harare, June 1995; Kathy Bond Stewart, 'Fostering Rights Awareness Through Community Publishing in Zimbabwe', in M. Schuler & S, Kadirgamar-Rajasingham, (eds), Legal Literacy: A Tool for Women's Empowerment, UN Development Fund For Women (UNIFEM), New York, 1992.
[67] Eddison Zvobgo, 'Removing Laws that Oppress Women', in Africa Report, March-April 1983, p. 46.
[68] Mary Maboreke, 'Women and Law in Post-Independence Zimbabwe', p. 220.

lives and by extension the well-being of society as a whole. However, those who tried to use the laws, such as demanding child maintenance from negligent fathers to maintain their children, met with social disapproval, and social sanctions could be applied. This is the light in which the impact of the laws should be viewed.

The *Legal Age of Majority Act* of 1982 gave men and women legal majority status at the age of 18.[69] In the past, women had been legal minors all their lives. The new law gave women contractual capacity, including the right to enter into a contract of marriage without having to seek parental authority.[70] The implications opened heated debate: fathers would not be able to claim damages for seduced daughters over 18 years of age, and women could now own and register immovable property in their own names, posing threats to male control.

Minister of Justice, Edson Zvobgo, had a tough time defending the legislation, because the majority of male Members of Parliament who participated in the debate argued that daughters would now marry without parental consultation and that they would not bother about *lobola* payments to their fathers. Zvobgo explained that the law had nothing to do with *lobola*. If daughters married without reference to their parents, that was a reflection of problems in that particular family rather than with the law.[71]

Thus the controversial *Legal Age Of Majority Act* (LAMA) was passed. For those women who were not economically independent (who were in the majority) however, the law did not make much difference: they still 'chose' to keep their heads bowed. Rudo Gaidzanwa explained that this law was maximally used by middle-class women with jobs, incomes and education.[72]

Other legal gains for women came with the *Customary Law and Primary Courts Act* of 1981. It contained provisions that reversed the terms under which men had borne no maintenance obligation towards their illegitimate children or former spouses.[73] It also enabled women to gain legal custody of children, whereas in the past custody had gone to the children's father or to their mother's male guardian (if *lobola* had not been paid). This was another major legal breakthrough for those women who did not mind being socially ostracised as they pursued their legal entitlements.

---

[69] Zvobgo, 'Removing Laws that Oppress Women, in *Africa Report,* March-April 1983, p. 46.
[70] *Ibid.*
[71] *Parliamentary Debates*, Zimbabwe House of Assembly, 17 June 1982, p. 82.
[72] Gaidzanwa, 'Bourgeois Theories of Gender and Feminism', p. 115.
[73] Maboreke, 'Women and Law in Post-independence Zimbabwe', p. 219.

The *Labour Relations Act* of 1985 gave working women maternity leave entitlements[74] and removed among other things, sex-based discrimination in the work place.[75] Again this stood to benefit those who were in employment.

The *Matrimonial Causes Act* changed property distribution practices in the event of divorce.[76] In the past, the bias towards 'tribal customs' had favoured men. The act also removed blame as a factor in determining distributing property after divorce.

Women ex-combatants: misleading images and realities

As the study of the camps revealed, many female fighters were 'custom-bound' in their perspective of life. However, this is not the immediate impression they created as they returned from the war. One former combatant reflected on how people viewed them then:

> *In those days we were feared. We had our time. It was comrade here... comrade there. But those were the times.*[77]

Another spoke of the way they had lived in the camps, where the basic concern was survival. She referred to their 'rough ways'.[78] Some of those habits lingered on after the war and confused the picture. Novelist Shimmer Chinodya attempted to capture society's view of the returning fighters in a scene outside a demobilisation office in the capital, describing the guerrillas as they appeared to most civilians, as 'tough and hardened':

> *To the quick eye of a passer-by, the women did not appear different from the men. They wore the same clothes and carried themselves with the same gait. They walked to go forward, to get where they wanted to go, their heads craned over tightly T-shirted busts and their behinds thrust out behind them.*[79]

Stories abounded in those early days of the unconventional breed of women:

> *sexually starved female guerrillas who 'prowled'... around their assembly point, abducting 'unfortunate' men and 'demanding' to be made love to.*[80]

Then, it was all over as they got to grips with the reality of their situation:

---

[74]   The maternity leave had no pay entitlements though. Now, they do.
[75]   Maboreke, 'Women and Law in Post-Independence Zimbabwe', p. 219.
[76]   Ibid.
[77]   Interview with Chido Tigere, Sunningdale, Harare, 16 March 1992.
[78]   Interview with Mildred Dengu, Sunningdale, Harare, 16 March 1992.
[79]   Shimmer Chinodya, *Harvest of Thorns*, Heinemann, Oxford, 1989, p. 13.
[80]   *Moto*, November 1990, p. 4.

The 'gangs' of 'nymphomaniacs' gradually shed their tight jeans, slipped into less eye-catching plain dresses and got down to the serious business of finding their places in life.[81]

By the time I started research for this study, more than a decade after the return of the fighters, I had problems finding where the haughty women, about whom so much had been said, had disappeared to. When I finally located them, they were very different women from their images of the early 1980s. They were ordinary urban township women, living in sections of houses still undergoing construction. Some brushed off my protests as they scrambled to get me somewhere clean to sit. In Dotito in rural Mt Darwin, I found mothers with babies on their breasts, waiting for their turn at the baby clinic.

These images collide with those of the not-so-revolutionary war period. For some female guerrillas, the deference civilians paid to them went to their heads. In the euphoria of the moment, some deluded themselves that certain social conventions did not apply to them any more. Those who whipped up emotions at the Women's League rallies, for example, were women who for the most part, had returned from the war and spoke as liberated women. The behaviour of the few, naive enough to think that things had changed, tarnished the other female ex-combatants. Soon, even their male comrades found excuses for abandoning them for civilian wives.

A former combatant left by the father of her two children recalled his insults as he walked out on her: 'Women from the bush, you are a problem.'[82] This was the man who had been with her in the bush! Several months before the same man had returned to her, full of apologies for running off with another woman. She thought he was genuinely regretful and took him back. She was five months pregnant when she learned her mistake. The man explained that he had accomplished his mission: he had returned solely to impregnate her. Leaving her with only two children after paying all that *lobola* was not enough, he said, as he left her to pick up the pieces of her shattered life.[83]

A former commander explained the comparisons men were now making between their war-ravaged wives and the pretty nurses in the urban hospitals and their smartly dressed office secretaries. He remarked light-heartedly how the nurses and the secretaries had stolen the show.

The Minister of Justice introduced a bill in Parliament in November 1984 to make wartime marriages binding.[84] Some argued, however, that those liaisons were merely com-

---

81   Ibid.
82   Interview with Alice Mukanga, (Challenge Chimurenga), Sunningdale, Harare, 14 March 1992.
83   Ibid.
84   See *Parliamentary Debates*, Zimbabwe House of Assembly, 9 November 1984.

mon-law unions rather than marriages and that they merited no special treatment.[85] Questions were asked how the male and female fighters had found time to fancy one another when they should have been fighting. If they wanted to be recognised as married, the argument went, they should follow the procedures everybody else followed.[86] Ruth Chinamano, the ZAPU female parliamentarian, agreed that the liaisons were improper and that they should have been deplored during the war. However, she argued:

> There must be strings to tie some raving bulls… these people who marry must marry lawfully and be recognised as married people so that they do not go about marrying every day.[87]

The debate also raised the problem of war-time unions involving men who already had other wives. The Minister of Justice responded that those who had previous marriages that legally allowed for polygamy could marry again, but those with church marriages could not marry a second time.[88] Ruth Chinamano asked what options were available to war-time wives who reluctantly found themselves in polygamous unions because they had been misled about their men's previous marital status. In response, the minister said that they were free to leave the men if they wanted to.[89] It was clear from the debate and the resulting law, the *War Marriages Validation Act of 1984*, that efforts to make war-time unions properly binding would only meet with limited success. Under the new act, Harare and Bulawayo were the only centres of validation for such marriages.[90] This meant that women living in remote areas of the country never benefited from the exercise. Thus, the majority of women who brought back children from the war found themselves in no better position than they had been in during the war.

If any of the former fighters had ever flirted with ideas of female emancipation, they, like civilian women, had to survey their economic position first. This, in most cases, was not secure. For those ex-combatants economically dependent on their husbands, their position was clear: '*Baba ndiBaba*', meaning their husbands were the heads of the house, in a sense, like their fathers. Others spoke of the men as 'the government of the household'.[91] Women had to abide by the rules and conventions set by that government. Some simply had to keep their mouths shut because in some instances, when they married, they brought with them a child from a previous war-time relationship. Such women considered themselves lucky, as women with such backgrounds found it difficult to secure husbands.

---

85   Ibid., p. 639.
86   Ibid.
87   Ibid., p. 642.
88   Ibid., p. 643.
89   Ibid.
90   *War Marriages Validation Act*, No. 34, 1984, Section 3.
91   Interview with Mai Winnie, Dotito, Mt Darwin, May 1992; interview with Jane Munikwa (Precious Takawira), Sunningdale, Harare, 14 March 1992.

Women's major concerns were about jobs, which had been hard to find given their lack of education. They had been the first to be demobilised by the Zimbabwe National Army, because that appeared to be the easiest way to cut down on numbers. Many women had not even considered joining the army, recognising that their prospects there did not look good. Most had held low ranks during the war and this grossly prejudiced their inclusion, let alone their ranking, in the new army.

Most women therefore 'opted' for demobilisation, receiving approximately Z$185[92] per month for about two years.[93] Few have anything to show for that money, which they either used to meet their immediate and extended families' needs, or they enthusiastically spent it on luxuries. Many said they thought government wanted them to have something of a good time after all the suffering they had endured. More would come, they thought. Those who pooled their resources to join co-operatives were regretful afterwards. The co-operatives succumbed to the calamities affecting other similar enterprises.[94]

Some female ex-combatants explained that some of their comrades never received their demobilisation pay. After agreeing to return to the country as 'refugees', they never managed to convince anyone afterwards that they had been soldiers. So they lost out.[95]

As for the progressive laws women fighters are supposed to have occasioned through their participation in the war, the majority have got nowhere close to accessing them. During my field research, I had trouble getting cleared to interview the female ex-combatants in the Mt Darwin area, from where most of the earliest recruits had come. An official in the Security Department of ZANU PF's Mashonaland Central Province alluded to the Party's fears, after I had explained my position. He said I was going to discover 'the neglected wives and children of the *chefs*' in this area, and 'open a can of worms' for people in top positions. As it happened, I did not encounter any senior men's wives but I did meet ex-combatant mothers with children who had dropped out of school. They had failed to get birth certificates so the children could register for Grade Seven examinations, to enable them to proceed to secondary school.

---

92 In January 1980, Z$1 equalled 65.4 pence (£0.65); in December 1980, it was worth 66 pence. Therefore the ex-combatants received what in December 2000 would be the equivalent of Z$9,200 i.e. the Zimbabwe dollar has devalued by approximately 5000 per cent.

93 All the female ex-combatants interviewed for this study had received it.

94 Muchaparara Musemwa, 'The Ambiguities of Democracy: The Demobilisation of the Zimbabwean Ex-combatants and the Order of Rehabilitation, 1980-1993', in Jakkie Cilliers, *Dismissed: Demobilisation And Reintegration of Former Combatants in Africa*, Institute For Defence Policy, South Africa, 1996. Also, Norma Kriger (Manuscript), 'Zimbabwe's Guerrilla Integration: Entitlement Politics', Department of Political Science, Johns Hopkins University, Baltimore.

95 The author did not meet any such women herself, perhaps because she asked for ex-combatants, which the 'refugees' were not. Probably they have now decided to keep a low profile after being told so many times that they are fakes, trying to steal what real fighters earned.

The children's fathers had either died or could not be found after the war, and the government did not offer assistance. In theory it is not necessary to present the father of the child to secure a birth certificate, but the bureaucracy that has to be overcome is daunting, time-consuming, and if you have to travel to a town, expensive.

One interviewee in Harare explained that a friend had written to her from Mt Darwin about the problem of securing this crucial document for her child. She was seeking her friend's assistance to locate the child's father who was known to be in the city. Chido Tigere explained how the woman's lack of education worsened the problem:

> I had to do a lot of guess work to understand what she meant. The spelling of birth-certifi-cate... it took me some time to work out what those jumbled-up symbols meant.[96]

This problem affects many other women apart from the ex-combatants. It remains, however, a major source of bitterness among some of the former combatants who feel they wasted their time in the war while civilians were studying.

Conclusion

Although a policy of education for all adopted at Independence enabled many women to go to school and achieve a higher education, the ZANU PF patriarchal establishment compromised the Zimbabwean women's movement. Nor have the educated women who have the potential to challenge the *status quo* fully exploited their position.

At Independence, the MCDWA employed several university graduates[97] who were instrumental in organising educational projects to familiarise women with their new legal position. Their impact, however, seems to have been neutralised by Party zealots. The following anecdote says volumes about the hurdles that need crossing.

A woman with a Masters degree working with the Ministry of Women's Affairs gave this account.[98] As leader of a group from her ministry attending a workshop out of the country, she arrived at the office dressed for the trip, sporting a nicely tailored jacket and matching skirt. But she soon learnt, she was 'inappropriately dressed'. Everyone else was wearing the 'national dress', the league's uniform, decorated with the Party President's picture. In the end, one woman reluctantly lent her a piece of cloth and went with her into a toilet where they hurriedly assembled the appropriate attire. Since she had no similarly deco-

96 Interview with Chido Tigere, Sunningdale, 16 March, 1992.
97 Gaidzanwa, 'Bourgeois Theories of Gender And Feminism', p. 115.
98 The woman's name is withheld as permission to use her account was not secured by the author.

rated clothes to change into, that was the only 'dress' she wore for the whole week they were away.

The woman said she could not relax and participate actively in the workshop sessions because the hurriedly done seams of her rather too small dress kept threatening to come apart with each movement she made. The evenings were spent mending the seams and laundering the garment for its next wear! Changing into anything else would alienate her from her colleagues, who could read a lot of things into her failure to observe Party etiquette. This, she could not risk. As she was the key person in her team, the workshop's potential was obviously not fully utilised.

Though anecdotal, that woman's account throws light on the restrictions frustrating those who seek to put social change in motion. This seems to be one of the main reasons why the majority of formidable feminist activists now work more with non-governmental organisations rather than with the government itself. In all likelihood, these women are trying to evade the patriarchal hold of the ruling party, ZANU PF.

Conclusion

The war brought many changes in the day-to-day lives of Zimbabwean people. While some left Zimbabwe for the guerrilla's rear base camps to train in the use of arms or sought refuge in neighbouring countries, others stayed behind, leading supposedly civilian lives in the countryside. But it was in rural Zimbabwe, then Rhodesia, where most of the military contests of the 1970s occurred. Thus, whether people joined the armed groups or remained in the war zones, life indisputably became militarised.

For women, the guerrilla war of the 1970s drove them into arenas of violence in an unprecedented way. In accordance with the new military demands of the day, young women who, prior to the war, had been tasked with carrying bundles of firewood and water for their families' domestic use, now also carried war materials from the guerrillas' rear base to supply the male fighters 'manning' the battlefront. Others abandoned their schooling, or their teaching jobs, to join the bush schools in Zambia or Mozambique where they lived under the constant threat of bombing raids. Still others perfomed similarly vital duties regarding the survival of the guerrilla army: treating the sick, instructing new recruits in how to use arms and familiarising them with the political objectives of the nationalist war, compiling and keeping ZANU and ZANLA's administrative records as clerks and secretaries, growing food crops, while helping to keep alive those values they considered essential to sustain the social fabric of life among the displaced population of the camps.

In the war zones inside Zimbabwe, women who had previously concerned themselves with growing food for their families' consumption now also produced enough to feed their 'extended family' in the bush, the guerrillas. The traditional cooking stick assumed a new symbolism. Like the guerrillas' gun, it became a weapon of war. Teenagers, who prior to the war had looked after cattle and goats, now combined such roles with watching for enemy movements. These young boys and girls became the 'ears and eyes' of the guerrillas. Relations with civilians were fairly harmonious in the early 1970s when the guerrillas operated in the north-eastern Zimbabwe, but by 1976 antagonisms were developing as the war spread out to cover the rest of the eastern half of the country. By 1979, there had developed what Terence Ranger termed 'a crisis of legitimacy', as increasing numbers of guerrillas used their powers arbitrarily in their conduct towards civilians, especially regarding their relations with women.

The Zimbabwean nationalist movement was a violent exercise, violating both men and women, but in ways that were specific to their gender. This study does not suggest that women monopolised suffering in the liberation war. Neither does it suggest that all men were privileged and that they all benefited from the war. Thousands died and some are still struggling to heal the wounds sustained in that struggle. Many men were also marginalised by virtue of their age, or of having joined the war later than the others, or by virtue of the inferiority or superiority of their educational credentials. Many did not measure-up to 'manly' duties and were demoted to 'feminine' roles. It is also true that a few women managed to break the barriers nad enter the male-dominated spheres. Similarly, in independent Zimbabwe some women, especially those with education, jobs, salaries and bank accounts, have moved a long way in comparison to their pre-war position, and in relation to those who are uneducated, unemployed and still under the patronage of their male relations. However, gender is still one of the major factors separating the 'haves' from the 'have-nots', clearly demonstrating that the sex-based prejudices of the pre-war period survived the war.

A scholar writing on nationalism, Robert H. Wiebe, could not be closer to the mark in his assessment. Although he sympathises in general with the nationalists' causes, he points out that: 'Nationalism can also be a trap fot those on the inside'.[1] His description of the family unit under nationalism as being 'male-dominated and female-dominated'[2] could well be applied to the nature of power relations in the whole structure. That Zimbabwe's war was male-led is doubtless. It cannot be contested that women served nationalist interests, and that the nature of their service was often detrimental to their own physical, social and political well-being. Women's roles were clearly as important important to the success of the nationalist struggle as men's roles. The women, however, did not participate in the as men's equals and this was most amply demonstrated by their absence in decision-making organs. The male leadership determined how and where women fought. Neither did Zimbabwean women share equally with men spoils of that war. In the same way that most of them were kept outside the decision-making organs of the armed struggle, they remain largely excluded from the power structures of the post-war state.

Finally it is impossible to draw definite conclusions about recent developments in Zimbabwe but it is clear that the struggles of the year 2000 – the farm occupations, the protests over the constitution, the violence before and after the election, to name but a few – are related to the current power elite's definition and understanding of the meaning of the struggle for Independence. Violent clashes have taken place on occupied farms, as well as in urban areas, where partisan struggles are becoming the order of the day. This

---

[1]   Robert H. Wiebe, 'Humanizing Nationalism', in *World Policy Journal*, Vol. 13, No. 4, Winter 1996-97, p. 87.
[2]   Ibid.

creates a quasi-military atmosphere in the areas affected. There have been news reports of women being raped and beaten up, and of young girls being molested. In many instances the alleged perpetrators of these crimes seem to think they are acting in the interests of the nation. As women have often been subjected to such indiginities by men who have claimed to be defending Zimbabwe's nationhood, the question is: what is the gender of that nationhood? As Wiebe postulates above, the gender of the nation is essentially male. So, turning his thesis around, we can also ask, if women were the citizens rather than the subjects of the nations to which they belong and for which they sacrifice so much, would men's national interests take priority all the time? Would the tactics of war, be used in peace?

Helie Lucas, a former fighter from the Algerian struggle ironically summarised the frustrations faced by women in an instructive way. She spoke for thousands of women in nationalists movements in colonised or former colonised countries the world over:

> We are made to feel that protesting in the name of women's interests and rights is not to be done NOW: it is never and has never been the right moment: not during the liberation struggle against colonialism, because all forces had to be mobilised against the principal enemy; not after independence, because all forces had to mobilised to build up the devastated country, not now that racist, imperialist Western government are attacking the Third World.[3]

Not now. Not ever.

Zimbabwean nationalists have every reason to be proud of their ability to rise against the injustices of the colonial system. It is their prerogative and no one can rightly deny them that. but after all the praises have been sung, the nation must be responsible enough to confront the vices of that period in order to see what lessons can be learnt for the present and for the future. Undesirable tendencies covered-up in the name of 'national solidarity' can mutate into monsters that will gobble up that hard-earned nationhood. Thus we need to take an honest look at the nationalist struggle and confront those ghosts from the past. As this study has tried to show, exploring women's experience is a fair starting point.

---

[3] Marie-Aimee Helie-Lucas, 'Women in the Algerian Liberation Struggle', in T. Wallace with C. March (eds.), *Changing Perceptions: Writings on Gender and Development*, Oxfam, Oxford, 1991, p.58.

Appendix

Some notes on sources

ZANLA records

After the war, former ZANLA commanders brought back with them to Zimbabwe, valuable documents from their Mozambican bases. These were the administrative records of the various organs of ZANU and ZANLA. They constituted reports and minutes of meetings held by members of the Central Committee, the High Command, the General Staff and the liberation movement's various administrative departments. The most useful records for this study emanated from the Departments of Women's Affairs, Education and Culture, as well as from the Political Commissariat. Reports from the operational zones were also very useful in throwing light on the situation inside war-torn Zimbabwe. Some of these precious papers are now housed at the ZANU PF Headquarters in Harare, following the leadership's decision to retain them as Party property rather than surrender them to the Zimbabwe National Archives. The documentation provides one of the wealthiest sources of information for historians of the war. The collection is a national heritage and it is the author's hope that in the future, ZANU PF will be able to complete cataloguing the papers and arrange for their proper storage. In the meantime, there is a dire need for both human and financial resources to carry out this task.

While these records contain a remarkable amount of detail for the last three years of the war, the period before 1977 is not so well covered. The fighters from that earlier period had very low literacy levels and this compromised record keeping. Although the mid-70s witnessed the recruitment of relatively well-educated fighters, who were conscious of the need to keep records, internal struggles and the assassination of Party Chairman Herbert Chitepo led to the imprisonment of the ZANLA High Command by their hosts, the Government of Zamba. Unfortunately, the documentation produced by the junior officers who took command of the war for that period were later destroyed in the purges that characterised the return of the senior commanders in late 1976. Although some attempts were later made to reconstruct the records from that unstable period, their accuracy was compromised by the lapse of time. In some respects, they were deliberately skewed to advance certain official arguments. However, these documents still constitute one of the most comprehensive sources of Zimbabwe's war history, as they throw light on both the situation in the liberation army's rear bases and in its operational zones inside Zimbabwe.

Oral evidence

Oral evidence helped to fill in the gaps and verify some of the issues highlighted in the documentation. Both former combatants and civilians were very important in this respect. Female ex-combatants from the Sunningdale residential area in Harare provided the first cluster of interviews. In their testimonies, the ex-combatants constantly referred the author to Mt Darwin in north-eastern Zimbabwe. Mt Darwin falls in the region which witnessed the earliest phase of intensive armed struggle and the majority of ZANLA's first recruits came from there. Interviews with former combatants and civilians in Dotito in rural Mt Darwin produced a remarkable wealth of information. The author also obtained interviews from ex-combatants in Mt Darwin town, as well as from those residing in Bindura, the capital of ZANU PF's current political bastion, Mashonaland Central Province. It was evident during the author's stay in both Mt Darwin and in Bindura that the communities were still trying to resolve the tensions which had characterised relations between the former fighters and the civilians, who had provided them with logistical support. Indeed, these tensions initially inhibited the author's ability to obtain interviews. However, once the former fighters relaxed, their testimonies revealed all too clearly how complex the war experience was for those involved.

Bibliography

AMADIUME, Ifi, *Male Daughters and Female Husbands: Gender and Sex in an African Society*, Zed Books, London, 1987.

BAUMHOGGER, Goswin and others (eds), The Struggle for Independence: Documents on the Recent Development of Zimbabwe (1975-1980) Vols. 1-7.

BEACH, David, *The Shona and Their Neighbours*, Blackwell Publishers, Oxford, 1994.

BERKIN, Carol R. and LOVETT, Clara M., (eds), *Women, War and Revolution*, Holmes and Meir Publishers, New York, 1980.

BHEBE, Ngwabi and RANGER, T. O., (eds), *Soldiers in Zimbabwe's Liberation War*, James Currey, London, with University of Zimbabwe Publications, Harare, 1995.

BOND-STEWART, Kathy, 'Fostering Rights Awareness Through Community Publishing in Zimbabwe', in Schuler M. and Kadirgamar-Rajasingham S., (eds), *Legal Literacy: A Tool for Women's Empowerment*, UN Development Fund for Women (UNIFEM), New York, 1992.

BOULDING, Elise, 'Warriors and Saints: Dilemmas in the History of Men, Women and War', in Eva Isaksson, (ed.), *Women and the Military System*, Proceedings of a Symposium Arranged by the International Peace Union, Harvester-Wheatsheaf, New York, 1988.

BOURDILLON, M. F. C., *The Shona Peoples, An Ethnography of the Contemporary Shona, with Special Reference to Their Religion*, Mambo Press, Gweru, 1987.

BRATTON, Michael, 'Drought, Food and the Social Organisation of Small Farmers in Zimbabwe', in Glantz, Michael H. (ed.), *Drought and Hunger in Africa: Denying Famine a Future*, Cambridge University Press, Cambridge, 1988.

CHAPKIS, Wendy, 'Sexuality and Militarism', in Isaksson Eva, (ed.), *Women and the Military System*, Proceedings of a Symposium arranged by the International Peace Union, Harvester-Wheatsheaf, New York, 1988.

CHEATER, Angela, 'The Role and Position of Women in Pre-Colonial and Colonial Zimbabwe', in *Zambesia, The Journal of the University of Zimbabwe*, Vol. 13, No. 11, 1986.

CHINODYA, Shimmer, *Harvest of Thorns*, Heinemann, Oxford, 1989.

CLARK, Christopher, 'The Wars of Liberation in Prussian Memory: Reflections on the Memorialization of War in Early Nineteenth Century Germany', in *The Journal of Modern History*, Vol. 68, No. 3, Sept. 1996.

COCK, Jacklyn, *Colonels and Cadres, War and Gender in South Africa*, Oxford University Press, Oxford, 1991.

DAVIDSON, Basil, CLIFFE, L. and SELASSIE, Bereket Habte, (eds) *Behind the War in Eritrea*, Spokesman, Nottingham, 1980.

DOLPHYNE, Florence Abena, *The Emancipation of Women: An African Perspective*, Ghana Universities Press, Accra, 1991.

ELSHTAIN, Jean B., *Women and War*, Basic Books, New York, 1987.

EHRENPREIS, Pia, *From Rhodesia back to Zimbabwe: All My Hopes Were to Go Home One Day: Refugee Stories*, UNHCR and SIDA, 1983.

FLOWER, Ken, *Serving Secretly: An Intelligence Chief on Record: Rhodesia into Zimbabwe, 1964 - 1981*, John Murray Publishers Ltd., London, 1987.

FREDERIKSE, Julie, *None But Ourselves, Masses Vs. Media in the Making of Zimbabwe*, Zimbabwe Publishing House, Harare, 1982.

GACIA-MORENO, Claudia, 'AIDS: Women are not Just Transmitters', in Wallace T. with March C., *Changing Perceptions: Writings on Gender and Development*, OXFAM, Oxford, 1991.

GAIDZANWA, Rudo, 'Bourgeois Theories of Gender and Feminism', in Meena Ruth (ed.), *Gender in Southern Africa: Conceptual and Theoretical Issues*, SAPES Books, Harare, 1992.

GAITSKELL, Deborah, 'Housewives, Maids or Mothers: Some Contradictions of Domesticity for Christian Women in Johannesburg, 1903-39', in *Journal of African History*, Vol. 24, 1983.

GROTH, Siegfried, *Namibia, The Wall of Silence: the Dark Days of the Liberation Struggle*, David Philip, Cape Town, 1995.

HAMMOND, Jenny and DRUCE, Nell (eds), *Sweeter Than Honey: Testimonies of Tigrayan Women*, Links Publications, Oxford, 1989.

HELIE-LUCAS, Marie-Aimée, 'Women in the Algerian Liberation Struggle', in Wallace, T. with March, C. (eds), *Changing Perceptions: Writings on Gender and Development*, Oxfam, Oxford, 1991.

HOOKS, Bell, *Ain't I A Woman: Black Women and Feminism*, South End Press, Boston, 1982.

ISAACMAN, Allen and ISAACMAN, Barbara, *Mozambique: From Colonialism to Revolution, 1900-1982*, Westview Press, Boulder, 1983.

JANCAR, Barbara, 'Women Soldiers in Yugoslavia's Liberation Struggle, 1941-1945', in Eva Isaksson, (ed.), *Women and the Military System*, Proceedings of a Symposium arranged by the International Peace Union, Harvester-Wheatsheaf, New York, 1988.

JEATER, Diana, *Marriage, Perversion and Power: the Construction of Moral Discourse in Southern Rhodesia 1894-1930*, Clarendon Press, Oxford, 1993.

KANOGO, Tabitha, 'Kikuyu Women and the Politics of Protest: Mau Mau', in Macdonald Sharon, Holden Pat and Ardener Shirley (eds) *Images of Women in Peace and War*, Macmillan Education, London, 1987.

KESBY, Mike, 'Arenas for Control, Terrains of Gender Contestation; Guerrilla Struggle and Counter-Insurgency Warfare in Zimbabwe 1972-1980', in *Journal of Southern African Studies*, Vol. 22 No. 4, Dec. 1996.

KRIGER, Norma, J., 'Zimbabwe's Guerrilla Integration: Entitlement Politics, Department of Political Science,' (Manuscript), Johns Hopkins University, Baltimore.

KRIGER, Norma J., *Zimbabwe's Guerrilla War: Peasant Voices*, Cambridge University Press, Cambridge, 1992.

LAN, David, *Guns and Rain, Guerrillas and Spirit Mediums in Zimbabwe*, James Currey, London, 1985.

LIKIMANI, Muthoni, *Passbook Number F.47927, Women and Mau Mau in Kenya*, Macmillan Publishers Ltd., London, 1985.

MABOREKE, Mary, 'Women and Law in Post-Independence Zimbabwe: Experiences and Lessons', in Suzan Bazilli, (ed.), *Putting Women on the Agenda*, Ravan Press, Johannesburg, 1991.

MAHAMBA, Irene, *Woman in Struggle*, ZIMFEP, Harare, 1986.

MALOBA, Wunyabari, O., *Mau Mau and Kenya: An Analysis of a Peasant Revolt*, Indiana University Press, Bloomington, 1993.

MAKANYA, Stella T., 'The Desire to Return: Effects of Experiences in Exile on Refugees Repatriating to Zimbabwe in the Early 1980s', in Allen, Tim and Morsink, Hubert (eds), *When Refugees Go Home*, United Nations Research Institute, Geneva, 1994; also by James Currey, London, 1994.

MARTIN, David and JOHNSON, Phyllis, *The Struggle for Zimbabwe: The Chimurenga War*, Zimbabwe Publishing House, Harare, 1981.

MAXWELL, David, *Christians and Chiefs in Zimbabwe: A Social History of the Hwesa People*, IAI, Edinburgh University Press, 1997.

MAZRUI, Ali A., 'Gandhi, Marx and the Warrior Tradition: Towards Androgynous Liberation', in A.A. Mazrui (ed.), The Warrior Tradition in Modern Africa, International Studies in Sociology and Social Anthropology, Vol. 23, 1977.

MCLAUGHLIN, Janice M.M., *On the Frontline: Catholic Missions in Zimbabwe's Liberation War*, Baobab Books, Harare, 1996.

MEENA, Ruth (ed.), *Gender in Southern Africa: Conceptual and Theoretical Issues*, SAPES Books, Harare, 1992.

MIKELL, Gwendolyn, 'African Feminism: Toward a New Politics of Representation', in *Feminist Studies*, Vol. 21, No. 2, 1995.

MOLYNEUX, Maxine, 'Mobilization Without Emancipation? Women's Interests, the State, and Revolution in Nicaragua', in *Feminist Studies*, Vol. 11, No. 2, 1985.

MUCHENA, Olivia N., 'A Socio-Economic Overview: Zimbabwean Women', African Training and Research Centre for Women, United Nations Economic Commission for Africa, Addis Ababa, 1982.

MUDENGE, S.I.G., *A Political History of Munhumutapa, c.1400-1902*, Harare, Zimbabwe Publishing House, 1988.

MUGABE, Robert G., 'The Role and History of the Zimbabwean Women in the National Struggle', in *Women's Liberation in the Zimbabwean Revolution: Materials From the ZANU Women's Seminar, Xai Xai, 21 May 1979*, ZANU, San Francisco, 1979.

MUSEMWA, Muchaparara, 'The Ambiguities of Democracy: the Demobilisation of the Zimbabwean Ex-combatants and the Order of Rehabilitation, 1980-1993', in Cilliers Jakkie, *Dismissed: Demobilisation and Reintegration of Former Combatants in Africa*, Institute for Defence Policy, South Africa, 1996.

NAIMAN, Joanne, 'Left Feminism and the Return to Class', in *Monthly Review*, June 1996.

NKOMO, Joshua, *Nkomo: The Story of My Life*, Methuen, London, 1984.

NYAMFUKUDZA, Stanley, *The Non-Believer's Journey*, Heinemann, London, 1980.

NYAMUBAYA, Freedom, *On the Road Again: Poems from the Liberation Struggle*, Zimbabwe Publishing House, Harare, 1986.

PANDYA, Paresh, *Mao Tse-Tung and Chimurenga: an Investigation into ZANU Strategies*, Skotaville Publishers, Braamfontein, 1988.

PANKHURST, Donna, *Women's Lives and Women's Struggles in Rural Zimbabwe*, Southern African Studies, University of Leeds, August, 1988.

PEEL, J.D.Y and RANGER, T.O. (eds), *Past and Present in Zimbabwe*, Manchester University Press, Manchester, 1983.

PRESLEY, Cora Anne, 'The Mau Mau Rebellion, Kikuyu Women, and Social Change', in *Canadian Journal of African Studies*, Vol. 22, No. 3, 1988.

RADHAKRISHNAN, R, 'Nationalism, Gender, and the Narrative of Identity', in Parker Andrew, Russo Mary, Summer Doris and Yaeger Patricia (eds), *Nationalisms and Sexualities*, Routledge, London, 1992.

RANGER, Terence, O., *Revolt in Southern Rhodesia, 1896-97: A Study in African Resistance*, Heinemann, London, 1967.

Idem, 'The Death of Chaminuka: Spirit Mediums, Nationalism and Guerrilla War in Zimbabwe', *African Affairs*, July 1982.

Idem, 'Tradition and Travesty: Chiefs and the Administration in Makoni District, Zimbabwe, 1960-1980', in Peel J.D.Y. and Ranger T.O., eds., *Past and Present in Zimbabwe*, MUP, Manchester, 1983.

Idem, *Peasant Consciousness and the Guerrilla War in Zimbabwe: a Comparative Study*, James Currey Ltd., London, 1985.

Idem, 'Guerrillas, Bandits and Social Bandits in the 1970s', in Crummey D., (ed.), *Banditry, Rebellion and Social Protest in Africa*, James Currey, London, 1986.

Idem, 'Violence Variously Remembered: The Killing of Pieter Oberholzer', *History in Africa*, 1997.

REYNOLDS, Pamela, 'Children of Tribulation: the Need to Heal and the Means to Heal War Trauma', in *Africa*, Vol. 60, No. 1, 1990.

RUDEBECK, Lars, (ed.), *When Democracy Makes Sense: Studies in the Democratic Potential of Third World Popular Movements*, AKUT, Working Group for the Study of Development Strategies, Uppsala University, Sweden, 1992.

SCHMIDT, Elizabeth, *Peasants, Traders and Wives: Shona Women in the History of Zimbabwe, 1870-1938*, London, James Currey, 1992.

SCHRAM, Stuart, *The Thought of Mao*, Cambridge University Press, Cambridge, 1989.

SCHRECKER, John, *The Chinese Revolution in Historical Perspective, Contributions to the Study of World History*, No. 19, Greenwood Press, New York, 1991.

SEIDMAN, Gay W., 'No Freedom Without Women: Mobilization and Gender in South Africa', 1970-1992', in *SIGNS*, Vol. 18, No. 2, 1993.

STAUNTON, Irene, *Mothers of the Revolution: The War Experiences of Thirty Zimbabwean Women*, James Currey, London, 1990.

STEWART, Julie, (ed.) Working Papers on Inheritance in Zimbabwe, Women and Law in Southern Africa Research Project, Working Paper No. 5, Harare, June 1995.

SWEETMAN, David, *Women Leaders in African History*, Heinemann, Oxford, 1984.

TUNGAMIRAYI, Josiah, 'Recruitment to ZANLA: Building up a War Machinery', in Bhebe, Ngwabi and Ranger, Terence, (eds)., *Soldiers in Zimbabwe's Liberation War*, James Currey, London, with University of Zimbabwe Publications, Harare, 1995.

URDANG, Stephanie, *Fighting Two Colonialisms: Women in Guinea-Bissau*, Monthly Review Press, New York, 1979.

URDANG, Stephanie, *And Still they Dance: Women, War and the Struggle for Change in Mozambique*, Earthscan Publications Ltd., London, 1989.

Voluntary Organisations in Community Enterprise, (VOICE) Directory of Non-Governmental Organisations, Voice, Harare, 1988.

WALKER, Cheryl, (ed.) *Women and Gender in Southern Africa to 1945,* James Currey, London, 1980.

WALLACE, T. with March, C. *Changing Perceptions: Writings on Gender and Development,* Oxfam, Oxford, 1991.

WEINRICH, A.K.H., 'Strategic Resettlement in Rhodesia', in *Journal of Southern African Studies,* Vol. 2, No. 3, April 1977.

WEINRICH, A.K.H., *Women and Racial Discrimination,* UNESCO, 1979.

WEINRICH, A. K. H., *African Marriage in Zimbabwe and the Impact of Christianity,* Mambo Press, Gweru 1982.

WEISS, Ruth, *The Women of Zimbabwe,* Kesho Publications, London, 1986.

WIEBE, Robert H., 'Humanizing Nationalism', in *World Policy Journal,* Vol. 13, No. 4, Winter 1996/97

YUVAL-DAVIS, Nira, 'Front and Rear: the Sexual Division of Labour in the Israeli Army, in *Feminist Studies,* Vol. 11, No. 2, 1985.

Women's Action Group, Zimbabwe, (WAG) 'Operation Clean Up', in Miranda Davies (Compiler), *Third World, Second Sex,* Vol. 2, Zed Books, London, 1987.

Government of Zimbabwe Publications

Parliamentary Debates, 17 Jun. 1982.

Parliamentary Debates, 6 Nov. 1984.

Parliamentary Debates, 9 Nov. 1984.

Parliamentary Debates, 15 Nov. 1984.

Rukuni Commission: 'Report of the Commission of Enquiry Into Appropriate Agricultural Land Tenure Systems', 1994.

War Marriages Validation Act, No. 34, 1984.

Zimbabwe-Rhodesia Government, Report of the Constitutional Conference, Lancaster
House, London, Sep. - Dec. 1979.

Magazines

Africa Report: African American Institute, 777 YN Plaza; New York, NY

Moto: Box 89, Gweru, Zimbabwe

Parade: Box 1683, Harare, Zimbabwe

Social Change and Development: Box 4405, Harare, Zimbabwe

Zimbabwe News: Box 4530, Harare, Zimbabwe

Other Publications

Church of the Province of Central Africa, Diocese of Mashonaland, 'Report of the Commission to Enquire Into the Legal Status of African Women', 1976.

Theses and Dissertations

MANUNGO, Kenneth D., 'The Role Peasants Played in the Zimbabwe War of Liberation,
with Special Emphasis on Chiweshe District', D. Phil. Dissertation, Ohio University,
1991.

MAXWELL, David, 'A Social and Conceptual History of North-East Zimbabwe', D. Phil.
Thesis, Faculty of Modern History, University of Oxford, 1994.

McLAUGHLIN, Sister Janice, 'The Catholic Church and the War of Liberation', Doctoral
Thesis, University of Zimbabwe, Department of Religious Studies, June 1991.

MUSHONGA, Munyaradzi, 'The Formation, Organisation and Activities of the Catholic
Commission For Justice and Peace in Rhodesia with Particular Reference to the Rho-
desian War, 1972-1980', B.A. Hons. Dissertation, University of Zimbabwe, History
Dept., 1990.

SCHMIDT, Heike, 'The Social and Economic Impact of Political Violence in Zimbabwe,
1980 - 1990', D. Phil. Thesis, Oxford, 1996.

STOTT, Leda, 'Women and the Armed Struggle for Independence in Zimbabwe, 1964-1979', M.Sc. Dissertation, University of Edinburgh, 1989.

Unpublished Seminar and Conference Papers

BEACH, David, 'Nehanda: An Innocent Woman Unjustly Accused', Seminar Paper, History Department, University of Zimbabwe, 1995.

CHUNG, Fay, 'Education and the Liberation Struggle', Paper Presented at the Conference on the Zimbabwe Liberation Struggle, University of Zimbabwe, 8-12 July, 1991.

MOORE, David B., 'The Zimbabwean People's Army: Strategic Innovation or More of the Same?', War and Religion Conference Paper, Uppsala, March 1992.

RANGER, T.O., 'Women in the Politics of Makoni District, Zimbabwe, 1890-1980', Manchester University Seminar Paper, 1981.

Archival Materials

National Archives of Zimbabwe

NAZ, IDAF File MS 308/40/3

NAZ, IDAF File MS 308/40/4

NAZ, IDAF File MS 308/40/5

NAZ, IDAF File MS 308/40/6

ZANU Archives, ZANU PF Headquarters

Documents were cited from the files in which they were located at the time of research. As they were still undergoing processing, some may since have been moved to different files. Also note that in some instances, two files could bear similar identification. They are simply cited as they appeared.

Defence Secretariat

Defence Secretariat (Women's Affairs)

Defence Dept., MMZ Province

Department of Women's Affairs

CC, HC and GS Minutes

Education and Culture Department

HC Minutes

Minutes of HC and GS Meetings

Operations MMZ Tete Province

Operational Reports, Manica

Party Communications (from 1965)

Political Commissariat

Southern Province, (Gaza)

Southern Province, (Gaza), Sector 4 Operational Reports.

Rhodesian Government Confidential Report, 'ZANLA Modus Operandi: Operation Repulse' 19 Dec. 1978.

Interviews
(all conducted by author) - arranged by dates

Margaret Dongo, Parliament House, Harare, 10 March 1992, (former combatant, former
MP)

Rwirai Nyika, (now late), Sunningdale, Harare, 11 March 1992, (former combatant)

Farai Dhlamini, Sunningdale, Harare, 11 March 1992, (former combatant)

Mary Mucheka, Sunningdale, Harare, 11 March 1992, (former combatant)

Muchaneta Mabhunu, Sunningdale, Harare, 12 March 1992, (former combatant)

Teedzai Mabhindauko, Sunningdale, Harare, 12 March 1992, (former combatant)

Mildred Dengu, Sunningdale, Harare, 14 March 1992, (former civilian aide/*chimbwido* who became combatant).

Precious Takawira, Sunningdale, Harare, 12 March 1992.

Helen Moyo (Ntombiyezwe Nyathi), Sunningdale, Harare, 14 March 1992.

Challenge Chimurenga, Sunningdale, Harare, 14 March 1994, (former combatant)

Chido Tigere, Sunningdale, Harare, 16 March, 1992, (former combatant)

Sifikile Masotcha, Kambuzuma, Harare, 20 April 1992, (former combatant)

Mrs Mavende, Dotito, Mt Darwin, 13 May 1992, (former civilian aide/*chimbwido* who became combatant)

Mai Fambai, Dotito, Mt Darwin, 13 May 1992, (former civilian aide/*chimbwido* who became combatant)

Mrs Mazarura Jnr. Dotito, Mt Darwin, 14 May 1992, (former civilian aide/*chimbwido* who became combatant)

Mai Winnie, Dotito, Mt Darwin, 14 May 1992, (former combatant)

Mrs Zurukwa/Nhanga, Dotito, Mt Darwin, 14 May 1992, (former civilian aide/*chimbwido* who became combatant)

Mai Matuwini, Dotito, Mt Darwin, 14 May 1992, (former civilian aide/*chimbwido*, who became combatant)

Mrs Mazarura Snr. Dotito, Mt Darwin, 13 May 1992, (civilian and former PV inmate)

Mr Mazarura, Dotito, Mt Darwin, 13 May 1992, (civilian and former PV inmate)

Molly Chipadza, Mt Darwin Town, 15 May 1992, (former combatant)

Chipo Moyo (not real name) London, 5 March 1994.

Mrs Joyce 'Teurai Ropa' Mujuru, Bindura, 2 November 1994, (former combatant, ZANU Secretary For Women's Affairs, Minister of Youth Sport and Culture, Minister of Community Development and Women's Affairs, Acting Minister of Post and Telecommunications, Governor for Mashonaland Central Province and now Minister of Rural Resources and Water Development.)

Maggie Chirata, Bindura, 3 November 1992, (former civilian aide/*chimbwido* who became combatant)

Tambudzai Chitseko, Bindura, 3 November 1992, (former combatant).

Julia Zvobgo, Kambanji, Harare, 10 January 1995, (former combatant, former Administrative Secretry For ZANU Department of Women's Affairs).